Disqualifying the High Court

Supreme Court Recusal and the Constitution

Louis J. Virelli III

University Press of Kansas

Published by the University Press of Kansas (Lawrence, Kansas 66045), which was organized by the Kansas Board of Regents and is operated and funded by Emporia State University, Fort Hays State University, Kansas State University, Pittsburg State University, the University of Kansas, and Wichita State University

Library of Congress Cataloging-in-Publication Data

Names: Virelli, Louis J., author.
Title: Disqualifying the high court : Supreme Court recusal and the constitution / Louis Virelli III.
Description: Lawrence, Kansas : University Press of Kansas, 2016. | Includes index.
Identifiers: LCCN 2016004961| ISBN 9780700622719 (hardback) | ISBN 9780700622726 (ebook)
Subjects: LCSH: Judges—Recusal—United States. | Judges—Disqualification—United States. | United States. Supreme Court. | Constitutional law—United States. | BISAC: LAW / Constitutional. | POLITICAL SCIENCE / Constitutions. | LAW / Judicial Power.
Classification: LCC KF8861 .V57 2016 | DDC 347.73/265—dc23 LC record available at http://lccn.loc.gov/2016004961
British Library Cataloguing-in-Publication Data is available.
Printed in the United States of America

10 9 8 7 6 5 4 3 2 1

For Meg, Gavin, and Ella. I love you more than words can tell.

Contents

Acknowledgments

I could not have completed this project without receiving significant help and support at every stage of the process.

I am enormously grateful to everyone at Stetson University College of Law. Dean Chris Pietruszkiewicz and the Highbaugh family provided me with valuable time and resources by awarding me the Leroy Highbaugh Sr. Research Chair. Michael Allen, Jason Bent, Jamie Fox, Roy Gardner, Marco Jimenez, Becky Morgan, Jason Palmer, Ellen Podgor, and Susan Rozelle helped by reading drafts, providing keen insights, and pointing me toward others who could help. Our crack team of librarians at Stetson, especially Rebecca Trammell, Wanita Scroggs, and Sally Waters, made my seemingly daunting research tasks more efficient and more fun. Cathy Rentschler was a patient and expert indexer. Stetson's Office of Faculty Support, in particular Shannon Edgar and Janice Strawn, always found ways to make things work better and more easily. I have been fortunate to work with a team of gifted, dedicated, and patient students over the years. This project particularly benefited from the talent and hard work of Jennifer McPheeters, Tara Petzoldt, and Melaina Tryon.

My friends and colleagues at other institutions also contributed in important ways. Ron Krotoszynski and Bill Araiza graciously and patiently shared their considerable wisdom and publishing experience. Brannon Denning, Joel Goldstein, and Eric Segall have been overwhelmingly kind with their advice and encouragement. My work is always better for their involvement with it. I am particularly indebted to Joel and to Chad Oldfather for their thorough and thoughtful review of an earlier version of the manuscript. Daniel Holt at the Federal Judicial Center was extremely helpful and responsive in my research. His willingness to share his historical knowledge of the federal courts helped make the book richer and more engaging. Andrew Ferguson has provided me with valuable advice, and invaluable friendship, since we were law school classmates. This project was no exception.

One of the most pressing challenges in completing this book was finding a quiet and comfortable place to work. I am indebted to the partnership of Banker Lopez Gassler, P.A., and especially Chuck Hall, for opening their doors to a relative stranger with a book to write.

Portions of the book were drawn from my previously published works, all of which have been significantly amended for inclusion here: "The (Un)Constitutionality of Supreme Court Recusal Standards," 2011 *Wis. L. Rev.* 1181; "Congress, the Constitution, and Supreme Court Recusal," 69 *Wash. & Lee L. Rev.* 1535 (2012); "What 'Stop and Frisk' Can Teach Us about the First Amendment and Judicial Recusal," 47 *Conn. L. Rev. Online* 13 (2014). I thank the journal editors for their contributions to the articles and for their permission, where required, to reprint those materials.

I would also like to thank my managing editor, Kelly Chrisman Jacques, as well as Chuck Myers, Jane Raese, and the University Press of Kansas for their help and guidance. Any errors are entirely my own.

Finally, and most important, is my family. My parents, Lou and Barbara Virelli, and my brother, Chris Virelli, have given me the gifts of education and confidence that made the decision to pursue a project like this possible. I am eternally grateful to them and the rest of my extended family for their love and support. My wife, Meghan Irmler, and children, Gavin and Ella, are quite simply the people who make everything else in my life worthwhile. Meg is my most trusted adviser and greatest champion, and Gavin and Ella provide me with a sense of joy and perspective that makes everything I do more purposeful. They made many sacrifices for me and this project. I am appreciative beyond words for all that they are and do.

Introduction

Many things interest Americans about the Supreme Court. Judicial recusal is not always one of them. This is unfortunate, because recusal, though not the highest-profile issue confronting the justices, directly impacts the Court's most persistent and fundamental challenge—its struggle to maintain its legitimacy in a democratic society.

The Supreme Court is inherently different from our other government institutions. In what is generally a representative democracy, where the power of government is entrusted to people who are elected, and reelected, by those they govern, the Court is an unelected, unreviewable body composed of justices who hold their positions for life and whose decisions have a profound impact on every aspect of our lives. Many Americans have never read Justice Harry Blackmun's decision in *Roe v. Wade* or Justice Anthony Kennedy's opinion in *Citizen's United v. FEC*, yet their mere mention sparks passionate debate. Even cases that are no longer good law linger in our collective memory. Names like *Plessy v. Ferguson* and *Dred Scott* are cultural shorthand for the failure of government institutions to protect the most vulnerable members of our community. What's more, the Court's influence over our political, social, and personal lives shows no signs of abating. In only the last few years the Court has taken on highly contested issues like gay marriage, gun possession, free speech, reproductive freedom, and campaign finance reform, to name just a few. As the country continues to grow more politically polarized, the Court finds itself increasingly on the cutting edge of American life.

But for all its power and independence, the Court is also vulnerable. It has the power to decide many of our most pressing and controversial national questions, but it has no power to enforce its decisions. In the words of Alexander Hamilton, the judiciary "has no influence over either the sword or the purse; . . . neither FORCE nor WILL but merely judgment."[1] This serves as an important check on the Court's authority, but it also threatens its effectiveness. The Court relies on the cooperation of the other branches of government, and by extension the people they represent, to fulfill its constitutional responsibilities. It earns this cooperation by remaining democratically legitimate, by exercising its judgment in a way that earns the faith and trust of the people it purports to govern. As Justice Sandra Day O'Connor famously stated in the landmark abortion case *Planned Parenthood of Southeastern Pennsylvania v. Casey*, "The Court's legitimacy depends on making legally principled decisions under circumstances in which their principled character is sufficiently plausible to be accepted by the Nation."[2] This requires not only that the Court's decisions themselves be defensible but also that they appear so to a watchful nation.

Enter judicial recusal. "Recusal," sometimes called "disqualification," is the exclusion of a judge or justice from participating in an individual case.[3] Recusal is regularly required when a judge has a monetary interest in the outcome of a case or when he or she may be, or may reasonably appear to be, biased against one of the litigants. Recusal serves at least two broad purposes. It protects litigants by helping to ensure an impartial decision maker for their claims. It also helps preserve the legitimacy of the judicial system as a whole. In many cases, even though a judge may be perfectly capable of acting fairly and objectively, recusal is nonetheless required because the judge's participation would create a reasonable appearance of bias. By guarding against the mere appearance of bias, recusal advances public confidence in the integrity and legitimacy of an otherwise unaccountable judiciary.

Perhaps because of its important role in defending the integrity of judges and the judicial system, recusal is as old as courts themselves. Early Jewish and Roman law both incorporated recusal, and it became part of the English common law system as early as the thirteenth century. It has continued unabated ever since, and American law is no exception. As direct descendants of the English common law system, pre-Revolutionary American courts employed recusal. Those practices were carried through the formation of the United States and the ratification of the Constitution. Recusal is currently practiced at all levels of the judiciary, in state as well as federal courts and from trial courts through appellate courts of last resort, including the U.S. Supreme Court.

Throughout this long history, recusal has been viewed almost exclusively as an issue of judicial ethics. This of course makes sense. The relationship of recusal to judicial ethics is obvious. When we think of judges in the American system, we think of people who are (hopefully) wise, but at minimum fair and independent.[4] We expect judges to resolve disputes objectively by applying the relevant law to the available facts. External pressures like monetary or political incentives are generally understood as disruptive to good judging. There are sound reasons for these preferences. Judicial fairness and independence are critical to the pursuit of justice. Recusal addresses the problem of unethical decision making by providing for the exclusion of potentially biased judges from individual cases.

Recusal is not, however, an exclusively ethical issue. Focusing solely on its ethical consequences overlooks the critical question of recusal's proper place in our constitutional system. Federal recusal standards are statutory. Congress sets the criteria for when federal judges must recuse themselves. This interaction between Congress and the judiciary raises critical constitutional issues that have so far been largely neglected. Do legislative commands to a coequal branch of government improperly interfere with that branch's own constitutional authority? Who should determine if violations have occurred? If violations are found, who should enforce them? Each of these questions implicates the separation of powers. The concept of separation of powers in America predates the Founding and is a fundamental principle of our constitutional system. It is based on the idea that the Constitution assigns each of the three coordinate branches authority over some aspect of government. At the same time, the branches' authority overlaps enough for each branch to prevent potential overreaching by the others. These checks and balances help legitimize our constitutional system. The ability of the government to effectively curb its own power is a compelling reason for the citizenry to support its governmental institutions. This is especially true with regard to the judiciary. Calling again on Alexander Hamilton, this time quoting the French political philosopher Montesquieu, "'there is no liberty if the power of judging be not separated from the legislative and executive powers.'"[5] Legislatively prescribed recusal raises significant questions about the intersection of legislative and judicial power that can only be addressed by treating recusal as a matter of constitutional law.

The constitutional stakes are magnified when we consider recusal at the Supreme Court. The Supreme Court is the only federal court mandated by the Constitution. While Article III of the Constitution *requires* the existence of the Supreme Court, it merely permits Congress to create the lower federal trial and appellate courts. The Supreme Court's constitutional mandate suggests that it also has a stronger claim to judicial power under Article III than the voluntarily created lower courts. As Michael Gerhardt explained, "Separation of powers concerns are at their most sensitive in those instances in which the removal, disqualification, and disciplining of the most powerful federal judicial officers are at stake."[6] The history and procedures relating to Supreme Court recusal are also different from those of the lower federal courts. As a procedural matter, the justices typically provide little or no explanation for their recusal decisions, and those decisions are not subject to review. Lower federal courts, by contrast, must defend their recusal decisions on appeal to a higher court, including the Supreme Court. Historically speaking, the first Congress enacted a recusal statute for the lower courts, but it took more than 150 years before the statute was made applicable to members of the Supreme Court. Since that time, the justices have shown little enthusiasm for applying the statutory standards to their own conduct. The combination of the Court's unique constitutional status as the head of the judicial branch and the justices' traditional refusal to apply statutory standards to their recusal decisions makes Supreme Court recusal a complex and significant constitutional issue.

It is also a very real one. Throughout the Court's history, the justices have been involved in a wide array of situations that raised serious questions about their recusal practices, including how those practices impact the constitutional separation of powers.[7] Supreme Court justices have had close personal relationships with sitting presidents, even going so far as to provide the chief executive with policy advice or campaign assistance while on the bench. Others have participated in cases reviewing legislation that they themselves played a significant role in drafting while members of Congress, or in cases in which they were also part of the reviewing court below. Several justices sat on cases that they had knowledge of and even involvement in while serving in the executive branch, and others had familial relationships or simply engaged in conduct that could be seen as projecting a lack of impartiality about an issue before the Court. Even where not invited by the justices' personal history or conduct, recusal has become a more frequent topic of public discourse about the Court, particularly as increasing partisanship fuels fears about the politicization of the justices and their decisions.[8]

Put simply, Supreme Court justices have faced difficult questions related to recusal since the opening of the Court, and their decisions in those cases have often been controversial. So in light of this long history of Supreme Court justices making questionable decisions about their participation in certain cases, the question must be asked: "Why now?" What is it about the modern Supreme Court that requires the first comprehensive constitutional analysis of its recusal practices? On one hand, the answer is nothing. The separation-of-powers questions raised by Supreme Court recusal are timeless. They were just as important in 1803 when Chief Justice John Marshall chose not to recuse himself from the landmark case of *Marbury v. Madison* as they are today. For more than a century, the Supreme Court has continually reiterated the importance of preventing even the most innocuous infringements on the separation of powers.[9] By that rationale, a constitutional treatment of Supreme Court recusal is long overdue but is not uniquely suited to the present.

On the other hand, this may be the perfect moment to discuss the constitutional ramifications of Supreme Court recusal. Although recusal may never rank as the public's most pressing concern about the Court, it is garnering more and more attention. As the Court faces growing public scrutiny across the entire range of its operations, that scrutiny more frequently manifests itself in discussions about the justices' recusal practices. Since 2010, multiple Supreme Court recusal statutes have been introduced in Congress, sitting justices have testified about recusal before Congress, the chief justice has published a Year-End Report on the Federal Judiciary that focused entirely on judicial ethics and recusal, and the conduct of several justices was questioned by members of Congress, the press, and the public in connection with recusal and other ethical issues. A cursory look at the environment surrounding the Court helps explain this growing interest in recusal. A divisive political climate and more frequent public appearances by the justices focus additional attention on the Court. Rick Hasen noted that "'the last decade in particular, has seen an explosion of Supreme Court justices being publicly reported on and being seen to some extent as celebrities.'"[10] With the trappings of fame come greater attention and, inevitably, criticism. The breadth of available information about the justices and the efficiency with which that information is communicated make it easier for political opponents to attack a justice's qualifications to participate in a particular case. All of these factors have contributed to an increasingly active and spirited public dialogue about recusal at the Court. As information about the justices and the Court continues to be readily and widely available, that dialogue is likely to continue, and the constitutional issues surrounding Supreme Court recusal are only likely to grow in importance.

This book examines recusal at the Court from a constitutional perspective, both to better understand recusal and to offer a framework for thinking more broadly about the constitutional separation of powers. Chapter 1 outlines the evolution of American recusal law from the expansive views espoused by ancient and medieval regimes, through the far narrower view held in the English common law, to a modern approach that more closely resembles its ancient ancestors. This account of how the underlying principles of recusal have changed over time provides a useful backdrop for understanding the ongoing tension between Congress and the Court that drives the constitutional issues around Supreme Court recusal.

Chapter 2 focuses on recusal at the Court since the beginning of the Republic. It highlights some of the more prominent recusal issues in the Court's history, from Chief Justice Marshall's decision not to recuse in *Marbury v. Madison* to Justice Clarence Thomas's and Justice Elena Kagan's decisions to participate in the Court's review of the controversial health care statute, the Affordable Care Act. It then examines the ongoing debate over recusal at the Court, including what I describe as the constitutional impasse between Congress and the Court over recusal. There are two primary purposes for this historical analysis. First, it highlights the long-standing and continuing relevance of Supreme Court recusal to American law and politics. This relevance shows no sign of fading and thus highlights the need to more closely examine all aspects of recusal at the Court. Second, some of the historical themes developed in chapter 2 bear directly on how the justices' recusal decisions fit within the separation of powers.

Chapter 3 explains the primary constitutional dilemma with Supreme Court recusal: the difficult answer to the question of who decides. It argues from constitutional text, history, practice, and structure that Congress's attempt to set mandatory recusal standards for the justices represents an unconstitutional infringement on the Court's inherent judicial power under Article III. It shows why the Constitution reserves Supreme Court recusal questions for the justices alone and offers some arguments for why this outcome is a net benefit to litigants, the Court as an institution, and our constitutional democracy writ large.

Chapters 4 and 5 target the most constitutionally acceptable solutions to the problem highlighted in chapter 3. Chapter 4 focuses on the impasse between Congress and the Court over recusal. There is an inherent conflict between the purportedly binding but utterly unenforceable federal statute governing the justices' recusal decisions and the Court's clear and open disregard for the statutory standard in its recusal practices. The result is a constitutional problem. Recusal creates a tension between the branches that draws their efficacy and legitimacy into question. Why would Congress enact a statute that it knows it cannot enforce and the Court will not abide by? How can the Court continue to act with open disregard for a validly enacted statutory mandate without any additional action or explanation as to why it feels entitled to do so? Chapter 4 seeks to resolve this inherent tension over recusal by applying separation-of-powers principles to suggest a course that both is faithful to those principles and acknowledges the Court's exclusive authority over its own recusal practices.

Chapter 5 moves from solving the interbranch impasse over recusal to determining how the Court should decide recusal questions in the absence of a statutory standard. The answer lies in the intersection of constitutional due process and the First Amendment. After outlining the history of the Court's due process recusal jurisprudence, I suggest a framework for the Court to apply due process principles to its own recusal decisions. This new framework seeks to balance the important ethical concerns that recusal is designed to address with the constitutional principle of separation of powers and the justices' right to free speech under the First Amendment. The result is a holistic view of the constitutional landscape confronting the justices' recusal decisions.

Chapter 6 relies on the preceding analysis to suggest applications beyond the Supreme Court, in particular how a constitutional view of recusal at the Court could better inform our understanding of recusal in the lower federal courts and in state supreme courts. In the case of the lower federal courts, it considers the (potentially significant) differences between the Supreme Court and other Article III courts within our constitutional structure and examines what constitutional limitations, if any, exist to constrain Congress's regulation of recusal in the lower courts. It argues that Congress's ability to regulate recusal in the lower courts depends on a set of related protections—such as the ability of federal judges to sit by designation on other courts—that would preserve the lower courts' ability to fulfill their judicial function even in cases where recusal was otherwise required.

Chapter 6 also considers the question of how treating recusal as a matter of constitutional law sheds light on recusal in state supreme courts and on the separation of powers in different constitutional systems. It relies on features of state constitutions that may distinguish them from the federal Constitution, such as their structure, their treatment of legislative power, their use of judicial elections, the breadth of state court jurisdiction, and their constitutional amendment procedures, to explore how the separation of powers affects legislative interaction with the judiciary over recusal at the state level.

Chapter 7 concludes by focusing on the broader lessons from Supreme Court recusal for interbranch conflict and the separation of powers. It recounts the major themes developed with regard to recusal in the federal courts and demonstrates how those themes are relevant to other separation-of-powers conflicts within the federal government. It relies on examples such as the interactions between Congress and the Court over quorum requirements, appellate jurisdiction, and impeachment, and between Congress and the president over the use of military force and the appointment and removal of federal officials to show how a constitutional view of recusal at the Court can shed light on other instances of imperfect interbranch relations.

So why should people be interested in Supreme Court recusal? The answer, I suggest, is twofold. First, the ethical integrity of the Court is vital to its ability to function as a legitimate part of a constitutional democracy. The second reason, and the primary focus of the following pages, is that the current structure of recusal at the Court raises a series of important and underappreciated constitutional questions that have an equal, if not greater, impact on its democratic legitimacy. These questions are critical to understanding how recusal decisions should be made and, more broadly, how our constitutional system should respond when two or more branches collide.

Disqualifying the High Court

1 | The Evolution of American Recusal Law

The Law of Recusal from the Ancients to the Common Law

The earliest legal systems understood the value of recusal to protect both individual litigants and the integrity of the judiciary. Recusal is not, however, a static concept. Although it has consistently reflected a commitment to core principles of fairness and neutrality, the law of recusal has varied widely over time and across different legal systems. American recusal law is a product of this history.

Ancient concepts of recusal took a broad view, endorsing the removal of judges based on the mere possibility that they would be unable to decide the case before them justly. Early Jewish law prohibited a judge from hearing a case involving a friend, relative, or someone he disliked.[1] In the sixth century AD, the Codex of Justinian allowed for recusal of a judge who engendered "suspicion" in a litigant.[2] The concept of suspicion in Justinian's time seemed to include concerns about the judge's attitude toward both the parties and the cause: "Although a judge has been appointed by imperial power yet because it is our pleasure that all litigations should proceed without suspicion, let it be permitted to him, who thinks the judge under suspicion to recuse him before issue joined, so that the cause go to another."[3] This early view remained the dominant European approach to recusal for roughly a millennium. In the fourteenth century, a Spanish statute—the Siete Partidas—adopted a standard nearly identical to that of the Codex. It permitted recusal in cases of fear and suspicion by the parties as well as personal hostility between the judge and the litigants.[4]

The leading statement about recusal from the medieval period, at least as it pertains to common law jurisdictions like England and, eventually, the United States, came from the English jurist Henry de Bracton. Bracton was a member of the King's Bench from 1247 to 1250, and then again from 1253 to 1257. He is best known for the treatise *On the Laws and Customs of England*, the most comprehensive attempt to describe the English *ius commune*, or common law, until Sir William

Blackstone's renowned *Commentaries* more than 500 years later.[5] The medieval common law of Bracton's time was a combination of Roman and canon law, so it is no surprise that his view of recusal is analogous to that of the Codex. Bracton took a broad view of recusal, agreeing with the Codex that judges should be removed for "suspicion," which he defined as including cases where the judge is related to a party, is a "friend, or enemy" of a party, or is a party's "dependent . . . counselor or narrator."[6] Bracton's views on recusal are important to a discussion of modern American recusal because of the close connection between English and American common law. In fact, his broad definition of "suspicion" can be seen in several aspects of the current law of recusal in America.

Bracton's view of recusal has not, however, always carried the day. It still reflects the law of recusal in many civil law countries,[7] but it was superseded in the English common law by the principle *nemo iudex in sua causa* (no man shall be a judge in his own cause). Despite the principle's Justinian pedigree, it took on a narrower meaning within the English common law system.[8] Lawyers and judges declined to reference Bracton's wider notion of judicial interest in a case, which included kinship and other personal relationships.[9] They instead took a more literal view, requiring recusal only in cases where the judge was a party to the suit.[10] The leading statement on common law recusal came from Chief Justice of the Court of Common Pleas Sir Edward Coke in 1608 in the famed *Dr. Bonham's Case*.[11] The case is best known for its support of judicial review of parliamentary acts, but it also provides a revealing account of the common law of recusal. Dr. Thomas Bonham brought suit against the London College of Physicians after being jailed and fined by the college for practicing medicine without a license. The college relied on an act of Parliament that empowered it to regulate and punish unlicensed practicing physicians. The statute also entitled the college to keep half of any fines it levied under the statute. Citing *nemo iudex in sua causa*, Lord Coke held that the college censors could not sit in judgment of Dr. Bonham because they stood to receive half of the fine they imposed on him. The judges' financial interest rendered them unfit to participate in the case.[12]

Later cases during Lord Coke's tenure confirmed that only a judge's financial interests, and not his personal relationships or biases, were grounds for recusal. In the *Earl of Derby's Case*, the court concluded that William Earl of Derby, as Chamberlain of Chester, could not sit as a judge in equity over a dispute involving the "trust and interest of a farm called Budshaw in the county of Chester" because Derby claimed an interest in the farm.[13] Some sixty-five years later, a subsequent Earl of Derby was again the subject of a recusal motion.[14] This time he was permitted to preside over a case in which his brother-in-law was a party and had a financial stake because although recusal is required "where a judge has an interest," that interest does not extend to personal relationships or biases, as "favour shall not be presumed in a judge."[15] This exclusive relationship between recusal and the judge's personal pecuniary interest persisted over the next century. In 1700, Lord Chief Justice John Holt explained that "the Mayor of Hereford was laid by the heels, for sitting in judgment in a cause where he himself was lessor of the plaintiff in ejectment."[16] In 1742, Parliament responded to a judicial decision requiring recusal where a judge's only financial interest in the case was due to his status as a taxpayer. It enacted a statute that expressly permitted judges to participate in such cases and limited recusal to cases where a judge's pecuniary interest is tangible.[17] Broader conceptions of economic interest were not sufficient to merit disqualification. Starting with Lord Coke and *Dr. Bonham's Case*, the common law standards for recusal in England began to contract from the broad view articulated by Bracton toward a more pointed doctrine designed to exclude only judges with a direct financial interest in the cases before them.

There was, however, an exception. If recusal would exclude all of the available judges from a particular case, one or more of the recused judges would be permitted to participate rather than deny the litigants a forum. This "rule of necessity" can be traced back as early as 1430, when the chancellor of Oxford was permitted to judge a case in which he was a party because "there was no provision for the appointment of another judge."[18] The rule was stated explicitly by Chief Justice of the King's Bench Henry Rolle: "If an action is sued in the bench against all the Judges there, then by necessity they shall be their own Judges."[19] As we will soon see, the concept of necessity continues to play a powerful role in American recusal law, especially as it pertains to recusal at the Supreme Court.

By the time of Blackstone's famed *Commentaries on the Laws of England 1765–1769*, the common law of recusal was firmly established as applying only when a judge had a pecuniary interest in the outcome of a case and there were other judges available to take his place. Blackstone confirmed that although "good cause" may have been grounds for recusal "in the times of Bracton and Fleta . . . now the law is otherwise."[20] He went further by stating that all other forms of interest are immaterial: "The law will not suppose a possibility of bias or favour in a judge, who is already sworn to administer impartial justice."[21] Rather than permit recusal of a non–financially interested judge, Blackstone was content to leave "a heavy censure from those to whom the judge is accountable for his conduct" as the (rather nebulous) remedy against judicial bias.[22]

Blackstone's characterization of the common law of recusal is exceedingly important to understanding the development of American recusal doctrine. First, it departs significantly from historical conceptions of recusal. Unlike Roman and medieval recusal requirements for suspicion or cause, Blackstone's standard is far more limited. It wholly overlooks any nonfinancial source of judicial interest or bias on the presumption that a judge's oath of impartiality must be adequate to protect against threats like personal animosity and the appearance of partiality. This extremely narrow construction of recusal is also consistent with the rule of necessity. Blackstone's account of recusal reflects an inherent trust in the integrity of the judiciary that is critical to the rationale behind necessity—that a hearing by a potentially biased judge is better than none at all.

Finally, Blackstone's *Commentaries*, including his description of the common law of recusal, was the definitive account of the common law at the Founding of the American Constitution.[23] As Daniel J. Boorstin put it, "In the first century of American independence, the *Commentaries* were not merely an approach to the study of law; for most lawyers they constituted all there was of the law."[24] Because the English common law of Blackstone's time effectively became the common law of the United States during the period leading up to and including the adoption of the American Constitution, it is a powerful source not only of the legal standards in place at the time but also of the meaning of other legal texts, including the Constitution, that were adopted within a similar regime.[25] Raoul Berger made the point quite elegantly in discussing Lord Coke's influence on the Founding Fathers' understanding of judicial review: "The animating force of an idea is not necessarily measurable by its verity. . . . The importance of Coke for judicial review does not therefore depend on whether he correctly stated the then existing law, but rather on the fact that at the time of the Constitutional Convention, Colonial America believed he did, and proceeded to act on that belief."[26] The same is true for Blackstone. The Founders' reverence for Blackstone's *Commentaries* makes its influence on American law immeasurable. Blackstone's "account of the British constitution and the common law was so comprehensive, so compendious, and so attractive that Americans were hardly tempted to make pretentious and dogmatic codifications of their own. The English tradition lived on and became the Anglo-American legal tradition."[27]

The Birth of American Recusal Standards

It comes as no surprise, then, that the law of judicial recusal in America around the time of the Founding looked very much like Blackstone's version. The American colonial courts adopted the pecuniary interest standard, which persisted through the ratification of the Constitution and the creation of the lower federal courts.[28] Soon after ratification, Congress codified the recusal standards for federal judges, changing federal recusal law from a purely common law doctrine to a matter of statutory construction. Congress's first recusal statute, in 1792, mirrored Blackstone's approach. It applied only to lower federal courts and included the familiar requirement that judges who were "concerned in interest" in the case must recuse themselves. It also added a prohibition for any judge who "has been of counsel for either party" in the case.[29] From 1792 through 1948, Congress revised the recusal standards for federal judges several times "with Congress enlarging the enumerated grounds for seeking disqualification almost every time."[30] In doing so, Congress moved American recusal law away from Blackstone's narrow conception toward the broader protection against potential judicial prejudice advocated by Bracton.

Congress first revised its 1792 recusal provision in 1821. In addition to the preexisting standards, it required disqualification when a judge's relative appears before him as a party.[31] In 1891, Congress added a new provision including, for the first time, judges presiding over appeals. It prohibited a judge from hearing an appeal of a case he had tried in the court below.[32] Twenty years later, Congress again revisited its recusal statutes. Section 20 of its 1911 act precluded judges from hearing cases in which they were a material witness.[33] Roughly 120 years since drafting its first recusal statute, Congress had identified five scenarios in which recusal was statutorily required—when a judge has a pecuniary interest in the proceeding, when he served as counsel for either party in the same case, when a relative appears before him as a party, when he is asked to decide an appeal from a case that he also presided over below, or when he was a material witness in the case before him.

Despite these seemingly clear standards, litigants still faced significant obstacles in seeking to recuse a judge. First, the statute was a "'challenge-for-cause'" statute.[34] It required litigants to initiate the recusal process and, in turn, neither mandated nor even appeared to anticipate that judges would independently assess their own fitness to preside over a case. Second, the statute did not provide any procedural mechanisms for initiating recusal proceedings. Parties seeking a judge's recusal under the statute had to devise their own vehicles for challenging the judge's participation. The statute also left judges with significant discretion to determine their own fate regarding recusal. The decision to recuse was, in the first instance, left to the judge himself.[35] The statute then required recusal only if the situation would "'render it improper, *in [the judge's] opinion,*'" to preside over the case.[36] This wide latitude for judges to decide their own recusal status continued on appeal, as a judge's decision not to recuse was reviewable only for an abuse of discretion.[37] What at first glance appeared to be an expanding objective standard for recusal was in fact, as of 1911, a subjective and largely unreviewable determination by a judge of his own qualifications to sit.

That same year Congress added a new provision to the recusal statute that appeared to offer the clarity that the existing regime lacked. Section 21 of the 1911 act allowed a party to remove a district judge by simply filing an affidavit stating that the judge has "'a personal bias or prejudice'" against the affiant.[38] Section 21, which is currently codified at 28 U.S.C. § 144, was the first federal statute to offer recusal on a peremptory basis. Under the plain language of the act, a judge had no choice but to recuse once a litigant submitted an affidavit containing the required allegations. More important, it marked the first time under federal recusal law that a judge's personal bias was deemed adequate to merit recusal. In short, section 21 appeared, at least on its face, to be a powerful new tool for litigants seeking recusal.

Soon after its enactment, the statute was severely limited by the courts. The Supreme Court considered the statute's scope in *Berger v. United States.*[39] *Berger* involved the trial and conviction in 1918 of multiple defendants of German descent under the Espionage Act. The defendants sought to recuse the trial judge, Judge Kenesaw Mountain Landis, under section 21 due to his alleged bias against Germans. The defendants' affidavit contained several allegations of racist statements by Judge Landis about Germans and German Americans. The decision came down to the question of whether an affidavit submitted under the new recusal statute would be sufficient, in and of itself, to trigger recusal. The Court held that judges could not question the veracity of the allegations in the affidavit, but that they may determine for themselves whether the allegations, taken as true, support a finding of actual bias or prejudice on their part as the presiding judge.[40] This decision confirmed the common law maxim that judges decide their own recusal motions in the first instance and limited section 21's effectiveness significantly. Rather than importing a broad notion of judicial suspicion and bias into the law of recusal, courts applying *Berger* construed the phrase "bias and prejudice" in section 21 narrowly, such that even allegations that on their face suggested a lack of impartiality could be read to fall short of requiring recusal under the act.[41]

At the time of the Court's *Berger* decision in 1921, American recusal law was showing signs of expansion. It required recusal in a greater number of circumstances than ever before and even allowed for peremptory recusal under section 21. It went well beyond the pecuniary interest standard articulated by Blackstone and the Founders. At the same time, the statutory standards included a high degree of judicial discretion, either explicitly in the subjective standard of section 20 or in the interpretive hands of the courts in the case of section 21, and they continued to exclude completely the justices of the Supreme Court.[42] Future attempts to reform the law of recusal would seek to protect against the entire range of judicial prejudice identified by Bracton and his civil law adherents and to do so across the full spectrum of the federal court system.

The first step in this process came from the American Bar Association (ABA) and again involved Judge Landis. The ABA adopted its Canons of Judicial Ethics in 1924. The canons were the first formal judicial code of ethics in the United States and were prompted, at least in part, by the perceived conflict of Judge Landis serving simultaneously as a federal judge and as the commissioner of Major League Baseball. Judge Landis had been asked to serve as baseball commissioner in 1920 in response to the scandal surrounding the alleged fixing of the 1919 World Series by the Chicago White Sox. He remained on the federal bench for two years after becoming commissioner, a position he held until his death in 1944. Judge Landis could not be found to have broken any existing legal rules by holding both jobs at once. As Attorney General A. Mitchell Palmer explained, "'There seems to be nothing as a matter of general law which would prohibit a district judge from receiving additional compensation for other than strictly judicial service, such as acting as arbitrator or commissioner.'"[43] Yet despite the apparent legality of his arrangement, Judge Landis encountered significant criticism. On February 2, 1921, a resolution was introduced in the House of Representatives calling for Judge Landis's impeachment.[44] On September 1 of that year, the ABA voted to censure him for maintaining dual employment while a member of the federal bench.[45] The controversy surrounding Landis's dual employment, particularly the concerns of the ABA, centered on the appearance of impropriety created by a federal judge receiving compensation from another employer. This was reflected in Canon 4 of the resultant ABA Canons, which stated that "a judge's conduct should be free from impropriety and the appearance of impropriety."[46] Canon 4 reflected a significant shift in at least the cultural understanding of recusal in the United States. It was the first time that the appearance of impropriety—what Bracton may have called "suspicion"—assumed a prominent role in the national conversation about recusal.

The 1924 canons expanded the bounds of recusal by incorporating concerns about the appearance of judicial impropriety, but they stopped far short of a legal revolution. For one, they were not legally binding.[47] As the law of recusal has developed throughout American history, the ABA's input has been highly influential, and in some instances adopted wholesale into legislation.[48] Standing on their own, however, ABA canons are not enforceable as a matter of law. They also failed to include the Supreme Court justices, thus leaving the Court free to develop and maintain its own recusal standards and procedures. Finally, the canons continued to leave the ultimate decision on recusal to the subjective judgment of the judge facing disqualification. The canons did not contain any procedural guidelines for how recusal matters should be decided and did not use mandatory language. Canon 4 stated that a judge's conduct *should* be free from the appearance of impropriety, implying that there are some instances in which an appearance of impropriety may be acceptable. The 1924 canons marked an important milestone in the development of recusal standards by formally introducing the concept of public perception as grounds for recusal. Yet by leaving the recusal decision to the subjective determination of the judge, and excluding the justices of the Supreme Court, the canons proved to be more suggestive than reformative.

Recusal Standards Reach the Court

That changed a bit in 1948, when Congress amended section 20 of the federal recusal statute to include the Supreme Court. The amended version of section 20 was recodified at 28 U.S.C. § 455, which has become the "principal" federal recusal statute. In fact, it is often (wrongly) referred to as the only federal recusal statute, largely because its primary competitors, sections 144 and 47, deal exclusively with trial courts and address only a narrow subset of the accepted grounds for recusal.[49] The 1948 amendments retained the same substantive grounds for recusal included in section 20, but they expanded the statute's scope to include Supreme Court justices.[50] The amendments required recusal where a judge or justice had been a material witness, had been of counsel, or was related to an attorney or party in the case.[51] They modified the personal interest standard to apply only in cases where a judge or justice had a *substantial* interest in the case. The amendments did not, however, limit judicial discretion in making recusal decisions or tighten the standard of review for those decisions on appeal. Recusal was still required only when it would be "improper, in [the judge's] opinion," for the judge to sit in the case, and a judge's recusal decision could still be reversed on appeal only when it represented an abuse of discretion.[52] Section 455 also did not offer any procedural guidance for litigants seeking recusal. Unlike section 144's detailed procedural framework for how and when a party may go about disqualifying a judge, section 455 operated in purely substantive terms. It set the standards for recusal but did not tell litigants how to go about enforcing those standards. The result was a one-dimensional expansion of federal recusal. The statute's reach was expanded in the sense that the Supreme Court was brought within the purview of federal recusal law. The substantive grounds for recusal remained at best the same, and likely even narrower than before, as only "substantial" financial interests qualified for recusal consideration under section 455.[53] Moreover, without explicit procedural guidelines, section 455's attempt to regulate the decisions of unreviewable

Supreme Court justices ran into problems of enforceability that did not exist in the context of lower courts subject to appellate review.

For approximately the next quarter century, section 455's recusal standards remained unchanged. But the absence of legislative activity regarding recusal did not prevent the federal judiciary from making its own contribution. In 1964, the Fifth Circuit Court of Appeals articulated what became known as the "duty to sit."[54] In *Edwards v. United States*,[55] a three-judge panel of the Fifth Circuit—Judges Hays, Cameron, and Rives—reversed defendants' convictions for failing to pay a federal gambling tax. The case was granted rehearing by the entire court (en banc), but the en banc hearing did not include the two judges who made up the majority of the panel decision under review. Judge Hays, who wrote the majority opinion, had been sitting by designation from another circuit and was thus statutorily precluded from participating in the en banc hearing.[56] Judge Cameron, who concurred with Judge Hays to form the panel majority, died before the en banc argument. In light of these unusual circumstances, the dissenting judge from the panel, Judge Rives, considered disqualifying himself and leaving the case to "be considered and decided by the remaining active judges of the Circuit" to avoid the appearance of unfairness to the parties at the rehearing.[57] After consulting with his colleagues on the bench, Judge Rives decided not to disqualify himself. Finding no statutory prohibition against his sitting in the case, Judge Rives concluded that "it is a judge's duty to refuse to sit when he is disqualified but it is equally his duty to sit when there is no valid reason for recusation."[58] Because the applicable statutes did not apply to Judge Rives's situation, he decided not only that he had no legal obligation to recuse himself but also that he had a countervailing obligation to participate in the case as part of his judicial duties.

The duty to sit concept described by Judge Rives has been a powerful influence on modern recusal law, especially at the Supreme Court. It created a presumption against recusal in an environment already heavily weighted toward judicial control. Judges who were previously empowered to exercise their own discretion over recusal were given an additional reason to read any applicable legal standards narrowly. The concept also had potential consequences for appellate review of recusal decisions, as appellate courts that recognized the duty to sit (which was all of them as of 1972) would find it even more difficult to conclude that a judge had abused their discretion by failing to recuse.[59]

As the duty to sit became entrenched in judicial attitudes toward recusal, there were several public controversies involving the perceived integrity of the Supreme Court and its members that brought federal recusal standards back into the spotlight. Justice Abe Fortas was the subject of two such events. The first involved President Lyndon Johnson's nomination of Justice Fortas to replace the retiring Earl Warren as chief justice. Justice Fortas asked President Johnson to withdraw his nomination when it became public that the justice had been paid $15,000— almost half of his salary as a member of the Court—to teach a summer seminar at American University. Even more important than the size of the payment was the fact that the money was raised by Justice Fortas's former law partner from three clients of Justice Fortas's former law firm.[60] The second event caused Justice Fortas to resign from the Court altogether due to his personal and financial relationship with Louis E. Wolfson, a businessman who had been convicted of illegal stock manipulations. Justice Fortas agreed to serve as a consultant to Wolfson's charitable foundation for an annual salary of $20,000, payable for the remainder of the justice's, and his wife's, life.[61] Justice Fortas was not suspected of breaking any laws in his relationship with Wolfson, and the full account of what happened was likely influenced by political issues beyond the justice's control,[62] but regardless of the precise reasons for Fortas's failure to become chief justice or to remain on the Court, the damage to his reputation and to the Court's perceived integrity and prestige proved too much for the institution and the justice to endure.[63] Justice Fortas's case did not explicitly involve a question of recusal, but it did bring into stark relief the importance of public confidence in the Supreme Court.

Recusal had a more direct impact on President Richard Nixon's scuttled attempt to appoint Justice Fortas's successor. President Nixon nominated Judge Clement Haynsworth to fill Justice Fortas's newly vacated seat on the Court. During Judge Haynsworth's confirmation process, it came to light that he had failed to recuse himself from several cases in which he held stock in one of the parties. As with Justice Fortas, it was generally accepted that Judge Haynsworth had not broken the law. Nevertheless, the backlash over his perceived lack of judgment and the resultant appearance of impropriety played a significant role in his failing to be confirmed by the Senate.[64]

The Fortas and Haynsworth controversies sparked a renewed focus on recusal standards, so much so that in August 1969, months after

Justice Fortas's resignation and contemporaneous with Judge Hayns-worth's nomination to the Court, the ABA convened a Special Committee on Standards of Judicial Conduct. The committee's task was to revise the existing ABA Canons of Judicial Ethics, which had remained virtually unchanged since their adoption in 1924.[65] The fruits of the committee's labor were revealed in 1972, when the ABA adopted new recusal standards in its Model Code of Judicial Conduct ("Model Code"). Canon 3C of the new Model Code prescribed recusal of a judge "in a proceeding in which his impartiality might reasonably be questioned, including but not limited to" cases of actual bias or personal interest in the case, or cases in which the judge had served as a lawyer or was related to the parties or their lawyers.[66] The enumerated grounds for recusal in Canon 3C closely resembled the statutory bases of section 455. The most prominent changes were the elimination of the "substantial" qualifier from the requirement that judges recuse when they have a "financial interest in the subject matter" before the court, and the suggestion that recusal could be based on an objective (reasonable) perception of judicial bias. Rather than seek to define quantifiable judicial interests or relationships that merit recusal, Canon 3C looked outward to the public's view of judicial impartiality in adopting the "reasonable appearance" standard for federal recusal.

The reasonable appearance standard was important for several reasons. First, it marked a renewed attempt to make judicial bias, or the appearance thereof, grounds for recusal. After the Court's limiting construction of section 144 in *Berger*, the ABA's return to a broad concept of impartiality as a touchstone of recusal law showed its commitment to incorporating a more rigorous set of ethical standards for America's judges. Although Canon 4 of the ABA's 1924 Canons did explicitly connect recusal to the public's perception of judicial behavior, it did so in a purely suggestive and subjective way by leaving the ultimate determination entirely to the judge.[67] The 1972 Model Code took a stronger position by measuring recusal independently of the judge's own feelings about how her conduct would be perceived.[68]

It also reflected a greater degree of skepticism about the judicial branch. Unlike Blackstone's maxim that "the law will not suppose a possibility of bias or favour in a judge,"[69] the Model Code made no presumptions about judicial impartiality and in fact did not even limit its recusal standard to actual bias. It called for recusal when a judge's impartiality "might reasonably be questioned."[70] Taken on its face, this "reasonable appearance" or "reasonable appearance of partiality" standard represented a move toward Bracton's concept of recusal based on suspicion. It prioritized the fairness and legitimacy of legal proceedings over deference to the judicial profession.

Despite its reformative qualities, the 1972 revisions to the ABA's Model Code were just that—revisions to a model code that neither carried the force of law nor applied to members of the Supreme Court. It took a more public experience with recusal to trigger more lasting change, and that experience came in the (rare) form of a memorandum from a sitting Supreme Court justice explaining his decision not to recuse himself from a specific case. Within months of the ABA code's adoption, Associate Justice William Rehnquist published a controversial memorandum explaining his decision not to recuse himself from the case of *Laird v. Tatum*.[71] Arlo Tatum, as representative of a class of anti–Vietnam War activists, challenged the constitutionality of the U.S. Army's domestic surveillance program.[72] The program was developed in response to growing instances of civil unrest in the country, such as the 1967 riots in Detroit, Michigan, and the widespread rioting and demonstrations that followed the assassination of Dr. Martin Luther King Jr. in 1968.[73] The surveillance program monitored the political activity of potential dissidents to provide the army with information that would enable it to more effectively aid local law enforcement in the event of future disturbances. When the program was revealed in an article in *Washington Monthly* magazine, Tatum and his co-plaintiffs filed suit attacking the program on First Amendment grounds.[74] They argued that the army's surveillance program had an unconstitutional chilling effect on the political speech of the program's targets, including Tatum.

When the case arrived at the Supreme Court, Tatum filed a motion to disqualify Justice Rehnquist due to his previous involvement with the surveillance program while an attorney at the Department of Justice. Prior to joining the Court, and during the period in which the surveillance program was instituted, Justice Rehnquist served as the head of the Justice Department's Office of Legal Counsel. The Office of Legal Counsel is one of the offices responsible for advising the president on the constitutionality of his conduct and, as such, would presumably have been asked to sign off on the surveillance program. While in the Office of Legal Counsel, Rehnquist testified before a Senate committee that was investigating the government's citizen data banks. He also allegedly made "speeches related to [the] general subject" of government surveillance before joining the Court.[75] On the strength of Justice Rehnquist's personal experience with the subject matter of the case, Tatum sought to recuse him. Justice Rehnquist refused and took the unusual step of explaining his decision in writing.

Justice Rehnquist began by citing the 1948 version of section 455, which was the version in effect at that time.[76] Recall that the 1948 version of section 455 required recusal only for judges (including Supreme Court justices) with a "substantial interest" in the case, or who had been "of counsel," a "material witness," or "related" to a party or lawyer in the case so "as to render it improper, in [the judge's] opinion, for him to sit."[77] Justice Rehnquist also noted that Tatum's recusal motion relied on the newly adopted language of the Model Code, in particular Canon 3C, which triggered recusal when a justice's "impartiality might reasonably be questioned."[78]

Although Justice Rehnquist stated that he was aware of the new ABA Model Code, he declined to address it formally in his memorandum because he concluded that it was not "materially different" from the statutory requirement of section 455.[79] After describing his previous involvement with the army surveillance program, he went on to apply the individual provisions from the 1948 version of the recusal statute. He did not address whether his prior involvement with the program could lead to his impartiality being questioned within the meaning of Canon 3C of the 1972 Model Code because he did not read Canon 3C as adding anything substantive to section 455. Applying section 455, he stated unequivocally that he was neither of counsel nor a material witness in *Tatum*.[80] He reasoned that his involvement did not violate the "so-called discretionary portion" of section 455 because he was not so closely related to the parties or their attorneys to render it improper, in his opinion, for him to participate. In support of this conclusion, Justice Rehnquist relied on the practice of other Supreme Court justices, especially those who also served in the Justice Department before taking the bench. He found that although previous justices had approached the recusal question differently, the precedents they set did not suggest that his relationship to the case in *Tatum* merited recusal. He also reiterated that under common law, recusal is an individual decision for a judge, and that to have preexisting knowledge and views about the law is a sign not of bias but of one's qualifications to serve.[81] He concluded by citing the duty to sit, which he described as "even stronger in the case of a Justice of the Supreme Court" due to the lack of both substitute justices and a higher court to review cases on which the Court is evenly split.[82]

Coming directly on the heels of the Model Code's suggestion that recusal be required where a judge's "impartiality might reasonably be questioned," Justice Rehnquist's memorandum in *Tatum* offers some important insights into the development of recusal law generally and recusal at the Court in particular. By interpreting away the Model Code's impartiality language, Justice Rehnquist reflected a sense of judicial prerogative over, and resistance to, more expansive recusal standards. Rather than engage in a true reasonableness inquiry, Justice Rehnquist took it upon himself to evaluate his conduct in comparison to his predecessors on the Court, all of whom made their decisions regarding recusal without the benefit of Canon 3C of the Model Code. He reiterated the individual nature of recusal decisions and relied on the duty to sit as a presumption against recusal, at least in close cases. Finally, he cited the unique orientation of the Supreme Court in the federal judicial system as an additional factor weighing against recusal, despite the fact that section 455 explicitly and without qualification included the justices.

Regardless of whether Justice Rehnquist's analysis in *Tatum* was correct, it had important consequences for the future of recusal law. In April 1973, soon after his memorandum was published, the Judicial Conference of the United States adopted the ABA Model Code as its Code of Conduct for United States Judges ("Code of Conduct").[83] The Judicial Conference is presided over by the chief justice of the United States.[84] Its Code of Conduct serves a similar function to the ABA's Model Code. Like the Model Code, it does not have the force of law and does not expressly include Supreme Court justices, yet it remains highly influential as a source of the legal profession's views on recusal. The Code of Conduct is arguably even more compelling than the ABA Model Code because federal judges voluntarily adopted it to govern their own behavior. The Code of Conduct's disqualification standards are effectively identical to those in the ABA Code. They, too, condition recusal on whether a judge's "impartiality might reasonably be questioned."[85] The fact that the practicing bar and the judiciary shared a unified position on recusal sent a clear message to Congress that, at least with regard to the lower courts, Justice Rehnquist's reading of the Model Code as indistinguishable from section 455 was inaccurate, and that the time had come for more restrictive standards.

That time came a year later, when Congress amended section 455 to reflect closely the requirements of the Model Code and the Code of Conduct.[86] The 1974 amendments to section 455 changed the definition of financial interest from the "substantial" financial interest that was grounds for recusal in 1948 to "ownership of a legal or equitable interest, however small," in the subject matter of the case at hand.[87] They also stated that a judge or justice *shall* recuse herself in any case in which her "impartiality might reasonably be questioned."[88] The use of the word "shall" went beyond even the Model Code and Code of Conduct, which stated that a judge "should" recuse under the same circumstances. By codifying the reasonable appearance standard, Congress rendered it legally enforceable on all federal judges and for the first time explicitly applied it to members of the Supreme Court. It also ostensibly overrode the duty to sit.[89] The clear, mandatory language of the amended statute *required* recusal in the face of an objective concern about a judge's impartiality. It did not offer any exceptions or grounds for judicial discretion in making that determination, nor did it suggest a presumption against recusal for any reason.

The 1974 amendments set the stage for a conflict in the area of Supreme Court recusal. Justice Rehnquist's memorandum in *Tatum* was rife with prudential considerations about the effective functioning of the institution, driven by the Court's unique status as the constitutionally mandated court of last resort. These issues are generally the focus of later chapters, but for now it is worth noting that the modern manifestation of section 455 grew out of public concern about judicial discretion over recusal decisions, and perhaps more significantly embraced questions of judicial legitimacy by focusing not just on actual judicial bias but on the very appearance of such bias. This move represents the clearest evidence that federal recusal law has adopted a Bractonian view of recusal as a bulwark against suspicious judging, rather than the common law approach of deference to judicial integrity and professional judgment. But the Supreme Court has not embraced this view of recusal with regard to its own members. The justices have a long history of involvement in controversial situations implicating recusal-related issues. That history confirms that the tension between Bracton's and Blackstone's views on recusal is still present on the nation's highest court.

2 | Recusal and the Supreme Court

Like all federal judges, the justices of the Supreme Court face challenging decisions about how their conduct on and off the bench impacts their ability to participate in certain cases. Perhaps due to the unique positioning of the Court at the top of the federal judiciary, or simply because federal recusal statutes did not include the justices for the first 150 years of the Republic, Supreme Court history includes a spate of controversies that reveal much about the justices' views of their own recusal practices. These controversies offer insight into the resultant tension with Congress over which branch has the authority to regulate recusal at the Court. They show the justices' willingness to depart from common law or statutory standards in favor of a more comprehensive, contextualized view of their own recusal. This approach, which more closely approximates a constitutional due process analysis than one based primarily on precedent or legislative command, has a pedigree dating back to the earliest days of the Court.[1]

Chief Justice John Marshall on Recusal

Chief Justice John Marshall, although the fourth chief justice of the United States, is widely regarded as the preeminent figure in early American law and the most influential justice to serve on the Court.[2] It is fitting, then, to look to Chief Justice Marshall's recusal practices to better understand the Court's institutional views on recusal. Three of the chief justice's decisions capture the range of recusal issues that have consistently occupied the Court. In *Marbury v. Madison*,[3] *Stuart v. Laird*,[4] and *Martin v. Hunter's Lessee*,[5] Chief Justice Marshall encountered circumstances that could have justified his recusal. His decisions in each case highlight the persistent questions that make recusal at the Court a matter of constitutional concern.

In *Marbury*, Chief Justice Marshall presided over a case questioning the validity of a presidential appointment to the federal bench. Pursuant to the Judiciary Act of 1801, which was passed in the waning hours of his presidency and created a long list of new federal judgeships,

President John Adams signed a commission appointing William Marbury to be a justice of the peace in Washington, DC. President Adams's secretary of state, Chief Justice John Marshall,[6] was responsible for delivering the commission to Marbury. But the commission was never delivered. When President Thomas Jefferson took office, he instructed his new secretary of state, James Madison, not to deliver Marbury's commission. Marbury brought suit claiming that his appointment became legally enforceable when President Adams signed his commission, and that the delivery was not a prerequisite to acquiring the position. Madison countered by claiming either that delivery was indeed a legal requirement for a successful appointment or that the Supreme Court lacked the authority to order a coequal branch of government, in this case the executive branch, to honor the appointment. *Marbury* was rife with novel and fundamental questions about the structure and authority of our federal government, including whether the judiciary had the power to review and invalidate, as a matter of law, conduct of the coordinate branches.

Marbury also raised several issues related to judicial recusal, and more specifically to the recusal of Chief Justice Marshall. The chief justice was heavily invested in the case prior to joining the bench. He was the person charged with making sure the commission was properly delivered. He was also a member of the Adams administration and a loyal member of the Federalist Party with a personal political interest in the appointment of Federalist judges, especially as the rival Republicans prepared to take control of the White House.[7] According to James Bradley Thayer, "It may reasonably be wondered that the Chief Justice should have been willing to give the opinion in [*Marbury*], and especially that he should have handled the case as he did. But he was sometimes curiously regardless of conventions."[8] Yet despite the obvious conflicts of interest, Marshall did not recuse himself from *Marbury*.

The chief justice took a different approach to recusal in another landmark case, *Stuart v. Laird*.[9] The Judiciary Act of 1801 was enacted by a lame-duck Federalist Congress and created many new federal judgeships (the famed "midnight judges"), including a new intermediate level of federal appellate courts.[10] These new circuit courts alleviated the need for Supreme Court justices to continue their practice of "riding circuit": traveling around the country to hear appellate cases with local district judges. In 1802, a Republican Congress repealed the 1801 act, eliminating the circuit courts and the new judgeships created by that act, and passed a new statute—the Judiciary Act of 1802—reinstating the requirement that Supreme Court justices ride circuit to hear intermediate appeals. Some prominent Federalists were outraged. They accused the Republicans of repealing the Judiciary Act of 1801 out of political vengeance and sought an opportunity to retaliate with the help of Federalist judges, including members of the Supreme Court.[11] *Stuart v. Laird* was part of that Federalist response.

John Laird, a resident of Maryland, brought a successful suit against Hugh Stuart, a Virginia citizen, in a federal trial court in January 1801. The appeal was originally set to be heard by a circuit court created by the Judiciary Act of 1801. When the 1801 act was repealed and the circuit courts abolished, Stuart's appeal was heard by an appellate panel consisting of a federal district judge and Chief Justice Marshall, who was riding circuit pursuant to the Judiciary Act of 1802.[12] The appellate tribunal ruled against Stuart, who appealed to the Supreme Court. Stuart's appeal made two constitutional claims: first, that the repeal of the 1801 act was unconstitutional because it deprived sitting circuit court judges of their positions, in violation of the life tenure provisions of Article III of the Constitution; and second, that the 1802 Act requiring the Supreme Court justices to ride circuit was unconstitutional because the justices did not hold commissions to sit as circuit judges, only as members of the Supreme Court.[13]

Stuart raised critical questions about the independence of the federal judiciary, in particular the power of Congress to create and abolish federal courts. As Sanford Levinson and Jack Balkin described it, "In terms of its viability as an institution, what the Supreme Court did in *Stuart* was every bit as important as what it did in *Marbury*, and probably more so."[14] Nevertheless, Chief Justice Marshall recused himself from the case. His official reason was that he had been part of the panel that had heard the appeal in the case below.[15] The chief justice was also deeply concerned that such a politically heated case "threatened to upend the nonpartisan stance the justices had adopted and, with it, the Supreme Court's legitimacy as the nation's highest tribunal."[16] Neither of these reasons, however, created a legal obligation for the chief justice to recuse himself. It was common at the time for Supreme Court justices to review cases that they had decided while riding circuit, and political ideology, even if openly acknowledged, was not yet a legal criterion for recusal of any federal judge, let alone a Supreme Court justice.[17] Chief Justice Marshall removed himself from a case that was critically important for the integrity and institutional viability of the Supreme Court even though the legal standards of the day did not require it. His decision reflected a broader understanding of recusal, more akin to Bracton's emphasis on suspicion than that articulated by either federal statute or Blackstone.

Chief Justice Marshall's views on recusal are also evident in *Martin v. Hunter's Lessee.*[18] *Martin* involved a dispute over a parcel of land in Virginia. The land had originally been granted by King Charles II and King James II of England to Lord Fairfax, who in turn bequeathed it to a nephew, Denny Martin. During the Revolutionary War, Virginia seized the land from Lord Fairfax and granted a portion of it to David Hunter, a citizen of Virginia. Hunter leased the property, and his lessee sued to eject Martin from the land. Martin objected on the grounds that a treaty between the new United States and England protected English loyalists' pre-Revolutionary claims to land in the United States. The primary issue before the Court was whether the U.S. Supreme Court had authority to review decisions of state supreme courts, like the Virginia Court of Appeals, which had awarded the land to Hunter's lessee in apparent violation of the applicable treaty.

Like *Marbury* and *Stuart*, *Martin* involved new and complex constitutional questions. It also raised a recusal issue for the chief justice. After the Revolutionary War, Chief Justice Marshall represented Lord Fairfax's heirs in their quest to regain title to the lands that had been confiscated by Virginia during the war.[19] In 1793, John Marshall and his brother James contracted to purchase 215,000 acres of those lands from Denny Martin. The sale was conditioned on Denny Martin receiving valid title to the land.[20] The question of Martin's title came before the Court in *Martin* and its predecessor case, *Fairfax's Devisee v. Hunter's Lessee.*[21] Chief Justice Marshall recused himself from both cases, but he did not formally explain his decision. His recusal was consistent with the common law standard that a judge should not participate in a case in which he has a financial interest, but it is not clear precisely why the chief justice decided to remove himself from the case. Is it a mere coincidence that he recused himself when the common law would have required it, or did he objectively apply the relevant legal standard to his own case? Could it be a combination of the two, where Marshall treated the common law requirement as a relevant, but not dispositive, factor in favor of his own recusal? We will likely never know for certain, but his ultimate decision does provide us with some valuable insight into the early Court's views on recusal.

Taken together, Chief Justice Marshall's recusal decisions in *Marbury*, *Stuart*, and *Martin* represent a snapshot of the ambiguity surrounding recusal at the Supreme Court. In *Marbury*, Marshall did not recuse himself despite his significant personal experience with the case prior to its arrival at the Court. Marshall was the secretary of state responsible for delivering Marbury's commission *at the same time* he was serving as chief justice.[22] This created a potentially powerful conflict of interest in the case and at minimum justified public suspicion about the chief justice's impartiality.[23] As a legal matter, however, there were no statutory requirements for Supreme Court recusal at the time (the federal recusal law did not include members of the Court), and the common law of recusal required removal only when a judge or justice had a direct financial interest in the case. Because Chief Justice Marshall had no financial interest in *Marbury*, his decision technically conformed with the prevailing legal standards, even if it raised obvious concerns about his fitness to preside over the case.[24] On a technical reading, then, *Marbury* does not seem to breed any uncertainty about recusal at the Court. In fact, the opposite appears true. Marshall's choice not to recuse when the law did not require him to looks like a straightforward legal analysis, made even easier by the fact that the case at hand was of high national importance and the jurist in question was the chief justice.

Yet as tempting as it is to see *Marbury* as simply the product of a conservative recusal standard, Marshall's decision to recuse in *Stuart* indicates that it is likely more than that. In *Stuart*, the chief justice recused himself despite the fact that it would have been neither legally required—there is no evidence that Marshall had any financial interest in the matter—nor particularly controversial for him to participate in the case under the judicial norms in place at the time of his decision.[25] In other words, he reached the opposite conclusion from *Marbury* without any clear legal basis for doing so. *Marbury* and *Stuart* thus make the chief justice's recusal analyses appear more like the sort of highly contextualized determinations that appear in the modern Court's due process jurisprudence than straightforward applications of black letter recusal law.[26] If Marshall was merely applying the common law standards in force at the time of his decision, he would have participated in *Stuart*. If he was applying an alternative, Bractonian view of recusal based on a broad definition of judicial suspicion, he almost certainly would have recused himself in *Marbury*. Finally, if he was opposed to recusal in important cases, he would not have removed himself from either *Stuart* or *Martin*.

The preceding examples are not offered to explain what drove Chief Justice Marshall to his decisions in any of the three cases, nor are they offered to endorse or criticize a particular outcome. The very fact that he employed contrasting approaches to recusal demonstrates the ultimate point of this chapter and the catalyst for the constitutional analyses that follow. In two of the cases, the chief justice reached different recusal decisions independent of the prevailing law. He was permitted to recuse himself in *Marbury* even though the common law did not require it, and he would have been permitted to sit in *Stuart* without violating the same common law standard. In *Martin*, he either applied the relevant legal standard or exercised his own discretion in favor of recusal. The variability in his decisions reflects the variability at play throughout the history of Supreme Court recusal. Since the Court's earliest days, the justices have found themselves in situations similar to those faced by Chief Justice Marshall, and their decisions have reflected a similar ambiguity in the prevailing standards for recusal at the Court.

A Tradition of Controversy at the Court

The difficult recusal questions faced by Chief Justice Marshall have remained a consistent feature of life on the Court. Although the justices do frequently recuse themselves, often for the same financial reasons articulated in Blackstone's common law standard, they also have a long history of highly controversial conduct and decisions related to recusal.[27] The fact that these events remain controversial decades later demonstrates the powerful impact of judicial recusal on the public perception and legitimacy of the Court. It also offers a foundation for the justices' modern view of their recusal obligations, which is critical to understanding the constitutional issues at stake in Supreme Court recusal.

Many of our most revered justices have found themselves confronted with questions analogous to those addressed by Chief Justice Marshall in *Marbury*, *Stuart*, and *Martin*. As in *Marbury*, justices have become intertwined with presidents and politics in ways that have drawn their impartiality into question. Not long after the Civil War, Justice Joseph Bradley was accused of "trading" his vote in the controversial *Legal Tender Cases* for his appointment to the Court by President Ulysses S. Grant.[28] The *Legal Tender Cases* were decided a year after Justice Bradley joined the Court and reversed the Court's previous ruling in *Hepburn v. Griswold* that only paper money that was secured by gold could be used to repay Civil War debts.[29] To the extent Justice Bradley in fact prioritized the policy preferences of the president over his independent legal judgment, and especially if he did so in exchange for a presidential appointment, his conduct raises grave questions about whether recusal, or even more severe sanctions, was warranted. Justice Bradley also drew negative attention for sitting on the Electoral Commission created to settle the disputed presidential election of 1876 between Republican Rutherford B. Hayes and Democrat Samuel J. Tilden.[30] The commission was created by Congress and was not a purely judicial entity—it consisted of five members each from the House and Senate, along with five members of the Supreme Court. It was responsible for resolving election disputes in four states with enough collective electoral votes to decide the election. Justice Bradley's vote for every contested Republican elector played a significant role in helping President Hayes secure victory and again created the untenable impression of a justice stepping outside the bounds of his judicial duties and allowing his political preferences to impact the affairs of the other branches.[31]

Almost a century later, then-representative Gerald R. Ford initiated impeachment proceedings against Justice William O. Douglas. The proceedings raised several issues regarding Justice Douglas's service and were ultimately closed without a vote. One of the points of contention in the final report of the subcommittee investigating Justice Douglas was his failure to recuse from cases relating to the war in Vietnam. Justice Douglas was an outspoken opponent of the war and issued several rulings (many of which were overturned by his colleagues) frustrating the war effort.[32] In light of the justice's record, Representative F. Edward Hébert sent multiple letters to members of the Court and the solicitor general requesting that they take the admittedly unprecedented step of involuntarily disqualifying a sitting justice from an upcoming case. The case, *United States v. Sisson*,[33] presented the question of whether the Constitution protected nonreligious conscientious objectors from prosecution under the Military Selective Service Act of 1967. Writing to Chief Justice Warren Burger, Representative Hébert called Justice Douglas's participation in cases involving the war effort "a mockery of justice because he has preconceived ideas on the subject and has repeatedly placed himself in the position of ignoring recognized Supreme Court practices."[34] In a letter to the solicitor general a month later, Representative Hébert stated that Justice Douglas "is morally and ethically unfit to sit on this crucial case" because he "has long been openly and vindictively opposed to the Vietnam war, the draft, and the so-called 'military industrial complex.'"[35] Representative Hébert's pleas were refused, but his letters appeared in the final report of the subcommittee investigating Justice Douglas, indicating that the justice's personal ideological biases were of sufficient interest to capture the subcommittee's attention.

Several justices have been scrutinized for their close personal relationships with sitting presidents. Of course, friendship alone between a president and a Supreme Court justice is neither uncommon nor necessarily grounds for concern. After all, the president is singularly responsible for nominating the justices. It stands to reason that presidents would have some affinity for their nominees, and that this affinity could naturally lead to additional interactions between them after a justice takes the bench. John Frank estimated in 1970 that "at least twenty-five percent of the Justices have at some time advised" the president after their appointment.[36] Controversy emerges, however, when personal friendship leads to collaboration between a president and a justice that threatens to run afoul of our ethical and constitutional expectations for the judiciary.

Two early examples of justices with close enough personal ties to sitting presidents to evoke controversy were Justice Samuel Chase, who was appointed by President George Washington at the end of his second term in 1796, and Justice William Johnson, President Jefferson's first appointee to the Court. Justice Chase actively participated in John Adams's campaign for president, which was seen as a significant enough dereliction of his judicial responsibilities to at least contribute to his impeachment by the House of Representatives (he was acquitted by the Senate).[37] Justice Johnson regularly engaged in lengthy correspondence with President Jefferson about matters relating to the Court, and he even authored legislation while a sitting justice, seemingly crossing the line between the judicial power assigned to federal judges and the policy-making authority granted to Congress and the president.[38]

More than a century later, Justice Louis Brandeis advised President Woodrow Wilson on a variety of matters while a member of the Court, but he made the formalistic distinction of refusing to do so in the White

House unless expressly invited by the president.[39] Chief Justice William Howard Taft was renowned for serving as an adviser to several presidents while on the bench, and Justice Harlan Fiske Stone was a close confidant and member of President Herbert Hoover's "Medicine Ball Cabinet" who "frequently responded to the President's requests for comment on drafts of speeches and executive messages."[40]

During the New Deal, Justice Felix Frankfurter enjoyed a very close and well-known relationship with President Franklin Roosevelt. Prior to joining the bench, he advised the president on major pieces of legislation and recommended many of the talented new public servants who would help to drive the engine of the New Deal. While Frankfurter was a member of the Court, however, his interest and perceived influence in the other branches of government appeared more controversial. He participated in a case interpreting the scope of the Norris-LaGuardia Act, despite playing "an important, perhaps dominant, part in [its] drafting."[41] He also engaged in frequent discussions with his former law clerk Philip Elman, then assistant solicitor general for civil rights cases in the Department of Justice. Justice Frankfurter shared information about internal Court deliberations and attitudes regarding segregation in an attempt to help the government devise a more successful desegregation strategy leading up to its landmark decision in *Brown v. Board of Education*.[42] Justice Frankfurter's willingness to seek social and political change outside the bounds of his judicial position raised some of the same questions that recusal seeks to address, namely, whether a judge or justice is able to treat a litigant fairly and impartially, and whether the Court retains its legitimizing status as the sole entity in our constitutional system that operates independent of the political process.

Chief Justice Fred Vinson's close personal relationship with President Harry Truman was also suspected of leading to some questionable interactions between the two leaders of their respective branches. The chief justice and president became friends "shortly after Truman assumed the presidency."[43] Their relationship grew to the point that "Truman included Vinson in almost every conference because he 'valued his judgment and advice highly.'"[44] President Truman appointed Vinson to his cabinet as treasury secretary in 1945 and then to be chief justice of the United States in 1946.[45] While on the Court, Chief Justice Vinson is reported to have advised President Truman on a wide variety of matters, including Truman's choice of his vice presidential running mate in 1948. The most controversial guidance from the chief justice was his alleged advice about the constitutionality of the president's decision to seize steel mills prior to the Court's decision in the landmark case addressing that issue, *Youngstown Sheet & Tube Company v. Sawyer.*[46] There is no direct evidence that the chief justice and president discussed the case in advance of the Court's decision—something that would have been highly irregular even under the more interactive standards of the day—but two of Chief Justice Vinson's law clerks suggested that such a conversation had occurred, and at least one chronicler has made the same (albeit disputed) claim.[47]

Similar issues arose several decades later due to Justice Abe Fortas's relationship with President Johnson. The two met when Fortas was working in President Franklin Roosevelt's Department of the Interior and Johnson was a relatively new congressman from Texas. They became close friends when Fortas represented Johnson in an appeal before the Supreme Court. The appeal involved an election dispute in the Democratic primary for a U.S. Senate seat from Texas. Representative Johnson and his opponent, ex-governor Coke Stevenson, were embroiled in an exceedingly close runoff election. When Johnson was named the winner by a margin of only eighty-seven votes (out of nearly a million cast), a contentious legal battle ensued over allegations of ballot stuffing and other improprieties. The case went all the way to the Supreme Court, where Fortas successfully represented Johnson and cleared the way for Johnson's successful ascension to a seat in the U.S. Senate, a key position on his way to the presidency.[48] Johnson developed a deep respect and affection for Fortas as a result of their work together, and the two became close friends. Seventeen years after winning his Senate seat, President Johnson appointed Fortas to the Supreme Court.[49] While on the Court, Johnson continued to seek Fortas's counsel frequently and on a wide range of executive decisions, including military and diplomatic issues, questions of race relations, the drafting of executive orders and presidential speeches, and Johnson's reelection campaign.[50] As the president was struggling with how to manage anti–Vietnam War protests around the country, Fortas published a pamphlet critical of those protests.[51] As Henry J. Abraham noted in his book *Justices, Presidents, and Senators,* while Fortas was certainly not the first Supreme Court justice to have a close relationship with a sitting president, that fact "does not gainsay the compromising of separation of powers attending such practices."[52] To that point, when the president appointed Fortas to succeed Earl Warren as chief justice in 1968, the closeness of their relationship became an important, albeit not dispositive, reason why the nomination ultimately failed and why Justice Fortas was ultimately forced to resign from the Court.

If *Marbury* was the first in a long line of controversies involving Supreme Court justices and their relationships with presidents, Chief Justice Marshall's experience in *Martin* foreshadowed controversies over various justices' participation in cases involving a former client or associate.[53] In arguably the most public ethical controversy ever to confront the Court, Justice Robert Jackson publicly questioned the decision of his colleague Justice Hugo Black to sit in a case in which one of the parties was represented by Black's former law partner. *Jewell Ridge Coal Corporation v. United Mine Workers of America* asked whether the "underground travel time" required for bituminous coal miners to get to the "working faces" of the mines constituted compensable work under the Fair Labor Standards Act.[54] Justice Black joined a narrow majority of the Court in voting that it did, and the losing party petitioned for a rehearing on the basis that Crampton Harris, a former law partner of Justice Black's, represented the victorious United Mine Workers before the Court. The Court denied the motion in a per curiam (anonymous) opinion, but Justice Jackson filed a concurrence in which he intimated that his reason for voting against rehearing was not because he thought it was unnecessary but because it would be fruitless. Because no member of the majority, according to Justice Jackson, was likely to "reconsider his position," Justice Jackson and the other dissenting justices in the case had "no voice as to rehearing, except [to] continue to adhere to the dissent."[55] This comment sparked controversy because it quite clearly implied—to Justice Black and others—that Justice Jackson thought Justice Black should have recused himself from the case. Justice Jackson would later explain in a public cable to members of the House and Senate Judiciary Committees that his real issue with Justice Black's participation in *Jewell Ridge* was the fact that Justice Black had apparently encouraged his colleagues in the majority to engage in the highly unusual practice of issuing their decision in the case "'without waiting for the opinion and dissent.'"[56] The only reason for this attempt to bypass normal Court procedure was, in Justice Jackson's view, to provide the United Mine Workers with an additional bargaining chip in their ongoing, yet stagnant, negotiations with mine operators.[57] The *Jewell Ridge* incident was far more damaging to the reputation of the individual justices involved (especially Justice Jackson) than to the public's long-term confidence in the Court's decision, but it did draw a lot of public attention and created a significant level of concern among the justices about its effect on the integrity of the Court as a whole.

Finally, like Chief Justice Marshall in *Stuart*, justices who have served as judges in other courts or as legislators found themselves confronted with cases involving issues that were not only familiar but also potentially personal. Justice Oliver Wendell Holmes sat on several cases for the Court that were appealed from decisions he had participated in while a justice on Massachusetts's Supreme Judicial Court.[58] Justice Black and Chief Justice Vinson both helped decide cases for the Court that involved statutes they had taken lead roles in passing as legislators. Justice Black participated in cases, like *Jewell Ridge*, that considered various aspects of the Fair Labor Standards Act, including the act's constitutionality,[59] despite the fact that he was the act's principal architect in the Senate. Chief Justice Vinson did not hesitate to sit on cases involving tax legislation that he "had been active in drafting and preparing . . . while a member of the House of Representatives."[60] Justice George Sutherland wrote an important opinion limiting the president's constitutional removal power despite having voted for the law under review while a senator.[61] Although not a member of Congress at the time, Chief Justice Burger engaged in "'vigorous and open lobbying for particular Bankruptcy Act amendments'" while on the Court and then dissented from a decision of the Court finding the Bankruptcy Act of 1978 unconstitutional.[62]

This consistent legacy of justices facing difficult questions about their impartiality reinforces the modern relevance of Supreme Court recusal. As federal recusal law evolved, the Court encountered another layer of concern about its recusal practices. They not only were potentially unethical or inappropriate but were arguably illegal. Before the 1974 amendments to the federal recusal statute, recusal at the Court was governed by very limited standards ranging from Blackstone's focus on financial interest to a lenient and highly subjective statutory mandate.[63] During this period, seemingly controversial decisions by the justices could almost always be justified by their technical compliance with the relevant law. Much as Chief Justice Marshall could claim that his decisions in *Marbury*, *Stuart*, and *Martin* were all permitted by the standards of his day, so too could Justice Black or Chief Justice Vinson justify their participation in cases involving legislation they drafted while members of Congress by relying on a recusal statute that depended on their own subjective opinion of their fitness to serve.[64]

The 1974 amendments to the federal recusal statute made the requirements for Supreme Court recusal more stringent by adding another dimension to recusal at the Court. Rather than merely arguing about whether their decisions were ethically sound, the justices faced criticism that they were acting unlawfully by failing to recuse. The adoption of tougher statutory recusal standards was thus a catalyst for the constitutional debate about who decides questions of Supreme Court recusal. Congress's position was clear. The plain language of the statute required recusal without exception whenever certain elements were met. The justices' position was more complicated. As Congress and the country moved toward more restrictive recusal requirements, the justices continued to pursue a more wide-ranging, contextual approach that was not always easy to reconcile with the statute's demands.

The Court's Modern Approach to Recusal

For roughly two decades after the 1974 amendments to section 455, the Court made no public statements regarding its views on recusal. A prominent example within the Court, however, revealed the full range of issues impacting the justices' recusal decisions. Justice Thurgood Marshall was confirmed to the Court in October 1967, after serving for four years as a judge on the U.S. Court of Appeals for the Second Circuit and for two years as solicitor general. Prior to his appointment to the Second Circuit, Justice Marshall spent twenty-five years in a variety of prominent roles with the National Association for the Advancement of Colored People (NAACP) and the NAACP Legal Defense and Educational Fund (LDF), which he founded in 1940.[65] In his roles with these organizations, Marshall won some of the most significant Supreme Court cases in American constitutional history, including perhaps the most famous, *Brown v. Board of Education*.[66] After he ascended to the Court, Justice Marshall voluntarily adopted a general policy of recusing himself from cases in which the NAACP or LDF was a party or intervenor. In 1984, more than twenty years after leaving the NAACP and seventeen years after joining the Court, Justice Marshall circulated a confidential memo to his colleagues in which he made the case that continuing with his blanket recusal policy was no longer necessary.[67]

Justice Marshall's decision to stop uniformly recusing himself from NAACP cases is not nearly as important to the present discussion as the reasoning he offered in support of it. Justice Marshall referred to "the statutory rules and ethical canons on judicial disqualification" and, in the last paragraph of the memo, to section 455 itself,[68] but his rationale for participating in future NAACP cases went beyond a straightforward interpretation of those provisions. It included analogies to the choices of former justices, many if not all of whom made their decisions before section 455 was amended to apply to them, and relied on arguments from common sense and prestatutory understandings of whether recusal is required when a former law partner appears before a judge. Finally, the memo was confidential, subject only to the review of his fellow justices. Justice Marshall felt no need, even in the face of a duly enacted statute, to treat his decision in the same publicly accountable way that the Court treats its other conclusions of law.

This is not meant to cast aspersions on Justice Marshall's decision or the way in which it was reached and announced. It had been twenty years since his last affiliation with the NAACP. All eight of his fellow justices appeared to concur that blanket recusal was no longer necessary, and none of them suggested that he should make his decision, or his reasons for it, public.[69] Justice Marshall's memo is relevant because it demonstrates that, even after section 455 was amended to include the Supreme Court, the justices' approach to recusal continued to be informed by factors beyond those typically associated with statutory interpretation.

The Court confirmed that section 455 has little, if any, real effect on its recusal practices in its 1993 Statement of Recusal Policy, its first public statement regarding recusal since the 1974 amendments to section 455. The Recusal Policy was signed by seven of the nine sitting justices. It explained that since the justices "have spouses, children or other relatives within the degree of relationship covered by [section 455] who are or may become practicing attorneys," it would be prudent for them to articulate their approach to recusal in cases where those relatives appear as counsel before the Court.[70] The justices were building on an earlier statement by Chief Justice Rehnquist that recusal is not required when a justice's relative is an associate at a law firm that is appearing before the Court but the relative did not participate personally in the case.[71] The justices went on to discuss what their policy would be in "additional situations," namely, where a justice's relative participated in the case below or is a partner in the firm appearing before the Court. They concluded that section 455's reference to relatives serving as counsel did not automatically apply to either of those situations, but that the justices would recuse, in the interest of caution, when a relative served as lead counsel in the case below or was a partner in the firm appearing before the Court.[72]

As with Justice Marshall's memorandum, the substantive positions in the Court's Recusal Policy are of limited interest here. Precisely when the justices believe they must recuse themselves tells us little about why they feel compelled to do so. What matters presently is how the Court approached the recusal issue. It did not approach it like a strict question of statutory interpretation. It relied on policy arguments wholly unrelated to the statutory language, such as the need to protect "the public interest" by preventing recusal from "impair[ing] the functioning of the Court."[73] It cited concerns about litigants "'strategizing' recusals" by hiring law firms that would trigger recusal for unsympathetic justices, and about recusals leading to tie votes in cases due to the lack of replacement justices.[74] Whether or not these arguments seem compelling, they are not rooted in a statutory analysis of section 455. They reflect the Court's consistent focus on institutional mission and effectiveness in its recusal decisions, often at the expense of statutory mandates. As Sherrilyn Ifill described it, "The Recusal Policy simply reflects the Justices' own sense of what to them would constitute a reasonable basis upon which to question a judge's impartiality."[75]

Chief Justice Rehnquist and Justice Antonin Scalia took a similar approach in individual statements about recusal at the Court. In 2000, Chief Justice Rehnquist followed his memorandum in *Tatum* with a second memo explaining his decision not to recuse in *Microsoft Corporation v. United States*.[76] Microsoft, a party to an antitrust suit before the Court, was represented in a different antitrust suit by a firm in which the chief justice's son was a partner. In considering whether to recuse himself on those grounds, the chief justice cited the relevant provisions of section 455, including the reasonable appearance standard. He concluded that there was no reasonable appearance of partiality because his son's "personal and financial concerns will not be affected" by the outcome of the case.[77] Recusal was not necessary, he reasoned, simply because the Court's decision could affect the outcome in other antitrust cases in which his son may be representing Microsoft. The chief justice closed with prudential reasons for not requiring recusal of a Supreme Court justice, such as the inability to replace a justice once she is recused and the potential for an equally divided Court.[78]

Justice Scalia issued perhaps the most famous recusal memo by a sitting justice four years later in *Cheney v. United States District Court*.[79] Justice Scalia was asked to recuse himself from the case because he had recently been on a hunting trip with Vice President Dick Cheney, a named party in the suit. In explaining his decision not to recuse, Justice Scalia relied almost exclusively on institutional reasons. He rejected the suggestion that he should "'resolve any doubts in favor of recusal'" because the "Supreme Court . . . is different."[80] He pointed to the lack of substitutes for recused justices and the potential problem of a "tie vote, [leaving the Court] unable to resolve the significant legal issue presented by the case."[81] He described recusal as "effectively the same as casting a vote against the petitioner"[82] and cited two prior recusal decisions by other justices—one of which occurred before section 455's reasonable appearance standard was even codified—as support for the proposition that no reasonable observer could question his impartiality.[83] He concluded by warning that his recusal would further "harm the Court" by effectively "giv[ing] elements of the press a veto over participation of any Justices who had social contacts with . . . a named official"[84] and by encouraging "so-called investigative journalists to suggest improprieties, and demand recusals."[85] Any question about the strength of Justice Scalia's convictions in *Cheney* were answered seven years later when, in a 2013 interview with *New York Magazine*, he responded to a question about his most "heroic" opinion for the Court by saying that his memorandum in *Cheney* was "the most heroic opinion—maybe the *only* heroic opinion I ever issued."[86]

Key members of Congress disagreed. During the *Cheney* controversy, Senators Patrick Leahy and Joseph Lieberman sent a letter to Chief Justice Rehnquist arguing that Justice Scalia should recuse himself from the case.[87] Citing section 455, the letter suggested that a reasonable person would "question" the impartiality of a judge who recently went on vacation with a litigant and reminded the chief justice that the statutory recusal standard is neither subjective nor dependent on the existence of actual bias.[88] In addition to relying on the statutory text, the letter reiterated section 455's institutional purpose to prevent even an appearance of judicial partiality, which it called a "threat to public confidence in our federal courts."[89] In closing, the senators shifted their inquiry to procedural questions. They asked what "canons, procedures and rules are in place" to guide the justices' recusal decisions, including "mechanisms . . . for obtaining advisory opinions" from the other justices and for the Court to disqualify one of its members, either on its own initiative or through reviewing an individual justice's decision not to recuse.[90]

Chief Justice Rehnquist responded four days later. He explained that each justice "strives" to comply with the requirements of section 455.[91] He also explained that, although justices often consult with one another on recusal matters, there is no formal procedure for the full Court to review an individual justice's recusal decision because "it has long been settled that each Justice must decide such a question for himself."[92] Perhaps most important, he defended Justice Scalia's decision in *Cheney* on the grounds that there is "no precedent" for recusal in such a case and that "any suggestion by you [Senator Leahy] or Senator Lieberman as to why a Justice should recuse himself in a pending case is ill considered."[93] The chief justice was not completely obstinate, however. On May 24, 2004, a few months after *Cheney*, Chief Justice Rehnquist appointed the Judicial Conduct and Disability Act Study Committee to "evaluate how the federal judicial system is dealing with judicial misbehavior and disability."[94] The committee became known as the Breyer Committee because Justice Stephen Breyer was the lone Supreme Court justice among the six committee members (the others were four federal judges and Chief Justice Rehnquist's chief administrative assistant).[95] The Breyer Committee published its report in 2006. Despite the fact that it was motivated by a dispute about Supreme Court recusal, the committee's report surprisingly declined to mention the justices' recusal practices.

The events around *Microsoft* and *Cheney* are a telling portrayal of the Supreme Court's attitudes about recusal in general and, more directly, about the power of Congress to influence the justices' recusal decisions. Chief Justice Rehnquist's and Justice Scalia's decisions did not depend on a rigorous analysis of section 455. They referenced the statute but employed few if any of the traditional tools of statutory interpretation in reaching their conclusions. They did not parse the statutory text, nor did they mention congressional intent, legislative history, or lower court interpretations of the statute. They instead relied heavily on institutional rationales and analogies to other justices' recusal decisions, regardless of whether they were made under the same statutory regime. Under normal circumstances of statutory interpretation—especially in the hands of Justice Scalia—the policy ramifications of a statute would be left to the legislature, and any negative consequences would be grounds for legislative amendment, not for judicial override.[96] The fact that this was not the case in *Microsoft* or *Cheney* demonstrates that recusal is not, at least in the eyes of these two justices, a normal circumstance. Faced with a validly enacted, mandatory recusal statute, both Chief Justice Rehnquist and Justice Scalia acted like judges faced more with a novel constitutional question than with one of statutory interpretation.

Chief Justice Rehnquist's rebuke of Senators Leahy and Lieberman's letter regarding *Cheney* reinforces this conclusion. The chief justice held his ground in the face of a direct request from high-ranking members of a coequal branch of government. He acknowledged the relevance of section 455 but did not concede that the justices were bound by it. "Striving" to comply with a statute is very different from being compelled to abide by it, and the difference was not likely lost on the chief justice. He also relied on an argument from precedent in supporting Justice Scalia's decision. This was telling because the use of precedent in Supreme Court recusal cases is often exclusive of statutory interpretation. First, there is very little of it. Justices almost never give reasons for their recusal decisions, so they must rely on a lack of precedent rather than on cases that affirmatively support a particular conclusion. Without prior cases to analogize to, a lawyer looking for a statutory answer would inevitably apply the language of the statute directly to the facts at hand. Relying on a lack of supporting precedent to make a decision, as the chief justice did, omits the critical step of independently applying the statutory recusal standard. The chief justice never did this because he was not, at the end of the day, performing a statutory analysis. Second, even when recusal precedents do exist for Supreme Court justices, they are very likely to be inapplicable because most of the available cases predate the current recusal standard. At the time of his response to the senators' letter, the only public explanation of a justice's recusal decision under the current version of section 455 was Chief Justice Rehnquist's own memo in *Microsoft*,[97] which involved a very different situation than the one facing Justice Scalia in *Cheney*. The scarcity of cases applying section 455 to members of the Court led the chief justice to rely on distinguishable precedents from other statutory or common law regimes.[98] His willingness to do so shows that the chief justice did not feel as if his or his colleagues' decisions were closely constrained by the federal recusal statute.

Recusal remained in the news after Justice Scalia's decision in *Cheney*, but the focus shifted from the justices' recusal practices to the relationship between recusal and the financing of state judicial elections.[99] Supreme Court recusal returned to the spotlight in 2011, fueled by the Court's pending review of the Affordable Care Act (ACA),[100] the sweeping health care reform signed into law by President Barack Obama in March 2010.[101] The case, which came to the Court as *National Federation of Independent Business (NFIB) v. Sebelius*,[102] was legally and politically divisive from the start, including with respect to recusal. Proponents of the ACA, including seventy-four congressional Democrats, called for Justice Clarence Thomas to recuse himself because his wife, Virginia Thomas, had allegedly received nearly $700,000 from the conservative Heritage Foundation as a direct result of her work in opposition to the act.[103] On the other side of the aisle, opponents of the ACA clamored for the recusal of newly appointed Justice Elena Kagan due to her service as solicitor general during the ACA's enactment. Senator Orrin Hatch stated publicly that Justice Kagan should recuse herself from any cases reviewing the ACA because "Kagan participated in discussions about the law and challenges to it while she served in the Justice Department as [solicitor general]."[104] Neither justice addressed the issue publicly, and they did not recuse themselves from the case, but the controversy served as a catalyst for what has proved to be a persistent national discussion about recusal at the Court.

The press responded to the controversy in *NFIB* with dozens of articles, opinion columns, and legal commentaries relating to Supreme Court ethics and recusal.[105] Six of the nine sitting justices—Justices Alito, Breyer, Ginsburg, Scalia, Sotomayor, and Thomas—were publicly criticized for their interactions with politically interested entities that either had been or were likely to come before the Court. Justices Scalia and Thomas were criticized for attending dinners sponsored by the conservative Koch brothers,[106] and Justice Thomas was chastised for his relationship with a wealthy conservative contributor who allegedly provided funding for projects of interest to the justice and his wife.[107] Justice Samuel Alito drew scrutiny for his attendance at fund-raising dinners for the conservative *American Spectator* magazine,[108] and Justices Breyer, Ruth Bader Ginsburg, and Sonia Sotomayor were singled out for having accepted paid trips from organizations with perceived political viewpoints.[109]

At the same time, Congress was working toward legislative reform of Supreme Court ethics and recusal. In March 2011, the House of Representatives introduced H.R. 862, also known as the Supreme Court

Transparency and Disclosure Act of 2011.[110] The act was inspired by a letter from 132 law professors to the House and Senate Judiciary Committees outlining the need for legislation to "protect the integrity of the Supreme Court."[111] It sought to make the Code of Conduct for United States Judges applicable to the justices and to establish formal procedures for the justices' recusal decisions. It required the justices to disclose "in the public record of the proceeding the reasons for the denial of [a recusal] motion" and established "a process under which . . . other justices or judges of a court of the United States" shall review a Supreme Court justice's denial of a recusal motion.[112]

Potential constitutional problems with the act aside, it did not appear to change the Court's view of recusal. The justices remained steadfast in their commitment to handling recusal matters internally and on their own terms. A little more than a month after H.R. 862 was introduced, Justices Breyer and Kennedy were called to testify before a House subcommittee regarding the Court's annual budget request and the status of ongoing updates to the courthouse.[113] During the hearing, they were asked about H.R. 862's attempt to apply the Code of Conduct to the Supreme Court.[114] Justice Kennedy explained that the justices effectively abide by the code in practice, and Justice Breyer concurred, noting that he consults the same ethics rules as other federal judges when faced with a difficult issue. Both justices rejected the idea, however, that the code should be legally binding on members of the Court. Justice Kennedy noted a potential "constitutional problem" in treating the code as binding because it is adopted by a conference of lower court judges.[115] More specifically, he explained that it would be "'structurally unprecedented for district and circuit court judges to make rules that Supreme Court judges have to follow.'"[116] Justice Breyer cited the complexity and uniqueness of Supreme Court recusal decisions—particularly the fact that recused Supreme Court justices cannot be replaced—as a reason for treating them differently than those of lower court judges.[117]

Six months later Justice Breyer was again before Congress, this time with Justice Scalia, to testify before the Senate Committee on the Judiciary.[118] The hearing was about the role of the judiciary in our constitutional system and included a short exchange between Senator Dick Durbin, Senator Leahy, and the justices about recusal at the Court. Justice Breyer responded to a general inquiry from Senator Durbin about judicial ethics by reiterating that the Court feels bound by the relevant ethical standards and that he and his colleagues on the Court consult a variety of sources in making their ethical determinations. Although he at one point described statutory ethical standards as binding the Court, he went on to explain that in deciding ethical issues he does not focus on the distinction between binding and nonbinding legal sources.[119] He then returned to the familiar territory of distinguishing the Supreme Court from the lower federal courts. He reminded Senator Durbin that because there are no available replacements for a recused justice, one justice's decision to recuse "could change the result" in that case, either by removing an influential vote from the process or by encouraging parties to "choose your panel."[120] As a result, Justice Breyer testified, members of the Court have "an obligation to sit . . . as well as an obligation to recuse," and the decision must be made by the individual justice.[121] When asked by Senator Leahy if retired justices could be used to replace recused ones, Justice Scalia objected on practical grounds, citing the difficulty in choosing a replacement and ultimately suggesting that the Court should just "stumble along the way we are."[122]

Chief Justice John Roberts offered his views on recusal at the Court in his 2011 Year-End Report on the Federal Judiciary. The Year-End Report is an annual public statement by the chief justice of the United States that typically includes some statistics from the previous year in the federal courts, as well as a discussion of whatever issues the chief justice wishes to address. Chief Justice Roberts chose to dedicate his entire Year-End Report in 2011 to Supreme Court ethics and recusal. In particular, he made the case for why the Code of Conduct for United States Judges should not bind the Court. He began by explaining that the Judicial Conference, the body that promulgated the Code of Conduct, was created by Congress specifically for the benefit of the lower federal courts, and as such "[the Judicial Conference's] committees have no mandate to prescribe rules or standards for any other body," including the Supreme Court.[123] He then addressed the specific question of how the Court should go about deciding recusal questions. He began by mentioning that the constitutionality of Congress seeking to regulate the Court's recusal practices remains an open question.[124] He went on to dispel the notion that the Court's recusal procedures are somehow lacking when compared with those of the lower federal courts. He pointed out that both lower court judges and Supreme Court justices make their own initial recusal decisions,[125] and that they rely on the same set of materials to do so, including "judicial opinions, treatises, scholarly articles, and disciplinary decisions."[126] He also noted that no court at any level of the federal judiciary reviews the recusal decisions of its own members.[127] This is especially important in the Supreme Court because it prevents the justices from affecting the outcome of a case through selective recusal. Selective recusal is not a threat in the lower courts because a recused judge may be replaced through the process of judicial assignment.[128]

The chief justice's perspective on recusal at the Court is consistent with that of his colleagues and predecessors. The justices continue to rely on long-standing historical practice for the proposition that they are entitled to make their own recusal decisions, and that those decisions are not reviewable by members of the same court. This latter point is controversial because, unlike in the lower courts, the justices' recusal decisions are not reviewable by anyone outside of the Court. Nevertheless, the Year-End Report maintained that the justices' recusal decisions are and should continue to be individual and unreviewable. It also reasserted the institutional point that recusal at the Court is materially different from that in the lower courts, even going so far as to build on Justice Breyer's Senate testimony by implying that the duty to sit may still apply in some instances:

> Although a Justice's process for considering recusal is similar to that of the lower court judges, the Justice must consider an important factor that is not present in the lower courts. Lower court judges can freely substitute for one another. . . . But the Supreme Court consists of nine Members who always sit together, and if a Justice withdraws from a case, the Court must sit without its full membership. A Justice accordingly cannot withdraw from a case as a matter of convenience or simply to avoid controversy. Rather, each Justice has an obligation to the Court to be sure of the need to recuse before deciding to withdraw from a case.[129]

The chief justice did not explicitly claim that the Court does not feel bound by the mandatory language of section 455 or any of the other relevant sources regarding recusal. But his rejection of recusal "simply to avoid controversy" and his reference to each justice's obligation to consider institutional factors in their recusal decisions suggests that members of the Court should be more reluctant to recuse than the reasonable appearance standard of section 455 may require.

The gravity of the chief justice's statements was not lost on Congress. Within two months of his Year-End Report, five senators sent the chief justice a letter requesting that the Court adopt a resolution "stating that Members of the Court abide by the Code of Conduct."[130] The chief justice responded four days later by stating that "for the reasons explained in my year-end report, the Court does not plan to adopt the Code of Conduct for United States Judges through a formal resolution."[131] Again, faced with direct inquiry from prominent members of the legislative branch, the Court remained committed to protecting its independence over recusal.

In 2015, Congress and the Court found themselves having the same conversation, and neither side had changed its tune. The House reintroduced the Supreme Court Ethics Act of 2013, which (again) sought to apply the Code of Conduct for United States Judges to the Court.[132] At an annual hearing to discuss the Supreme Court's budget, Justices Kennedy and Breyer were asked yet again about the Court's recusal practices, including the possibility of the Court formally adopting the Code of Conduct and making "recusal decisions by the justices more transparent for the public."[133] As they have throughout, the justices held fast. Justice Breyer repeated that the Court is different due to the lack of replacement justices. He reminded the senators that the Court's unique status imposes a duty on the justices to sit as well as to recuse, and that concerns about strategic recusals affect the Supreme Court differently than the lower courts.[134]

Justice Kennedy's response shed new light on the Court's approach to recusal. He explained that he thinks recusal decisions "should never be discussed," even with other members of the Court, because "that's almost like lobbying."[135] His answer echoed the statements of several of his colleagues, who have explained that they do not like to reveal the reasons for their recusal decisions because they do not want the other justices to feel pressure to recuse in the same situation.[136] This is a very powerful point. As the justices well know, reaching similar conclusions based on similar facts is the very essence of law. A statutory approach to recusal, particularly by a small, relatively static group of actors like the Supreme Court, would cause all of the justices to reach the same decision regarding recusal when faced with the same facts. By stating that they do not want to publish their reasons for fear of influencing their colleagues to follow their lead, the justices are effectively admitting either that they have no confidence in their decisions (which, based on their status and occupation, is highly unlikely) or that they do not feel closely bound by the applicable recusal statute.

The Court's resolve has not discouraged the public from continuing to focus on Supreme Court recusal, especially in high-profile cases. In 2014, Justice Ginsburg was criticized for her public comments on an abortion case that eventually came before the Court.[137] In anticipation of a Court decision on the constitutional status of same-sex marriage, both sides of the political aisle found grounds for recusal. Proponents of same-sex marriage called for Justice Scalia's recusal based on his apparent moral opposition to the idea and comments that have been described as disparaging homosexuals.[138] Opponents argued that Justices Kagan and Ginsburg were unfit to participate because they had officiated at same-sex weddings and, in Justice Ginsburg's case, commented publicly on the issue.[139] Even after *NFIB*, Supreme Court recusal has proved resilient in maintaining the public's attention. Based on this recent history, it is fair to say that recusal's relevance to American law and politics shows no sign of abating. It also shows few signs of generating any consensus about its proper scope and role at the Court. From scholarly panels to public calls for reform by leading academics to reporting on the justices' recusal practices in specific cases,[140] Supreme Court recusal appears to be permanently established as an issue of both public and legal consequence—and conflict.

The Interbranch Impasse over Supreme Court Recusal

The modern debate over recusal at the Supreme Court can be described in terms of two distinct viewpoints, both of which can be traced to different points in the history of American recusal law. The first is a reformist view. The overwhelming majority of commentary from legal academics, members of Congress, and journalists supports some measure of recusal reform for the Court. Proponents of reform express concern about the impact of the justices' recusal practices on the public perception of the Court and on the due process rights of individual litigants. They consistently call for more rigorous congressional regulation of Supreme Court recusal practice to protect the integrity and legitimacy of the Court.[141] The opposing view is focused on judicial independence. It is primarily represented—and increasingly put forth—by the justices themselves. It is grounded in concerns about constitutional structure and function, and thus centers on the unique role and nature of the Court within our constitutional system. The interaction of these differing perspectives has created not only a heated controversy but also a potential impasse in the conversation about recusal at the Court.

Reformists argue that the justices' failure to submit their decisions to more traditional legal processes has damaged the integrity and reputation of the Court. The fact that recusal decisions at the Court are not reviewable has raised concerns about the quality of those decisions, especially because recusal inquiries are fact-specific and depend on the justices to serve as both fact finders and adjudicators.[142] Advocates of recusal reform have suggested mandating review of an individual justice's decision not to recuse by the remainder of the Court or by a special committee of federal judges assembled specifically for that purpose. Jeffrey Stempel has proposed a standard of review—since echoed by other commentators—under which "any party aggrieved by the refusal of a Supreme Court Justice to disqualify himself may, on timely motion, obtain review by the full Supreme Court."[143] The proposed 2011 Supreme Court Transparency and Disclosure Act went further by allowing for review of a justice's decision not to recuse by "other justices or judges of a court of the United States, among whom retired justices and senior judges . . . may be included."[144]

The most compelling criticism of Supreme Court recusal practices involves the justices' reluctance to explain their decisions. The Court offers public explanations of most of its decisions as a means of remaining accountable and protecting its own legitimacy. The justices' general failure to explain their recusal decisions imperils that accountability and legitimacy, even more so because the practice is out of step with judicial behavior more broadly. This failure has been described as indefensible in a modern democratic society. In an age where other information about the justices' practices is so readily available, the relative dearth of information about the justices' recusal decisions has inspired calls for statutory requirements that they publish their reasons for denying a recusal motion.[145] Debra Lyn Bassett has advocated for greater disclosure of the justices' reasons for recusal through "statements of interest."[146] William Yeomans and Herman Schwartz have argued: "The courts' fundamental legitimacy rests on the notion that judges . . . explain what they have done in reasoned opinions for all to read. . . . This same transparency is even more essential when justices apply the law to themselves. . . . Courts obviously need secrecy for their deliberations and decision making. But there can be no harm in a justice explaining why he or she withdraws from a case or refuses to withdraw."[147]

Finally, the preceding complaints evoke a common concern about the effects of the justices' recusal practices on public perception of, and confidence in, the Court. The effectiveness of the Court depends heavily on public confidence in its integrity, and it has recently experienced a historic decline in its public image. According to a 2014 Gallup poll, only 30 percent of Americans have confidence in the Supreme Court, the lowest number since 1973, when such data were first recorded.[148] This may be explained by a general mistrust of government, or it may be the product of a growing concern that the Court and its activities—regardless of the results obtained in specific cases—are becoming increasingly politicized.[149] A 2014 *Rasmussen Reports* poll found that 55 percent of Americans believe the justices have their own political agendas.[150] As the public becomes more and more skeptical of the justices' ability to be apolitical, those concerned may naturally turn to recusal reform as a bulwark against politically driven decision making by the Court.

The responses to these arguments for recusal reform come principally from the justices themselves. They focus, perhaps not surprisingly considering their source and the historical development of the Court's recusal practices, less on the nature of individual recusal decisions and more on the effects of those decisions on the Court's institutional mission. The central theme of this viewpoint is derived from the common law "duty to sit" or "rule of necessity," under which a judge's decision to recuse is overridden by the lack of an adequate replacement to hear the case.[151] In the words of the famed English legal historian and jurist Sir Frederick Pollock, "Although a judge had better not, if it can be avoided, take part in the decision of a case in which he has any personal interest, yet he not only may but must do so if the case cannot be heard otherwise."[152] In the context of the lower federal courts, the rule of necessity is basically a nullity. Congress has provided for replacement judges in the event a judge is recused.[153] But the Supreme Court is different. The constitutional mandate that there be one Supreme Court creates significant (if not impenetrable) barriers to the availability of replacement justices.[154] According to Chief Justice Charles Evans Hughes, "The Constitution does not appear to authorize two or more Supreme Courts or two or more parts of a Supreme Court functioning in effect as separate courts."[155] A lack of replacements means that a single recusal could lead to a tie vote in a case. A tie results in a nonprecedential affirmance of the decision below that is inconsistent with the Court's responsibility to "resolve the significant legal issue presented by the case."[156]

Recusal is also problematic for the litigants, the argument goes, because a decision by an irreplaceable justice to recuse is "effectively the same as casting a vote against the petitioner" on the merits[157] or at the certiorari stage. A petitioner must garner a larger percentage of the available votes (five out of eight rather than five out of nine for a victory on the merits, and four out of eight for a certiorari petition) in cases involving at least one recusal.[158] The recusal of multiple justices is even more problematic for the Court, as it could defeat quorum in a specific case and thus make the Court powerless to exercise its constitutional function as the final adjudicator of "cases" or "controversies" properly before it.[159]

There are other reasons to support the Court retaining control over its own recusal questions that are not grounded in concerns about a lack of replacement justices. Justice Scalia has argued that reducing the justices' independence over recusal decisions could lead to politically motivated attacks designed to influence the outcome of cases by forcing unsympathetic justices to recuse themselves.[160] Channeling Blackstone, he explained that "the people must have confidence in the integrity of the Justices, and that cannot exist in a system that assumes them to be corruptible by the slightest friendship or favor, and in an atmosphere where the press will be eager to find foot-faults."[161] The justices have also raised constitutional concerns about congressional attempts to influence recusal at the Court. While testifying before the House Subcommittee on Financial Services and General Government,[162] Justice Kennedy pointed out that "'there is a constitutional problem'" with making statutory recusal standards binding on the Court.[163] In his 2011 Year-End Report, Chief Justice Roberts made a point of explaining that "the limits of Congress's power to require recusal [of Supreme Court justices] have never been tested. The Justices follow the same general principles with respect to recusal as other federal judges, but the application of those principles can differ due to the unique circumstances of the Supreme Court."[164] In sum, the justices treat their recusal decisions as being too complex to be governed by objective statutory standards. They prefer to rely on a wider range of considerations, including the institutional mission of the Court. The result is that the justices' recusal decisions more closely approximate highly contextualized due process analyses than instances of traditional statutory interpretation.

The conflict over the proper role of legislative involvement in Supreme Court recusal practice reflects a constitutional impasse between Congress and the Court. Although proponents of statutory recusal standards generally acknowledge the important differences between recusal in the lower courts and the Supreme Court,[165] concerns over the Supreme Court's integrity, both internally and in the eyes of the public, have caused them to look to Congress to standardize and strengthen the Court's recusal standards. But Congress's attempts to regulate the Court's recusal practices have inspired both direct and indirect resistance from the justices. The Court's most direct public statements about recusal and the separation of powers have also been among its most recent. In February 2012, for instance, Chief Justice Roberts rejected a request from five members of the Senate Judiciary Committee asking the Court to formally adopt the Code of Conduct for United States Judges.[166] The chief justice's response came in the wake of his Year-End Report, in which he made clear that the justices consider their ethical and recusal obligations to be individual and independent.[167]

These recent (and defiant) comments are the most explicit in a long list of indications that the justices do not feel bound by congressional attempts to regulate recusal at the Court. The Court has never conceded that Congress has the constitutional authority to set recusal standards.[168] Moreover, although recusal remains a relatively common practice at the Court,[169] the justices rarely explain their decisions.[170] When explanations are proffered, institutional concerns about the effective functioning of the Court predominate over the statutory standards put forth by Congress. In the words of Sherrilyn Ifill, "The Justices encourage and protect a fiercely independent approach to their recusal determinations."[171] Most important, because the statutory standards are practically unenforceable against the Court and because the Court's decisions are not reviewable, there is no coercive legal action available to Congress to force the justices to change their practices. As Jeffrey Stempel so aptly described it, "Supreme Court recusal practice provides an almost unique illustration in American government of substantive law without force when applied to a certain institution."[172] The Court appears determined to keep it that way, resulting in an ongoing tension between Congress and the Court.

The impasse is more than a legal abnormality or inconvenience. In many ways, it is the source of much of the public frustration with and criticism of the Court and Congress over recusal. On a small scale, the impasse makes it more difficult to achieve any sort of lasting resolution or thoughtful treatment of the recusal question as the two sides effectively talk past one another. On a much grander scale, the impasse over recusal raises the same systemic problem as any seemingly irreconcilable dispute between two coequal branches—doubts about the legitimacy of our constitutional democracy. As the two branches continue to appear at odds over when and how Supreme Court justices should refrain from participating in specific cases, both sides appear to be obstinate, arbitrary, ineffective, or some combination thereof. This promotes an air of lawlessness around the issue that weakens confidence in our public institutions and creates problems for our constitutional structure. Finally, the recusal impasse is significant because it represents the first step in what Eric Posner and Adrian Vermeule call "constitutional showdowns"—interbranch disputes over constitutional authority that end in the development of new constitutional precedents.[173]

The harmful effects of the impasse over recusal are the culmination of the long history of American recusal law. They also represent a serious and heretofore unappreciated problem with Supreme Court recusal. The debate over what the Court should be required to do and whether those requirements would lead to untenable consequences largely misses the point. The impasse between Congress and the Court over recusal is, at its core, a constitutional separation of powers problem. It must be viewed that way in order to properly contextualize the entire range of tensions and issues at stake. Only then can we envision a set of solutions worthy of a conflict among coequal branches of government.

3 | The Constitutionality of Supreme Court Recusal Standards

Casting the ongoing tension over Supreme Court recusal as a matter of constitutional law and structure raises several new questions: What does the Constitution tell us about who decides recusal issues at the Court? If legislative reform is not constitutionally permitted, how do constitutional principles suggest the ongoing impasse between Congress and the Court should be resolved? Without legislative guidance, what other constitutionally designed limits exist to channel the justices' discretion in recusal cases? Do the answers to these constitutional questions have any implications for recusal in the lower federal or state courts? Each of these questions will be taken up in the following chapters, beginning here with the issue of which branch has the constitutional authority to decide matters of Supreme Court recusal.

The question of who decides matters of recusal at the Court is unavoidably tied to the history of American recusal law. Because Congress has set recusal standards for the justices, the issue of constitutional authority over recusal boils down to whether Congress has the power to enact a recusal statute that binds the members of the Court. This question necessarily implicates the principle of separation of powers. The concept of the separation of powers was adopted by the Framers from the work of the French political philosopher Montesquieu.[1] At its core, it reflects the idea that the three coordinate branches of government retain at least some measure of substantive authority separate and apart from one another. This literal "separation" of power takes advantage of the specific strengths and competencies of each branch and provides for "checks and balances" among the branches by empowering each branch to protect against the overreaching or aggrandizement of power by another branch. This concept of divided power has remained a foundational principle of American government. As Chief Justice Roberts explained for the Court in *Stern v. Marshall*, a case interpreting the scope of Article III judicial power:

Under "the basic concept of separation of powers . . . that flow[s] from the scheme of a tripartite government" adopted in the Constitution, "the 'judicial Power of the United States' . . . can no more be shared" with another branch than "the Chief Executive, for example, can share with the Judiciary the veto power, or the Congress share with the Judiciary the power to override a Presidential veto." . . . In establishing the system of divided power in the Constitution, the Framers considered it essential that "the judiciary remain[ ] truly distinct from both the legislature and the executive." As Hamilton put it, quoting Montesquieu, "'there is no liberty if the power of judging be not separated from the legislative and executive powers.'"[2]

Chief Justice Roberts went on to acknowledge, however, that "the three branches [of the federal government] are not hermetically sealed from one another."[3] The principle of separation of powers can thus assume different forms. A formalist view prefers strict divisions between executive, legislative, and judicial functions based largely on the Constitution's text.[4] A functionalist approach accepts more flexible divisions of labor among the branches in the interest of promoting sound policy outcomes.[5] Both formulations, however, depend on the branches being able to limit one another's accumulation of power. This balance cannot be achieved without each branch possessing at least some core or inherent authority that is completely protected from interference by any other branch.[6]

This basic premise provides the starting point for the following two-part constitutional analysis of Supreme Court recusal standards. The first question looks to constitutional history, practice, and structure to determine whether a justice's recusal decision is part of the judicial power assigned to federal judges under Article III.[7] Article III unequivocally vests the "judicial Power of the United States" in the Supreme Court and "in such inferior Courts as the Congress may . . . ordain and establish."[8] It does not, however, offer any further explanation of the scope or substance of the judicial power, much less whether and to what extent that power includes the authority of Supreme Court justices to decide questions of their own recusal. With such limited opportunity for textual analysis, constitutional history, practice, and structure become important tools in determining who decides Supreme Court recusal questions.

The second question is whether a justice's use of her judicial power to make a recusal decision is constitutionally protected from congressional interference by the separation of powers. This latter question draws on our understandings of constitutional structure and the inherent powers of the judiciary to determine whether the justices' recusal authority is exclusive of congressional power under, for instance, the Necessary and Proper Clause of Article I.[9] While the two questions overlap somewhat—particularly in their reliance on constitutional structure—treating them as conceptually distinct offers additional insight into the relationship between the Supreme Court's recusal practices and the separation of powers.

Founding Era Historical Evidence

James Liebman and William Ryan have offered compelling evidence of the meaning of various terms in Article III based on the records of the Constitutional Convention and the subsequent ratification debates in the state legislatures.[10] Little if any of the information in those records, however, deals specifically with the phrase "judicial Power."[11] There is no record of recusal being discussed at either the Constitutional Convention or the state ratification debates, let alone Supreme Court recusal. A historical analysis of Supreme Court recusal under Article III must therefore be based on the sources of information most commonly understood to have been relied upon by the Framers in fashioning the judicial power—the "business of the Colonial courts and the courts of Westminster when the Constitution was framed,"[12] as well as "early congressional and judicial precedent" interpreting Article III.[13]

This historical information provides an important perspective on the relationship between Article III judicial power and the recusal of federal judges, in particular Supreme Court justices. Prior to the Founding, recusal was, both procedurally and substantively, a purely judicial question. In pre-Revolutionary England and America, recusal decisions were the product of judge-made common law; the standards for establishing whether a judge could participate in a case were developed and applied within the judicial branch.[14] In fact, in English common law and throughout the history of federal recusal law in America, judges at every level of the federal judiciary have been empowered to make the initial ruling as to their own recusal.[15]

Substantively, the common law of recusal in England and America before the Founding was also highly deferential to the judiciary. Under English common law only a direct pecuniary interest in the outcome of a case was grounds for recusal,[16] and then only where another judge was able to hear the case in place of the recused judge: the "rule of necessity."[17] This was not only a departure from the more stringent Bractonian requirement of recusal for "suspicion"[18] but also a rejection of the narrower grounds of recusal for personal bias, including bias deriving from familial relationships.[19] American colonial practice was essentially the same prior to and immediately after the Founding.[20]

After the Founding, the political branches continued to leave federal judicial recusal—and especially the recusal of Supreme Court justices—largely to the judicial branch. Congress passed its first judicial recusal provision for the federal courts in 1792.[21] It codified the common law requirement that judges not have a pecuniary interest in the outcome of the suit and preserved judges' practice of ruling on their own recusal status. It added only that a judge may not preside if he "had been counsel for either party."[22] This additional basis for recusal was at best a minor departure from the narrow common law procedural and substantive framework articulated by Blackstone and in place at the time the Constitution was drafted and ratified.[23] Moreover, even if the statute is seen as an attempt by Congress to take more control over judicial recusal, the statute by its terms applied only to judges, not justices of the Supreme Court.

Founding era evidence thus supports, albeit indirectly, the idea that recusal was largely a question for an independent judiciary. Judges developed the common law standards for recusal and used them to decide their own recusal motions.[24] With regard to the Supreme Court in particular, the political branches chose not to intervene in the justices' exercise of their recusal power even after they chose to do so for the lower federal courts.[25] The persistence of these ideas at the time the Constitution was drafted indicates that Supreme Court recusal was, in the minds of the Framers and their contemporaries, a matter for the Court pursuant to its judicial power under Article III.

Long-Standing Practice and Supreme Court Precedent

The original understanding of the relationship between Article III judicial power and Supreme Court recusal is not, however, the only relevant

source of information on the topic. Long-standing governmental practices have frequently been relied upon to help delineate constitutional
boundaries in difficult separation-of-powers cases. In the words of then
professor Felix Frankfurter and his student James Landis, "The scope
and qualities of a power which has been voluminously exercised since
1789 must be looked for in the cumulative proof of its exercise."[26] This
approach is most frequently used in disputes between the legislative and
executive branches, and perhaps the most well-known statement regarding the division of authority between Congress and the president is in
Justice Jackson's concurrence in *Youngstown*.[27] Justice Jackson's famous
three-tiered system in *Youngstown* considers evidence of Congress's historical "inertia, indifference or quiescence" to executive action in determining the proper balance of power between the branches.[28] Although
congressional intent regarding the conduct of a coordinate branch can
be difficult to determine, its relevance in Justice Jackson's framework
highlights the important fact for present purposes—that constitutional
meaning in separation of powers disputes can be gleaned from prior
interactions between the branches. Justice Frankfurter made this clear
in his own *Youngstown* concurrence: "A systematic, unbroken, executive practice, long pursued to the knowledge of the Congress and never
before questioned, engaged in by Presidents who have also sworn to
uphold the Constitution, making as it were such exercise of power part
of the structure of our government, may be treated as a gloss on 'executive Power' vested in the President by . . . Art. II."[29] Despite being the
most frequently cited example of the Court's use of historical practice
to understand constitutional language, *Youngstown* was not the first case
to employ that methodology.

Chief Justice Marshall articulated the relevance of historical practice
to constitutional meaning as early as 1819 in *McCulloch v. Maryland*.[30]
McCulloch involved a challenge to Congress's creation of the Bank of
the United States. It was in fact the second time Congress had created
the Bank, which was first authorized by statute in 1791. The initial char-
ter expired in 1811 and was renewed by statute in 1816.[31] *McCulloch* began in 1818 as a suit to enforce a Maryland tax on the Bank, but it grew
into a challenge to the constitutionality of the Bank itself. Maryland
argued that Congress did not have the constitutional power to create a
national bank, while the parties representing the federal government,
including McCulloch, maintained that the Bank was constitutional and
that Maryland's taxation of it was not. Chief Justice Marshall's opinion

for a unanimous Court in *McCulloch* is best known for its exposition on Congress's power under Article I's Necessary and Proper Clause.[32] Prior to discussing the necessary and proper power, however, the chief justice made an argument in support of the Bank's constitutionality from historical practice and congressional acquiescence. He explained that a "doubtful question, . . . in the decision of which . . . the respective powers of those who are equally the representatives of the people, are to be adjusted; if not put at rest by the practice of the government, ought to receive a considerable impression from that practice."[33] He went on to note that the power to create a Bank of the United States "was exercised by the first congress" after a fully informed and robust debate and in the face of resistance from the legislative and executive branches, only to be exercised again after a "short experience of the embarrassments to which the refusal to revive it exposed the government."[34] Chief Justice Marshall concluded his argument from historical practice by suggesting that "it would require no ordinary share of intrepidity, to assert that a measure adopted under these circumstances, was a bold and plain usurpation, to which the constitution gave no countenance."[35] While certainly not the sole justification for the Court's position in *McCulloch*, Chief Justice Marshall's opinion highlighted the potential power of historical practice—even within a relatively short period of time—as a source of constitutional meaning.

More than a century later, in *Myers v. United States*,[36] the Court relied heavily on congressional acquiescence to long-standing executive practice to resolve a dispute between the executive and legislative branches. The case involved the scope of the president's power to remove executive officials, more specifically President Woodrow Wilson's power to remove a postmaster of the first class named Frank Myers. An 1876 statute required the president to get Senate consent before removing "Postmasters of the first, second, and third classes."[37] The United States (litigating on behalf of the presidency after President Wilson's death in 1924) objected on the grounds that historical practice supported the president's sole authority to remove executive officers, and that the 1876 statute was thus constitutionally invalid because it was inconsistent with that historical record. The government's position was supported by the fact that the first Congress, as early as 1789, recognized the president's sole removal authority over executive officers.[38] Starting in 1863, however, and first materializing in a statute in the Tenure of Office Act (1867), a movement took hold in Congress to "subject the power of removing executive officers appointed by the President and confirmed by the Senate to the control of the Senate."[39] The 1876 statute limiting President Wilson's power to remove Myers was a product of this movement. The Court was thus forced to determine whether a congressional change of heart altered the historical record enough to modify the preexisting constitutional relationship between the legislative and executive branches over removal. The Court was not persuaded that Congress's more recent position answered the constitutional question. It held that because the president's exclusive removal power had already become firmly established under the Constitution prior to 1876, the statute was an unconstitutional infringement on that power.[40] As Rebecca Brown described it, "Congress had given its consent by long-standing practice, and that consent gave the executive's position constitutional validity."[41]

The Court similarly applied long-standing governmental practice to resolve a separation-of-powers question in the *Pocket Veto Case*.[42] Article I of the Constitution states that if the president does not wish to sign a bill presented to him by Congress, he shall return it to Congress with his objections within ten days (excluding Sundays) of its being presented to him. If he does not return a bill to Congress within those ten days, the bill automatically becomes law "as if he had signed it" unless Congress managed to "prevent" the president from returning the bill by "their Adjournment."[43] The *Pocket Veto Case* involved a dispute over this adjournment exception. Congress presented President Calvin Coolidge with a duly enacted bill on June 24, 1926. On July 3, 1926, Congress adjourned for the summer. It remained adjourned until after July 6, the tenth day, not counting Sundays, after the bill was presented to the president. The question posed to the Court was whether a legislative adjournment constituted congressional prevention of the president's return of a bill to the Congress when the adjournment occurred within the ten-day return period mandated by Article I.[44] Traditionally, a congressional adjournment had been treated as congressional prevention of the return of the bill and thus the bill's demise, rather than as presidential inaction resulting in the bill becoming law.[45] The Court relied, at least in part, on the fact that constitutional meaning had already been established by long-standing practice and could not later be overridden by a congressional change of heart: "For a long series of years, . . . all the Presidents who have had occasion to deal with this question have . . . [concluded] that they were prevented from returning the bill to the House in which it originated by the adjournment of the session of Congress; . . . this construction has been acquiesced in by both Houses of Congress."[46]

There are myriad other examples of historical practice influencing constitutional interpretation. In *Dames & Moore v. Regan*,[47] the Court relied on the president's traditional power to settle claims with foreign nations to uphold an executive order suspending claims by U.S. nationals against the government of Iran without explicit congressional authorization.[48] In *United States v. Midwest Oil Company*,[49] the Court allowed the president to prevent the purchase of public lands by private individuals despite a statute permitting the acquisition of those lands by U.S. citizens. The Court reasoned that because Congress was aware of the long-standing executive practice of acquiring public lands, it could not have intended to nullify that traditional practice by statute.[50]

Long-standing governmental practice is even relevant to interbranch disputes that were not brought before the courts. President Obama's 2011 decision to engage in hostilities in Libya without congressional authorization, for example, reignited a long-standing debate about the applicability and constitutionality of the War Powers Resolution, a Vietnam-era statute designed to restrain presidential use of force without congressional approval.[51] The courts have consistently refrained from getting involved in war powers disputes, characterizing such disputes as beyond the courts' authority to decide.[52] This did not stop commentators from invoking the long-standing government practice doctrine in debates over President Obama's use of force in Libya. Scholars, journalists, and political actors repeatedly invoked long-standing executive practice in engaging in hostilities (at least on a limited, temporary basis) and congressional acquiescence in those decisions as support for their constitutionality.[53]

Historical practice arguments are less common in separation-of-powers disputes between the legislative and judicial branches, perhaps due to the judiciary's reticence to take up its own cause against the legislature. Nevertheless, enough examples exist to confirm the role of governmental practice in informing our constitutional understanding of the judiciary's power to act under Article III. In *Chambers v. NASCO, Inc.*,[54] the Court upheld the judiciary's authority to impose sanctions for bad faith conduct despite a lack of statutory or regulatory authority to do so. NASCO sued G. Russell Chambers for breach of contract, alleging that Chambers had contracted to sell NASCO a television station and then attempted to renege on the deal. The district court ruled in favor of NASCO and in the process concluded that Chambers had engaged in several unethical acts during the litigation, including trying to fraudulently deprive the court of jurisdiction, filing "'a series of meritless motions and pleadings and delaying actions,'" and participating in "other tactics of delay, oppression, harassment and massive expense."[55] The court sanctioned Chambers accordingly, ordering him to pay NASCO nearly $1 million, or the "entire amount of NASCO's litigation costs paid to its attorneys" in the case.[56] Chambers objected on the grounds that there was no legal basis under which to sanction him. He contended that the most relevant statutory provisions and rules of civil procedure did not cover at least two of the three categories of allegedly sanctionable conduct, and that this omission reflected Congress's intent to displace the courts' inherent power to sanction litigants. The Supreme Court disagreed, relying on the courts' historical practice of sanctioning bad faith as proof of their constitutional power to do so. It explained that "'we do not lightly assume that Congress has intended to depart from established principles' such as the scope of a court's inherent power" to impose sanctions for bad faith.[57]

The Court again relied on long-standing practice to uphold judicial power in *Link v. Wabash Railroad Company*.[58] William Link's car had been in an accident with a train owned by the Wabash Railroad Company. Link filed suit but as of six years later had failed to do much more than respond to a motion for judgment on the pleadings. When Link's counsel failed to appear for a pretrial conference six years after the initial filing date, the trial court dismissed the case on its own motion, citing its inherent judicial authority to do so. Link objected on the grounds that Federal Rule of Civil Procedure 41 implicitly prohibits the court from dismissing a case *sua sponte*, without a motion from the defendant. The Court disagreed, ruling in favor of the dismissal because

> the authority of a court to dismiss sua sponte for lack of prosecution has generally been considered an "inherent power," governed not by rule or statute but by the control necessarily vested in courts to manage their own affairs so as to achieve the orderly and expeditious disposition of cases. . . . It would require a much clearer expression of purpose than Rule 41(b) provides

for us to assume that it was intended to abrogate so well-acknowledged a proposition.[59]

More recently, the Court held that Congress may not reopen final judgments of the judicial branch. *Plaut v. Spendthrift Farm, Inc.*,[60] involved a constitutional challenge to a statute allowing plaintiffs to reopen a group of securities fraud cases that had been previously dismissed for being outside the applicable statute of limitations. The Court explained that, in cases that have completed their journey through the hierarchy of the federal judiciary, the separation of powers protects the judicial branch from being retroactively overruled by legislative fiat. The *Plaut* Court explained its decision by stating that the judicial power of Article III includes the exclusive power to decide cases, and that long-standing congressional practice was consistent with the Court's view. "Apart from the statute we review today, we know of no instance in which Congress has attempted to set aside the final judgment of an Article III court by retroactive legislation. That prolonged reticence would be amazing if such interference were not understood to be constitutionally proscribed."[61]

Long-standing government practice is thus an important source of information in separation-of-powers cases.[62] It helps courts understand the constitutional limits on the power of the individual branches as well as the proper constitutional balance among them. In the case of Supreme Court recusal, long-standing legislative and judicial customs indicate that the decision to recuse a Supreme Court justice is not only a judicial decision but also one that is constitutionally protected from legislative interference.

Congress has been regulating the recusal of lower federal court judges since 1792. Neither the original federal recusal statute nor any of the amendments to it for the next 150 years applied either explicitly or in practice to Supreme Court justices.[63] It was not until 1948 that Congress amended the federal recusal statute to include, in addition to lower court judges, "any justice . . . of the United States."[64] Although the justices occasionally claimed to feel constrained by the statutory standards for the lower courts, their conduct in specific cases belies these claims. Chief Justice Harlan Fiske Stone testified before a House committee in 1943 that "it has always seemed to the Court that when a district judge could not sit in a case because of his previous association with it, or a circuit court of appeals judge, it was our manifest duty to take the same position."[65] Only three years later, the chief justice recused himself from *North American Company v. Securities and Exchange Commission (SEC)*, a case challenging the constitutionality of an SEC order under the Public Utility Holding Company Act of 1935.[66] He reversed his decision, however, when it became clear that his recusal would deprive the Court of a quorum to decide the case.

The current federal recusal statute does nothing to disrupt the historic (and ongoing) practice of judges resolving questions about their own recusal. With regard to the Supreme Court, although section 455 purports to impose substantive recusal requirements, its failure to prescribe procedural requirements has led to a continuation of the same historical recusal practices at the Court—unreviewable, individualized determinations by each justice of his or her own qualification to sit in a particular case, without any obligation to justify or otherwise explain those decisions.[67] The ultimate result is an entirely unenforceable recusal regime. Nevertheless, in light of ample evidence of the Court's controversial recusal decisions, Congress has not taken any definitive steps to strengthen section 455 or to indicate that it considers the Court's ongoing recusal practices constitutionally problematic.[68] In fact, Congress's most recent attempts at recusal reform, the Supreme Court Transparency and Disclosure Act of 2011 and the Supreme Court Ethics Act of 2013, died in committee with the Court publicly questioning their appropriateness and constitutionality.[69]

While Congress has appeared largely content to acquiesce to the Court's views on recusal, those views are evident in the justices' recusal practices. The preceding chapter outlines the Court's long history of controversial recusal decisions and the justices' reliance on nonstatutory factors in deciding whether to recuse. The justices' recusal practices changed little, if at all, after Congress applied the federal recusal standards to members of the Court.[70] Supreme Court recusal decisions were still only tangentially faithful to the statutory standard, and the Court has yet to apply section 455 to one of its own members.[71] In *Laird v. Tatum*,[72] then–associate justice Rehnquist's argument against recusal depended heavily on the precedent set by other justices. He explained that "different Justices who have come from the Department of Justice have treated the same or very similar situations differently" from one another,[73] and that his "impression is that none of the former Justices of this Court since 1911 [more than thirty-five years before the recusal statute included members of the Court] have followed a practice of disqualifying themselves" in cases analogous to *Tatum*.[74] He reminded the reader that "under the existing practice of the Court disqualification has been a matter of individual decision" and pointed out that the lack of substitutes for recused justices and the potential for equally divided decisions of the Court make Supreme Court recusal uniquely difficult as an institutional matter.[75]

Justice Scalia took a similar approach more than twenty years later in *Cheney*,[76] when he chose to focus on the institutional consequences of his recusal for the Court rather than the text of the federal statute. He mentioned that the lack of substitute justices and the potential for tie votes could compromise the Court's ability to fulfill its judicial responsibilities. He cited precedents set by other justices—one of which occurred before section 455 was enacted—as support for his conclusion that no objective observer could question his impartiality[77] and concluded by suggesting that more demanding recusal standards could embolden interested parties to use recusal as a sword to strategically remove justices in certain cases.[78]

Justices Rehnquist's and Scalia's analyses of their own recusal decisions are important because they are representative of the entire Court's views on recusal. Neither justice focused on the statutory requirements pertaining to his recusal decision—they paid little or no attention to the statutory text or legislative intent. The only judicial precedents they relied on were those of their predecessors on the Court, many of whom made their recusal decisions before section 455 was amended to include the justices. Neither justice cited lower court interpretations of the statute, despite the fact that such interpretations are far more common. Instead of their recusal decisions reflecting the fact that there is a binding statute on the books, the justices offered explanations based on institutional and prudential factors that were more at home with an analysis under the Due Process Clause than a traditional statutory analysis.

This feature of Supreme Court recusal practice was corroborated by the Court's 1993 Statement of Recusal Policy.[79] As Debra Lyn Bassett observed:

Rather than applying an objective reasonable person standard on a case-by-case basis, as § 455(a) requires, the Recusal Policy simply reflects the Justices' own sense of what to them would constitute a reasonable basis upon which to question a judge's impartiality and applies that standard across the board. In the Statement of Recusal Policy, the Justices "re-emphasized their negative view of recusal in cases where actual bias is not at issue." Thus, the Supreme Court has made it clear that it has no intention of following the strict proscriptions of section 455, and instead believes that the Court's unique nature justifies a less-demanding recusal standard.[80]

More recently, Justice Kennedy testified before a House subcommittee that "there is a constitutional problem" with making the rules binding on the Court.[81] Chief Justice Roberts noted in his 2011 Year-End Report on the Federal Judiciary that "the limits of Congress's power to require recusal have never been tested" and that the justices have "an obligation to the Court to be sure of the need to recuse before deciding to withdraw from a case."[82] When five senators wrote him a letter in response to his Year-End Report, the chief justice confirmed that the Court would not respond to pressure from the legislative branch to limit the justices' independence or discretion in deciding their own recusal questions.[83]

The point of reviewing governmental practice in the area of Supreme Court recusal is to provide insight into who is best suited to decide recusal questions at the Court under our separation-of-powers regime. The constitutional balance required by the separation-of-powers is often determined by reference to the historical compromises between the competing branches. In the case of Supreme Court recusal, the evidence reveals a long history of congressional indifference prior to the enactment of section 455, followed by acquiescence to the Court's traditional approach to resolving recusal questions. The Court's resultant autonomy over its own recusal practice is a strong indicator that Supreme Court recusal not only is part of the judicial power assigned to the Court by Article III but also is the exclusive province of the justices.

Constitutional Structure and Inherent Power

The most difficult analysis regarding the Supreme Court's control over its own recusal standards comes from constitutional structure. Whereas constitutional history and practice provide relatively straightforward support for the conclusion that Article III grants the Court authority to control its own recusal jurisprudence, the structure of the Constitution requires more detailed consideration.[84] Article III vests the judicial power in the federal courts.[85] Read in isolation, or in conjunction with only the vesting clauses of Articles I and II,[86] Article III appears to assign all things judicial exclusively to the federal courts. A more complex picture of the meaning and scope of the judicial power emerges when Article III is read along with other relevant provisions of the Constitution, including Article I's affirmative grants of power to Congress, but the conclusion remains the same; the Constitution commits Supreme Court recusal to the justices and only the justices.

Article III contains two provisions that are commonly thought of as qualifying the judicial power vested in the federal courts: the provision empowering Congress to "ordain and establish" the inferior courts,[87] and the Exceptions Clause, which empowers Congress to make "exceptions" to the Court's appellate jurisdiction.[88] Neither of these provisions has any significant bearing on the Court's power over recusal. While the power to create the inferior courts has been interpreted to provide Congress with sweeping power to regulate those courts,[89] it simply does not apply to the Supreme Court and as such cannot be used as a source of congressional authority over the Court in any context, let alone one like recusal that has an exclusively judicial history.[90]

Congressional Power over the Court's Appellate Jurisdiction

The Exceptions Clause, by contrast, clearly does apply to the Court. It does not, however, provide Congress with constitutional authority to regulate the justices' recusal practices. This is true for several reasons. First and most directly, the Exceptions Clause grants Congress authority to limit only the Court's appellate jurisdiction, a process commonly referred to as "jurisdiction stripping."[91] Jurisdiction, however, is not recusal. James Liebman and William Ryan have demonstrated that the Framers did not equate judicial power with jurisdiction,[92] and this is consistent with our common understanding of judicial authority. Jurisdiction is the power to decide issues of law and fact. It does not explain how those issues should be decided or whether the judicial branch must share its authority to render such decisions with the political branches. In fact, there are many instances in which judges exercise their judicial authority without implicating their power to decide the case before them. Taking jurisdiction for what it purports to be—a prerequisite to the exercise of judicial power over a case or class of cases by a particular court or court system[93]—shows that authority over a court's jurisdiction does not necessarily extend to authority over questions arising before the court under the proper exercise of that jurisdiction. Recusal is one of those questions, and as such is outside the jurisdictional authority assigned to Congress by the Exceptions Clause. Moreover, recusal is just as likely to arise in cases under the Court's original jurisdiction, which is expressly not subjected to congressional influence under the Exceptions Clause or any other part of Article III. For these reasons, it would be an overreading of the Exceptions Clause to assume that it grants Congress authority to regulate the Court's recusal decisions.

But even if the Exceptions Clause does not directly empower Congress to pass a recusal statute for the justices, what about the fact that Congress could use its jurisdictional authority to strip the Court of appellate jurisdiction in cases involving recusal? Envision a statute that reads, for instance, "The Supreme Court shall not have appellate jurisdiction over any case in which at least [fill in some number between one and nine] justices are recused under § 455." Relying on jurisdiction stripping is different from using the Exceptions Clause to justify a simple recusal statute because empowering Congress to regulate recusal directly requires reading the Clause to include direct congressional power over recusal. By enacting a jurisdiction-stripping statute that uses recusal as its substantive trigger, Congress would at least be within the plain language of the Exceptions Clause, and thus closer to validating its exercise of legislative authority. If Congress can link recusal to its jurisdictional authority, why doesn't that imply the power to regulate recusal directly? Or, more to the point, if jurisdiction stripping allows Congress to achieve the same results as a recusal statute, doesn't that answer the question about who decides recusal issues for the Court? For both legal and policy reasons, the answer is no. There are several problems with linking recusal and jurisdiction stripping, such that the original question of who decides matters of recusal at the Court cannot be answered by resort to the Exceptions Clause.

As a legal matter, tying jurisdiction stripping to recusal (of any number of justices) may run afoul of the limits of the Exceptions Clause. The Court has offered very limited guidance regarding the scope of the Clause, but the information it has provided indicates that Congress has a robust, yet not unbounded, authority to limit the Court's appellate jurisdiction. The Court has upheld nearly every congressional attempt to limit its appellate jurisdiction,[94] yet it has consistently stopped short of allowing Congress to wholly insulate a class of cases from Supreme Court review. In *Felker v. Turpin*,[95] the Court considered a statute that precluded the Court from hearing appeals from circuit courts' decisions whether to authorize Supreme Court review of a prisoner's successive habeas petition. The Court unanimously held that the statute was permissible under the Exceptions Clause. It also made clear, however, that the statute did not totally shield the Court from hearing the case. The Court retained the power (despite not having exercised it since 1925) to hear the case as an original habeas petition brought directly to the Supreme Court.[96] *Felker* is the most recent of a very short, but long-standing, line of cases to reach a similar conclusion.[97]

In addition to potentially eliminating a wide range of cases from Supreme Court appellate review, a jurisdiction-stripping statute incorporating substantive recusal standards could also face constitutional challenges on the basis that it improperly uses jurisdiction stripping to influence the substantive outcome of particular cases. *United States v. Klein*[98] involved a statute dealing with claims by former Confederates to retrieve property seized from them by the Union during the Civil War. Many of the parties seeking to retrieve property had received presidential pardons for their wartime activities. In an attempt to prevent them from recovering their property, Congress enacted a statute removing the Supreme Court's appellate jurisdiction over cases in which a defendant had received a presidential pardon, on the grounds that the pardon was evidence that the recipient had in fact aided the rebellion. In its only opinion striking a statute for violating the Exceptions Clause, the Court invalidated the statute, explaining that

> the language of the proviso shows plainly that it does not intend to withhold appellate jurisdiction except as a means to an end. . . . The court has jurisdiction of the cause to a given point; but when it ascertains that a certain state of things exists, its jurisdiction is to cease and it is required to dismiss the cause for want of jurisdiction. It seems to us that this is not an exercise of the acknowledged power of Congress to make exceptions and prescribe regulations to the appellate power. The court is required to ascertain the existence of certain facts and thereupon to declare that its jurisdiction on appeal has ceased, by dismissing the bill. What is this but to prescribe a rule

for the decision of a cause in a particular way? . . . We must think that Congress has inadvertently passed the limit which separates the legislative from the judicial power.[99]

Requiring the Court to dismiss for want of jurisdiction because one or more justices met the recusal standards sounds very much like what the Court in *Klein* called "prescrib[ing] a rule for the decision of a cause in a particular way."[100] If that is true, then a jurisdiction-stripping approach to recusal would be unconstitutional. It would represent Congress "inadvertently pass[ing] the limit which separates the legislative from the judicial power."[101] But because the facts related to recusal are likely not part of the underlying cause of action before the Court, relying on recusal as a trigger for jurisdiction stripping is less of an infringement on the judicial power that was present in *Klein*. Stripping jurisdiction based on recusals may be too attenuated from the merits of the case to constitute the unconstitutional deck stacking by Congress that the *Klein* Court sought to prevent. The problem with this position is that the separation-of-powers consequences are the same regardless of which facts Congress determines are sufficient to trigger a loss of jurisdiction. *Klein* and our hypothetical recusal-based jurisdictional statute both remove jurisdiction when a specific fact is present in a case, and do not threaten jurisdiction when that fact does not exist. According to the Court in *Klein*, this goes beyond a mere jurisdictional realignment and instead amounts to an interference with the disposition of an individual case, a project that is beyond Congress's constitutional purview.[102]

There is thus a viable argument that jurisdiction stripping is not a constitutional means of imposing recusal standards on the Court. Even if such a statute would be constitutionally permissible, for several practical reasons recusal-based jurisdiction stripping is not a satisfying answer to the question of whether Congress may regulate Supreme Court recusal. Put simply, it may not be possible to fashion a jurisdiction-stripping statute that would work. Jurisdiction stripping is institutionally focused. It necessarily precludes the entire Court from functioning in specific cases. Recusal operates individually by determining the fitness of a particular justice in a particular case. The result is that an attempt to enforce individual recusal standards through an institutional remedy like jurisdiction stripping is inherently both too broad and too narrow. Recall our hypothetical statute stripping the Court of jurisdiction over cases involving a certain number of recusals. The statute is too broad when the number of recusals is small because it enhances Congress's ability to affect the Court's recusal practices at the expense of making the entire Court unavailable to perform its duties. It seems rather draconian—and potentially inconsistent with the *Klein* Court's interest in protecting its power to decide cases—to deny Supreme Court review because a small subset of the justices were not, in the eyes of Congress, fit to participate in that particular case. Conversely, unless the statute stripped jurisdiction from every case with a single recusal, it would be conceding that cases with some unfit justices are permissible, while those with more are not. This may be a reasonable position to take as a policy matter, but it highlights the awkward fit between jurisdiction stripping and recusal. Congress must decide between potentially prohibiting the Court from deciding some of its docket (thereby raising the constitutional concerns that come with such a severe intrusion) and allowing cases to go forward where a subset of justices are otherwise unfit to participate. In the meantime, it creates a powerful disincentive for individual justices to recuse themselves. A single justice will undoubtedly be reluctant to recuse where doing so could imperil the entire Court's ability to address a legal issue that it had already deemed worthy of review. A case in point is Chief Justice Stone's decision to reverse his own decision to recuse in *North American Company v. SEC*, where doing so would have deprived the Court of a quorum.[103] Without any suggestion that his initial recusal decision was flawed, he chose to participate in order to preserve the Court's ability to resolve the case.[104] There is no reason to believe that having the rest of the Court review the chief justice's decision would have made recusal more likely, as the other justices are just as likely to be concerned about protecting the Court's power to decide a case properly before it.

On the other end of the spectrum, jurisdiction stripping based on recusal seems easier to justify in cases where the number of recusals is relatively high. If a majority or strong plurality of the justices merit recusal in a given case, it may be worth interrupting the traditional appellate hierarchy in favor of protecting the litigants and the system at large from potentially widespread partiality on the bench. Yet such a statute would likely be too narrow. It would permit the entire Court to preside over a case when several of its members, but not enough to meet the threshold in the statute, should have been recused. The worst scenario for Congress is a case where one fewer justice than the statutory minimum merits recusal. In that case, there are still several justices who should be recused, but not enough to strip the Court's jurisdiction under the statute, so the case continues before several "unfit" justices. Too broad a recusal standard, however, could lead to cases being excluded from consideration by the Court too easily, without a defensible ethical reason for doing so. This has serious practical implications in terms of preventing the Court from serving as the ultimate arbiter of federal law, and potential legal consequences due to its effect on the Court's inherent judicial power, a topic that will be discussed in greater detail later in this chapter.

Finally, Congress could try to utilize its authority under the Exceptions Clause to control the procedures employed by the Court in its recusal decisions. More specifically, it could remove the Court's appellate jurisdiction over cases in which the justices failed to review—ostensibly as an appellate court—a single justice's recusal decision. There are a number of reasons, however, why this is neither troubling nor of significant interest to the present analysis. As a practical matter, this approach seems more like a grant of appellate jurisdiction over recusal decisions than a removal of the Court's appellate jurisdiction, and as such it would be outside of the Exception Clause's scope and purpose. There is also a long history within federal recusal law of judges not reviewing the recusal decisions of their colleagues on the same court.[105] This long-standing practice would counsel heavily against Congress creating a new review structure within a single level of the judiciary. It is also not clear that the Court, in reviewing its own members' recusal decisions, would in fact be exercising its appellate jurisdiction. The Court's appellate jurisdiction has traditionally been thought of as jurisdiction over decisions rendered by courts or government entities that have a lesser authority to make legal pronouncements than the Supreme Court. An internal review of a justice's recusal decisions would run afoul of the traditional, and to date uninterrupted, hierarchical structure of appellate review.

This is true even if we compare review by the entire Court to en banc review at the federal appellate level. Unlike circuit courts of appeal, the Supreme Court cannot be subdivided. Article III expressly requires that there be one Supreme Court, and this has been widely understood to mean that the Court cannot perform its function as the judicial tribunal of last resort unless all of the available justices are eligible to participate. Review of an individual justice's recusal decision would require treating that initial recusal decision as an appealable judgment by a single justice, which is inconsistent with both Article III's one Supreme Court mandate and its jurisdictional requirements. It is inconsistent with the one Supreme Court mandate because it represents a single justice acting alone to issue a final judgment that her colleagues on the Court can only participate in on appeal. It is outside the Court's jurisdiction because treating a justice's recusal decision as an appealable judgment would require granting the justice original jurisdiction over the claim, something that is prohibited by the language and subsequent interpretations of Article III.

If Congress cannot order review by the full Court under the Exceptions Clause, it is unlikely that the Clause is a viable basis for Congress to impose any procedural requirements on the justices. A jurisdictional remedy is a rather blunt way to deal with recusal procedure; removing jurisdiction over an entire category of cases is a steep price for both the public and the Court to pay for procedural reforms, especially for reforms that will likely have no impact on the substantive outcome of any recusal decision. If the analysis were to progress this far, and for the reasons already stated that seems unlikely, an additional separation of powers issue may arise regarding the ability of the Exceptions Clause to influence the Court's internal procedures on appeal. There may well be other provisions that permit Congress to regulate the Court's internal procedures—such as the Necessary and Proper Clause, which is discussed later in this chapter—but the Exceptions Clause does not seems like a proper source of that authority.

The Exceptions Clause has been interpreted sparingly and remains the subject of much controversy and confusion. When we consider it as potential authority for congressional regulation of the Court's recusal practices, two things become increasingly clear. First, jurisdiction stripping comes with its own set of constitutional obstacles. The few cases in which the Court has considered the limits of Congress's power under the Exceptions Clause have all indicated that it does not consider the clause to be a vehicle for Congress to totally exclude the Court from the appeals process, and that Congress may not use its jurisdictional authority to prescribe the outcomes in specific cases. A recusal-based jurisdiction-stripping statute could run afoul of the Court's Exceptions Clause jurisprudence on both counts. Second, even if a jurisdiction-stripping statute based on recusal would be constitutionally valid, it would be sufficiently cumbersome and imprecise to make it at best an unattractive option for Congress in its interactions with the Court over recusal. Removing the Court's jurisdiction in a case is very different from the decision to remove a specific justice. The consequences to the judicial system and the challenges of finding the appropriate balance between excluding the right justices and continuing to enable the Court to fulfill its constitutional duty make jurisdiction stripping at best a seriously flawed method for achieving the fairness and integrity that recusal seeks to guarantee.

Congress's power to limit the Supreme Court's appellate jurisdiction does not include congressional authority over recusal. But Article III alone cannot tell us whether power over recusal at the Court is granted exclusively to the justices. The question remains whether some other constitutionally enumerated power allows for extrajudicial involvement in Supreme Court recusal decisions. To answer this (far more difficult) question, we must look to those provisions in Article I that speak directly to Congress's power to interfere with the Court's authority—the Impeachment Clauses[106] and the Necessary and Proper Clause.[107]

Impeachment and Recusal

There are three constitutional provisions that relate to the removal of federal judges *from office*, including Supreme Court justices. Article III guarantees federal judges their offices "during good Behaviour,"[108] and Article I states that the House of Representatives "shall have the sole Power of Impeachment" and that the "Senate shall have the sole Power to try all Impeachments."[109] The common understanding of these three provisions is that federal judges are removable only by means of impeachment, and generally only for conduct that would rise to the level of the "high crimes and misdemeanors" required for impeachment of members of Congress or the president. There is some notable disagreement with this view, based primarily on divergent views about the original understanding of the Impeachment and Good Behavior Clauses,[110] but this debate is inapposite to the current discussion. Historical practice has established that impeachment is the constitutionally prescribed mechanism for removing judges from office, and that impeachment must be justified on a standard akin to high crimes and misdemeanors.[111] As Michael Gerhardt, author of the definitive work on federal impeachment, explained, "Both the relevant text and original understanding support viewing impeachment as the only political means for judicial removal. . . . [T]his conclusion is consistent with analogous Supreme Court opinions on the separation of powers."[112] Moreover, even if impeachment is not the only way for Congress to remove a federal judge, permanent removal from office is sufficiently distinct from recusal that the impeachment power cannot be understood to include the lesser and more readily available remedy of recusal.

The Good Behavior and Impeachment Clauses are relevant to understanding the relationship between the Article III judicial power and Supreme Court recusal because they are the only textual references in the Constitution to the removal of federal judges.[113] They do not, however, grant Congress the power to set legally binding recusal standards for the Court. As a purely textual matter, "impeachment" and "recusal" are not synonyms. This implicates the interpretive canon of *expressio unius est exclusio alterius* (to state the one is to exclude the other). Recusal is not listed alongside impeachment as one of Congress's powers over the judiciary, the argument goes, so it should not be treated as such.[114] While there are inherent dangers in relying on specific canons of construction in interpreting constitutional provisions,[115] the fact that Article I refers only to impeachment and, most important, that impeachment is substantively and procedurally distinct from recusal offers strong support for the idea that the power to impeach does not include the power to recuse.

Impeachment is substantively different from recusal in at least three ways. First, the two concepts are aimed at entirely different types of conduct. Impeachment is available only in instances of culpable misconduct by Article III judges, while recusal does not depend on any judicial wrongdoing—it can be based on a judge's financial interest in a case or an objective appearance of impropriety.[116] None of the historical grounds for recusal, including Bractonian suspicion, require any finding of judicial misconduct or culpability. This is a far cry from a constitutionally impeachable event and in fact does not even amount to a similar category of offense.

Second, they serve different purposes. Impeachment is both punitive and prophylactic. It threatens to permanently remove judges from office in order to protect the system from unscrupulous individuals and to deter sitting judges from engaging in such behavior in the first place. It is not, however, designed to benefit a specific set of litigants or improve the integrity of judging in a particular case. That could be the effect in the sense that an impeached judge will be unable to continue her misconduct in future cases, but it is not necessarily true that impeachment applies only to judges who are expected to act badly *again.* Impeachment is backward-looking. It is justified by prior bad acts and is not dependent on a finding of potential future misconduct. In fact, it will likely be difficult in most instances of impeachment to predict which future cases, if any, were saved from judicial misconduct.

Recusal has neither the punitive nor the deterrence goals of impeachment. Recused judges do not experience any monetary or other penalty based on their recusal, and the only other "cost" of exclusion is reputational. This cost is high for impeachment, which is a rare and permanent mechanism for ending a judge's career, but is likely to be extremely low for recusal. This is due to several factors, the most obvious of which is that recusal is an individual decision that does not require any public filings or hearings. It is therefore less potentially embarrassing and damaging to a judge's reputation than the public impeachment process, even in cases where a judge is impeached but not convicted or removed from office. Recusal is also less of a threat to a judge's reputation, and thus less punitive, than impeachment because recusal operates on a case-by-case basis. Any reputational damage from recusal would have to be derived from the exclusion of a judge from a single case. It is not impossible to think of circumstances unique to a single case that would require recusal and be personally or professionally embarrassing to a judge, but unless those circumstances taint the judge's participation in a wide range of cases, any embarrassment associated with the decision to recuse in a small subset of cases is likely to be diluted by the judge's performance in the remainder of her docket. That said, even serial recusals are not likely to have the same long-term reputational effects as impeachment. A long history of bad recusal decisions could rise to the level of culpability necessary to constitute "high crimes and misdemeanors," but such a situation would be at minimum rare. American recusal law requires recusal for conduct that would not imply any culpability on the part of the recused judge, let alone sufficient culpability (even when aggregated) to compare to the standards for impeachment. When considered in both the short and the long term, the reputational cost of recusal—and in turn its punitive effect—pales in comparison to that of impeachment.

The reputational effect of recusal is further tempered by the fact that judges make their own recusal decisions. Even if the circumstances giving rise to recusal would be stigmatizing to the recused judge, the fact that judges have the authority to make their own recusal decision gives them an opportunity to redeem themselves by recusing in the face of an embarrassing situation. It is true that lower court judges are subject to appellate review of their recusal decisions, and a reversal on appeal of a decision not to recuse could be embarrassing for the judge facing recusal. Reversals are difficult to achieve, however, as appellate review depends on a factual record that was created by the same judge who is deciding whether to recuse, and appellate courts are highly deferential to lower court fact-finding. In most cases, the standard of review on appeal is abuse of discretion.[117] Therefore, even if it is potentially embarrassing, the prospect of reversal on appeal still does not make recusal punitive in the same way as impeachment because the recusal process invests judges with ample opportunity to avoid harmful outcomes.[118] This is particularly true in the context of Supreme Court recusal, where the justices maintain total control over their recusal decisions by making their own factual and legal determinations independent of any further review.

The third factor that differentiates recusal from impeachment is that they employ vastly different remedies. Impeachment results in a judge being permanently removed from the bench. The removal is explicitly insulated from presidential pardon under Article II and can thus be reversed only by reinstituting the appointment and confirmation process, which in the case of an impeached judge or justice would almost certainly be ineffective.[119] It is a drastic, unwieldy remedy that amounts to a severe burden on the independence of the judiciary, as the threat of such dire consequences could have a tremendous influence over how federal judges exercise the judicial power granted to them by the Constitution. Recusal, by contrast, is discrete and temporary. It precludes judges from participating in a specific case but does not threaten either their ability to participate in the Court's other business, including other cases, or their job security. The nature of the two remedies is so different that it stands to reason that they are not synonymous. According to Gerhardt:

> Both the relevant text and original understanding support viewing impeachment as the only political means for judicial removal. The Constitution erected and the framers understood the federal impeachment process as a highly deliberative, cumbersome decision-making mechanism. It defies

common sense for the framers to have taken great pains to have purpose-
fully designed such an awkward system for remedying judicial misconduct
but then implicitly left Congress and the president free to remove judges on
identical or more lenient grounds through some other, nonspecified, more
efficient devices.[120]

In addition to the substantive differences between them, impeachment and recusal employ vastly different procedures. Impeachment
requires a politically charged, two-part process. In the first part, the
House of Representatives must vote to pass articles of impeachment
against an official, including a federal judge.[121] Once those articles are
passed, the Senate conducts a trial of the impeached official, asking
its members to vote on whether there is sufficient evidence to convict
the impeached person of "Treason, Bribery, or other high Crimes and
Misdemeanors," or in the case of federal judges, for failing to exhibit
"good Behaviour."[122] Provided two-thirds of the senators concur, the impeachment process empowers Congress to remove an individual from
federal office. It does so, however, at significant cost in terms of political
capital, time, and public money. This is not an accident. The awkward
and costly nature of the impeachment process represents a deliberate
choice by the Framers to make impeachment a less attractive vehicle
for Congress to exercise control over the coordinate branches. This is
consistent with their feelings about judicial independence, as frequent
judicial impeachments or any other interference with the functioning
of the judiciary would leave too much power in the hands of Congress
and offer the public too little protection from the potential excesses of
government.[123]

Recusal, however, results in changes to the makeup of the bench
on a case-by-case basis in a way that costs Congress very little, especially
when compared with impeachment. Recusal is by definition temporary
and can be achieved through, at most, the normal adjudicative process.
In the case of the Supreme Court, recusal decisions are made through a
truncated process by which an individual justice makes an unreviewable
decision about whether to recuse herself. Recusal is thus more readily available than impeachment as a legislative check on the judiciary.
To read the impeachment power to include the lesser (but more easily
employed) recusal power would give Congress a much broader constitutional basis upon which to interfere in individual judges' exercise of
their constitutionally granted authority under Article III. This level of

intrusion into the judicial power is neither anticipated nor sanctioned by the principle of separation of powers or the Impeachment Clauses. As a result, Congress's impeachment power should be read to accord proper respect for the federal judiciary's role in our constitutional scheme. When read this way, the Impeachment Clauses offer structural support for the proposition that recusal is sufficiently distinct from impeachment to be understood as a feature of judicial, rather than legislative, authority.

The Necessary and Proper Clause and Inherent Power

The structural analysis becomes much more difficult, however, when viewed through the lens of the Necessary and Proper Clause.[124] The Necessary and Proper Clause grants Congress power to "make all Laws which shall be necessary and proper for carrying into Execution . . . all other Powers vested by this Constitution in the Government of the United States, or in any Department or Officer thereof."[125] Since the earliest days of the Republic, courts and commentators have struggled to reconcile this seemingly broad grant of congressional authority with the vesting clauses of Articles II and III, which unequivocally assign the executive power and the judicial power to the president and Supreme Court, respectively.[126] The same challenge is presented by the question of which branch retains constitutional authority over Supreme Court recusal.

As an initial matter, because Congress's necessary and proper power is derivative of other enumerated powers, Congress cannot justify its recusal standards by claiming that they are necessary and proper for carrying into execution constitutional provisions that are completely inapposite to the issue at hand. For example, the preceding arguments from constitutional structure demonstrate that neither Congress's impeachment power—as manifest in the good behavior requirement of Article III—nor its power to limit the Court's appellate jurisdiction under the Exceptions Clause is a potential source of the power to set recusal standards for the Court. If these provisions are indeed inapposite to the question of Congress's constitutional authority over recusal, then there is likewise no foundation for Congress to claim that it may regulate recusal in a way that is necessary and proper to the execution of those powers. The Due Process Clause is likewise not a basis for legislative control over the justices' recusal decisions. The Fifth Amendment does not contain a legislative enforcement clause, and there is no reason to believe that the Necessary and Proper Clause includes the power to legislate in support of due process. Due process is not a "power" for Congress to "carry into execution" within the meaning of the Necessary and Proper Clause. Even if the Necessary and Proper Clause were deemed relevant to due process, the Court has made it clear that Congress would be limited in its legislative powers by the Court's construction of the Due Process Clause, thereby making any recusal legislation purportedly based on enforcing litigants' due process rights redundant with the Court's own interpretation of that Clause.[127]

Recusal standards could, however, help the courts carry into execution their *own* assigned powers. In that case, the Necessary and Proper Clause appears to provide Congress precisely the authority it needs to enact a recusal statute for the Supreme Court. All that is left is to weigh this apparent grant of legislative authority against any independent and conflicting source of constitutional authority that is exclusive to the federal courts. Congress's incursion into the Court's recusal practices could violate the separation of powers by unconstitutionally interfering with the inherent power of the federal courts under Article III.

The fact of inherent judicial power, at least in some form, should not be particularly controversial. In general, inherent power under the Constitution can be described as the range of authority constitutionally reserved to one branch of government either in addition to or at the expense of the other branches. Our tripartite system of government demands that all three branches have some measure of independence and influence over one another. Whether this is described as separate powers or checks and balances, the upshot is that none of the three branches can be in a position of ultimate power over the others, else the promise of divided government fails. This broader premise about our constitutional structure effectively guarantees the existence of some inherent power in all three branches of government. Take Congress's necessary and proper power as an example, both because it is the provision most relevant to the question of Supreme Court recusal and because it is among the most explicit grants of power to one branch at the expense of the others. It is easy to read the Necessary and Proper Clause to effectively permit Congress to influence nearly every manner of executive and judicial power. Congress could claim, for example, that it is necessary to the proper functioning of interstate commerce to enter into a treaty with Canada to build a transcontinental oil pipeline. Regardless of how one feels about the policy decision, it would seem like a rather blatant infringement on the president's Article II treaty power to have Congress negotiate and ratify a treaty pursuant to its authority under the Necessary and Proper Clause. The same is true of Congress's relationship with the judiciary. If the Necessary and Proper Clause reaches all manner of judicial function, then there is no power that is uniquely judicial. The independence of the courts would be lost. Imagine another scenario involving the earlier pipeline example. This time Congress relies on its necessary and proper power to reopen a decision by the Court interpreting the language of a duly ratified pipeline treaty. If Congress can rely on its necessary and proper power to undo otherwise binding judicial decisions in individual cases, then the judicial power no longer appears separate in any meaningful way, and the judiciary's power to act as a check on Congress is effectively lost.[128] Assuming that the constitutional structure was not created to anoint a single, all-powerful branch (an assumption that is confirmed by the overwhelming weight of constitutional history and practice), then some measure of inherent power must reside in all three branches of government. Once we reach this largely unsurprising conclusion, the remaining, and far more difficult, endeavor is determining the proper scope of that power.

The scope of inherent judicial power under the Constitution is a controversial and complicated subject for both judges and commentators. The Court has on a number of occasions indicated that Article III reserves some quintessentially judicial powers to the courts alone.[129] Picking up on these references, commentators have considered which specific exercises of judicial authority qualify as inherent under Article III.[130] Judicial recusal has not been the subject of any of these prior discussions.

The issue for Supreme Court recusal is whether the Necessary and Proper Clause empowers Congress to regulate the Court's recusal practices, or whether recusal is within the Court's "inherent power" under Article III such that Congress (and any other governmental actor, for that matter) is precluded from doing so. The inherent powers literature offers a number of theories that bear on the question, ranging from the Necessary and Proper Clause acting as a "one-way ratchet" to permit only congressional enhancement of judicial power,[131] to the judicial power protecting only those choices that are indispensable to the functioning of a court.[132] The Supreme Court has likewise indicated that, at minimum, there are some features of judicial power that are so fundamental to the character and nature of a court, such as litigation management and sanctions and supervisory power over the lower courts, that they are completely insulated from the other branches by Article III.[133]

It is not enough that theories of inherent judicial power recognize that Article III reserves at least some subset of judicial authority to the courts. We must identify the content of inherent judicial power to determine if it is infringed by legislative recusal standards. The full range of this authority is the subject of ongoing debate, but a common reed (however slender) has emerged.[134] In addition to agreeing at least in principle that there is such a thing as inherent judicial power and that it protects some core of judicial activity from extrajudicial control or interference, it is also common wisdom among courts and commentators that this core of judicial conduct must include the ability to independently and completely decide cases. As Liebman and Ryan explained in their comprehensive and influential study of inherent judicial power:

> "The judicial Power" means the Article III judge's authority and obligation, in all matters over which jurisdiction is conferred, independently, finally, and effectually to decide the whole case and nothing but the case on the basis, and so as to maintain the supremacy, of the whole federal law. By "independently, finally, and effectually decide," we mean dispositively to arrange the rights and responsibilities of the parties on the basis of independently developed legal reasons, subject to review only by a superior Article III court. By "case," we mean a court action that can be resolved on the basis of enforceable law, and by "whole case," we mean not only the "construction" of applicable provisions of law but also their actual application to the facts to reach a decision.[135]

As a court of last resort, and one that is singled out in the text of Article III as unique among the federal judiciary, the Supreme Court provides the strongest constitutional case for retaining some inherent judicial power, including the power to decide cases properly before it. Even when viewed in this limited way, the Court's inherent judicial power includes recusal.

The details of how recusal interacts with the inherent power of the courts are more complicated. Recusal is distinct from other issues that come before the Court because it involves a decision by an individual justice, rather than the Court as a whole. This individual conception of recusal suggests that if recusal standards interfere with some inherent judicial power, they must do so with respect to the power of the individual justice being recused. Recusal is not, however, a purely individual issue. It affects the inherent power of the Court as a whole. In order to fully understand the intersection of recusal and judicial power, we must therefore address the question of recusal's impact on the Court's ability to decide cases by viewing inherent judicial authority as both an individual and an institutional matter.

AN INDIVIDUAL CONCEPTION OF JUDICIAL POWER AND RECUSAL

The decision to recuse has a direct (and potentially fatal) effect on an individual justice's ability to decide a case. Recusal is, on an individual level, analogous to removal from the bench. But removal through recusal is not a remedy granted to Congress by the Constitution. Impeachment is the only textually prescribed remedy by which Congress may remove a justice from the bench. It is a far more severe and procedurally cumbersome remedy than recusal, and there is no constitutional authority for reading Congress's impeachment power to include the lesser power of recusal. It would seem absurd to think of Congress legislatively singling out a specific justice and prohibiting her from participating in a case before the Court. But that is precisely the point. If we are to treat recusal as part of an individual jurist's inherent power under Article III, then any statutory requirement that infringes on that jurist's ability to decide a case is effectively indistinguishable from impeachment.

The fact that recusal is limited to a single case at a time does not change the analysis, because any inherent judicial power will attach equally to every case over which the Court has jurisdiction. It is thus no answer to say that recusal presents only a discrete infringement on inherent judicial authority because there is no constitutional basis for claiming that Congress may partially abdicate inherent judicial power. Inherent power under the Constitution is by definition sacrosanct—any infringement by a coordinate branch, however small, is prohibited.[136] Furthermore, a separation-of-powers question like this one is rarely comprehensive. One branch rarely, if ever, threatens the entirety of another branch's constitutional prerogative. The Court's most famous pronouncements on the scope and limits of governmental authority all involve discrete encroachments by one branch or another. Granted, these cases often deal with particular substantive issues rather than specific cases, but they are still subject to the denominator problem of how to characterize the scope of the potential infringement. In

Plaut v. Spendthrift Farm, Inc.,[137] the Court rejected Congress's revision of the Court's rulings in a fixed set of securities cases. At issue was whether the statutory reopening of several cases that had been finally decided by the courts was an infringement of their inherent power. Congress's influence over specific recusal decisions could similarly be viewed as a constitutionally prohibited infringement on the authority of individual justices to decide individual cases.

Even if case-by-case infringements are somehow deemed less intrusive on inherent judicial power than, for example, impeachment, it is important to remember that the current exercise is being performed in the context of the hypothetical universe where Article III judicial power is conferred upon and exercised by individual justices. In this environment, every act of deciding a case rises to the level of a direct exercise of a constitutionally assigned power. Even if the cumulative argument is made that recusal standards seriously threaten a justice's constitutional power to decide cases only when spread out over a critical number or percentage of those cases, the problem remains that there is no principled way to limit the number of cases in which statutory recusal standards will affect a justice over time. Any attempt to cap the number of recusal cases for a specific justice will necessarily result in at best strategic, and at worst arbitrary, recusal decisions. Any argument for a compromise between a justice's Article III power and effective judging is therefore lost, as recusal requires at least some infringement on an individual justice's constitutionally assigned power, while attempting to limit the total number of recusals fails to guarantee any measurable improvement in either the quality or the rationality of recusal decisions.

The severe and permanent nature of the impeachment remedy and the cumbersome procedures required to effectuate removal by impeachment are carefully designed to create a legislative check on the judiciary without sacrificing the judicial independence embodied in Article III.[138] Allowing Congress to remove justices from a particular case by a simple legislative mandate—rather than the full impeachment process laid out in Article I—violates the separation of powers by infringing on the independence of the judiciary in a way not anticipated by constitutional text or structure. For these reasons, a view of recusal as an individual justice's exercise of judicial power reveals a corresponding authority to decide cases that is unconditionally protected under Article III.

There are two additional objections to this formulation of individual judicial power that are of interest but ultimately fail. The first is that a recusal decision is not a "case" such that congressional interference with a justice's decision to recuse does not strike at a core judicial power to decide cases under Article III. There are practical and historical responses to this argument. Practically speaking, it is important to remember that treating recusal as an exercise of individual judicial power under Article III necessarily requires some extrapolation from the inherent powers literature and Article III itself, which do not treat justices as individual agents of judicial power but instead focus—quite rightly, outside of the recusal context—on the Court as an institution. If Article III's core function is to protect the Court's ability to decide cases, any understanding of that same power on an individual basis would have to consider removal from a case as the equivalent of prohibiting a decision by that individual justice, and hence an interference with that justice's core judicial power. It is only when we compare the *individual* consequences of recusal to the power of the Court *as an institution* that the power to decide is not necessarily implicated. But that conflation of individual and institutional power is either a mistake or fiction. From a historical perspective, it has been assumed that individual judges and justices have the power to resolve their own recusal questions even when there is little if any authority for them to decide other legal issues on an individual basis. It would be a mistake to simply say that recusal decisions are not the resolution of a case by an individual justice, and therefore are not part of that justice's core constitutional authority, when the consequences for that justice are identical to removal from the Court for purposes of that case and the justices have always—in plain view of Congress—exercised their recusal power on no more authority than their status as jurists.

A second objection to treating recusal as an exercise of inherent constitutional power by an individual justice is that a case cannot be considered "properly before" an individual justice who is subject to recusal. In other words, an individual justice is not deprived of her inherent authority to decide a case by virtue of her being subject to external recusal standards because an individual justice who meets such recusal standards does not have authority to decide that case in the first instance. This is a theory of individual jurisdiction and, as such, is a nonstarter. First, jurisdiction is an institutional concept, as a matter of both constitutional text and practice. Second, even if one were to assume that jurisdiction is a concept that could be applied to an individual judge or justice, it would improperly conflate jurisdiction and substantive rules of decision to claim that the enumeration of substantive recusal standards deprives a justice of the prerequisite authority to decide the issue. If that were the case, the recusal standards would have to be treated as jurisdictional rules, which are limited to the Court's appellate jurisdiction by the plain language of Article III.[139] Finally, judges have been deciding their own recusal questions for centuries, and the practice was considered part of the core power of the judiciary at the time of the Framing.[140] This long-standing historical practice would have to be either ignored or turned completely on its head to conclude that individual justices lack jurisdiction to make recusal decisions. An individualistic view of recusal and judicial power thus leads to the conclusion that substantive recusal standards infringe on the justices' inherent power to decide cases properly before them. This view requires some assumptions about the nature of judicial power and individual justices, however, that are not entirely consistent with actual practice, in which judicial power affixes to courts as institutions, rather than to individual jurists.

An Institutional Perspective on Judicial Power and Recusal

The more natural approach to thinking about judicial power and recusal is to treat recusal as an exercise of a court's *institutional* authority to decide cases. Treating recusal as an exercise of institutional authority leads to the conclusion that recusal qualifies as part of the Supreme Court's inherent judicial power under Article III because recusal has the power to interfere with or even wholly preclude the Court's ability to decide cases. A mandatory recusal statute could result in there not being enough justices to resolve a case that is otherwise properly before the Court, the phenomenon referred to here as "complete recusal." Consider the easy hypothetical of a case in which an intimate friend of all nine justices was either a party or counsel to a party. If the current statute would not require recusal of all nine justices in that case (and it is not clear what the statute's "impartiality might reasonably be questioned" standard would require),[141] it is entirely possible that Congress could enact a statute that would require complete recusal based solely on the laudable and sensible goals of protecting the fairness and integrity of the judicial system and of avoiding the appearance of partiality at the Court. Justice Scalia said as much when he explained in *Cheney* that "a rule that requires Members of this Court to remove themselves from cases in which the official actions of friends were at issue would be utterly disabling."[142] There are two clear implications to be drawn from Justice Scalia's comment. First, it is indeed possible for Congress to draft a statute that could, if enforced, render the Court unable to perform its core duties, and second, the justices would never let that happen against their will. What Justice Scalia left out is the next logical step—that legislative "disabling" of the Court in this way is an unconstitutional infringement on the Court's inherent authority to decide cases.[143]

This complete recusal argument is often met with strong resistance, primarily because those who object rightly consider it extremely unlikely that complete recusal would ever occur on the Court. This statement is of course true. It is extremely rare for a majority of justices, let alone the entire Court, to recuse themselves from a single case. But this argument misses the point. The fact that a recusal statute rarely causes the recusal of all nine justices has little if anything to do with the fact that under the current statutory standard it is entirely plausible that recusal could be statutorily required for any number of justices, including all nine, in the same case. This is particularly true in light of Congress's historic trend of expanding the range of recusable conduct and its recent (failed) attempts to pass more stringent recusal legislation for the Court.[144]

Take the earlier example of a close friend of all nine justices representing a party before the Court. Is it far-fetched to assume that having a close friend appear before the Court would cause a reasonable person to question the justices' impartiality? Recall that since 1974, actual bias has not been a requirement for recusal. Remember also the public outcry (from reasonable people) over Justice Scalia's choice to participate in *Cheney*. Monroe Freedman, a renowned scholar of judicial ethics, thought recusal could have been justified in *Cheney* based on the fact that "a reasonable person might nevertheless question whether ex parte communications . . . occurred" during the justice's trip with the vice president.[145] Justice Scalia himself admitted that friendship with a litigant is grounds for recusal when the litigant is sued personally.[146] The justices are an elite group of people who come from an increasingly narrow segment of society. They are virtually assured to have friends, or at minimum professional acquaintances, in common. Many of them have close relationships with high-ranking government officials, and they tend to have similar educational backgrounds.[147] During the October 2015 term, the nine sitting justices had attended a grand total of three law schools among them.[148] Compare this with the members of the Warren Court that decided *Brown* in 1954. That Court hailed from no fewer than seven different law schools in six states. This is not meant to suggest that the justices of the Warren Court were a more diverse group than the Roberts Court—they almost certainly were not. It merely suggests that the modern Court may be even more vulnerable to large-scale personal conflicts of interest than its predecessors. Nevertheless, the argument persists that concerns about recusal of multiple justices in a single case are overblown. Why are we comfortable assuming that a broad statutory standard, and one that is under political pressure to expand even further, is not able or even likely to implicate many or all of the justices in a specific case? If the answer is simply that it almost never does, we need look no further than the Court's own recusal practices for an explanation.

As an initial matter, it is not true that recusals never affect the Court's ability to achieve a quorum. Prior to the recusal statute being amended in 1948 to include Supreme Court justices, there were at least three cases in which enough justices felt they met the prevailing recusal standard to defeat a quorum and render the case unresolvable by the Court. Since 1948, a search of Supreme Court cases citing the quorum statutes[149] reveals at least eighteen cases in which the Court determined that recusals rendered the Court unable to act due to a lack of a quorum.[150] The most high-profile example was the 1988 case of *Haig v. Bissonette*, in which four justices recused themselves from a case brought on behalf of several participants in the 1973 civil uprising in the village of Wounded Knee, South Dakota, on the Pine Ridge Indian Reservation.[151] More than 200 Pine Ridge residents and other Native American activists seized control of the village of Wounded Knee on February 27, 1973, in protest of alleged treaty violations by the United States.[152] The U.S. government surrounded and laid siege to the town for seventy-one days, making the incident the longest-lasting "civil disorder" in American history.[153] In *Bissonette*, residents of Pine Ridge brought suit challenging the government's use of the military to quell the domestic uprising. The Court was prevented from hearing the case due to a lack of quorum.[154] Although they never explained their decisions publicly, four justices—Rehnquist, Kennedy, O'Connor, and Scalia—recused themselves from the case, almost certainly due to their prior relationships with various members and offices of the U.S. Justice Department that were involved in the case.[155] The Court's failure to achieve a quorum in *Bissonette* is emblematic of the potential for recusal to interfere with the Court's ability to fulfill its judicial function. At minimum, this (likely incomplete) list of cases, including *Bissonette,* demonstrates that it is not impossible for recusal to interfere with the Court's ability to decide cases.

It does not, however, explain how serious a threat complete recusal presents to the effective functioning of the Court. The answer to that question remains largely theoretical but not entirely so. Because the justices do not typically include a public explanation for their recusal decisions, it is difficult to track the frequency with which recusal has in fact threatened the Court's ability to resolve a case over which it has jurisdiction. Because we do not know when the justices may have had reason to recuse but decided against it, it is virtually impossible to quantify the number of cases in which recusal could have threatened the Court's ability to function. There is evidence, however, that the Court has been willing to engage in self-help in order to prevent recusal from interfering with its institutional mission. Remember that the justices retain virtually unlimited control over their decisions to recuse, even where the standards for recusal clearly apply. In order to see whether the existence of statutory recusal standards constitutes a meaningful threat to the Court's functionality, we should look at those cases where the justices had reason to recuse but chose not to. The Court's management of the potentially conflicting problems of quorum and recusal, coupled with the fact that the justices almost never explain their recusal decisions, can help reconcile the strong theoretical case for complete recusal as an obstacle to the Court deciding cases with the fact that the Court has rarely allowed recusal to be such an obstacle.

Several early cases offer a peek into the potential disruption recusal creates for the Court. In 1920 the Court decided *Evans v. Gore,*[156] a case by a federal judge challenging the constitutionality of an income tax statute. The judge challenged the statute on the grounds that it was a diminution of his salary in violation of Article III's Compensation Clause, which guarantees that federal judges' "compensation . . . shall not be diminished" while in office.[157] The statute applied to all federal judges and as such created an obvious conflict of interest throughout the federal courts, including at the Supreme Court. The justices simply ignored this clear conflict apparently for reason of necessity—the question of whether Congress could tax the federal judiciary required a final answer that only the Court could provide.

Recusal issues threatened the Court's ability to garner a quorum in three cases from the 1940s. Two of the cases were never heard by the Court, thereby confirming recusal's potential to interfere with the Court's judicial function and bringing to life the separation of powers dilemma that inspired this analysis; a congressional statute rendered the Court unavailable to perform the core constitutional function of deciding cases properly before it. The first, *Chrysler Corporation v. United States*, involved the modification of a consent decree in an antitrust case. It was simply dismissed for a lack of quorum.[158] The second, *United States v. Aluminum Company of America*, was a direct appeal from a district court ruling that defendants did not violate antitrust laws by entering into a conspiracy to restrain trade in aluminum.[159] Pursuant to a federal statute to that effect, the case was "transferred to a special docket and . . . postponed until such time as there is a quorum of Justices qualified to sit in it."[160] Nearly eight months after the initial postponement, a quorum still did not exist, and the Court finally transferred the case to the Second Circuit for decision.[161] The Court ultimately decided the third case, *North American Company v. SEC*, which involved the constitutionality of the Public Utility Holding Company Act.[162] Chief Justice Stone, who had previously determined that he should recuse himself, reversed his decision without explanation in order to preserve a quorum.[163]

Without relying too heavily on cases from more than seventy years ago, these pre-1948 cases shed at least some light on why recusal has not been a particularly disruptive force for the Court. First, it is worth noting that the justices in those cases were applying a more fluid recusal standard than currently exists; all four cases occurred before the federal recusal statute had been amended to include members of the Court. So under less restrictive standards, recusal was still enough of an issue to imperil the Court's ability to decide certain cases. In the most important cases, however, the two involving the constitutionality of federal statutes, the Court found a way to prevent recusal from interfering in its ultimate authority to render a decision. It refused to exclude itself from *Evans* on institutional grounds, and in *North American Company* the chief justice reversed his previous decision to recuse without any apparent reason other than to establish a quorum.[164]

The Court expressed a similar view regarding recusal and its power to decide cases some thirty years later in *United States v. Will*.[165] Several federal judges challenged the constitutionality of statutory cost-of-living reductions under the Compensation Clause of Article III.[166] On review, and despite the fact that no objections had been raised by the parties to the suit, the Supreme Court acknowledged the sensitivity of its resolving a case that could directly affect its members' compensation. It thus proceeded from the point of view that "§ 455 mandates disqualification of all judges and Justices without exception."[167] Notwithstanding its default position that the statutory standard alone would require recusal of the entire Court, the Court held that recusal was not necessary in the present case due to the rule of necessity, which it described as having "its genesis at least five and a half centuries ago" and being "consistently applied in this country in both state and federal courts."[168] It cited its 1920 decision in *Evans* as dealing with the rule "by clear implication" but admitted that it had so far never expressly invoked the rule, apparently because it "so took for granted the continuing validity of the Rule . . . that no express reference to it . . . was needed."[169]

Because *Will* arose more than three decades after section 455 had been amended to apply to members of the Court, the justices were forced to reconcile section 455 with the common law rule of necessity. The Court noted that "the congressional purpose [of section 455] . . . gives no hint of altering the ancient Rule of Necessity, a doctrine that had not been questioned under prior judicial disqualification statutes." It went on to note that "the public interest would not be served by requiring disqualification under § 455"[170] and that the Court, citing *Marbury v. Madison*, "would not casually infer that the Legislative and Executive Branches sought by the enactment of § 455 to foreclose federal courts from exercising 'the province and duty of the judicial department to say what the law is.'"[171] Regardless of whether the justices were correct in concluding that they should not recuse themselves in *Will*, their explanation for their decision offers insight into why recusal is not a regular problem for the Court in meeting its quorum requirements. Armed with common law rules protecting its right to hear cases and constitutional arguments about its responsibility to be the final arbiter of questions of federal law, the Court approached its recusal decisions from a wider berth than the plain words of the statute. Just as it did in the 1940s, this allowed the justices to protect their power to decide cases from potential infringement by Congress's recusal standards, even in cases where the plain language of the statute would require recusal.

The fact that the Court in *Will* successfully maintained a quorum in the face of challenging recusal issues does not mean, however, that recusal standards are not a threat to the Court's ability to fulfill its constitutional duties. On the contrary, the Court's reliance on the rule of necessity depends upon its reading the statute to not clearly foreclose the use of that common law rule. The statute, however, says rather clearly that a judge or justice "*shall* disqualify himself" when one of the enumerated conditions applies. It offers no exceptions for conditions of necessity, despite the fact that legislators would have been well aware of a rule that "had its genesis at least five and a half centuries ago . . . [and] has been consistently applied in this country in both state and federal courts" when they drafted the statute.[172] Even if the current statute did lend itself to a reading that incorporated the rule of necessity, if Congress has the constitutional power to regulate recusal, there is no constitutional reason—except perhaps a due process objection where there is literally no judge in the country to hear a case, a question addressed in later chapters—why a future recusal statute could not clearly prohibit the use of necessity as an excuse.

Moreover, necessity may not be a broad enough justification to protect the court's power to decide cases in every instance where complete recusal is a possibility. Envision a case involving an interpretation of a federal statute, for instance, in which the Court has jurisdiction over the case and would like to make a final pronouncement on the topic. Also assume that the case is being argued for one party by a close friend of the justices such that complete recusal would be statutorily required. It is hard to imagine that the Court could claim that it is necessary for it to hear the case, especially if it was decided below by a competent court and that decision was not contradicted by a court of equal authority, for example, a circuit split. For the rule of necessity to protect against complete recusal, it would have to be read so broadly as to include all instances in which the Court would like to participate in a case but is stopped from doing so. This reading would provide the justices with so much discretion in their recusal decisions that it would effectively eviscerate the federal recusal statute, thereby resolving the tension over complete recusal at the expense of de facto invalidating a duly enacted statute. This creates its own separation-of-powers problem, which I take up in the next chapter, but it also reveals how the Court's use of a common law exception to statutory recusal requirements is better understood as a defense of its own inherent power. The Court's opinion in *Will* is a more recent reminder of how statutory recusal requirements present a meaningful threat to the Court's ability to decide cases.

These examples collectively offer a snapshot both into the technical impacts recusal can have on the Court, as seen by the actual disruption of Supreme Court review in several cases, and into the Court's feelings about whether recusal law should be permitted to interfere in cases that the justices feel strongly about deciding. They show both that it is possible for recusal to disrupt the constitutional functions of the Court and that the justices themselves feel empowered to prevent that from happening. Taken with the fact that the current recusal statute covers a wider range of the justices' conduct than ever before and that mounting political pressure seeks to expand it even further, Congress's interference with the Court's power to decide suddenly seems very real, and the reasons why it has not been a frequently recurring problem are just as plausibly due to the justices' own recusal practices as to the rarity of the problem.

Congress's Other Powers over the Court

A few other constitutional arguments have been made in support of congressional involvement in Supreme Court recusal, albeit primarily as smaller parts of broader discussions. First, there are no exceptions that Congress could insert into the recusal statute that would solve the constitutional problem of complete recusal. For example, if Congress limited the total number of recusals in a certain case to preserve adequate participation to render a decision, it would result in an unconstitutional choice as to which justices should stay and which should go. On one extreme, Congress would encounter the same constitutional problems with making individualized removal decisions described earlier. On the other, Congress would be acting arbitrarily in allowing some justices who meet the recusal standard to sit and prohibiting others from doing so. Justices Scalia and Breyer noted as much in Senate testimony about the role of judges under the Constitution. In response to a question from Senator Patrick Leahy about the wisdom of having retired justices fill in for recused ones, both justices resisted the idea.[173] Justice Scalia was concerned about who would pick the replacements. He explained that the chief justice would be an unpopular choice to act alone and then wondered what would happen if the full Court split evenly on the choice, ultimately concluding that the justices "can stumble along the way we are."[174] Justice Breyer showed a similar lack of enthusiasm, stating only that "there might be problems" with the idea in practice.[175]

It is equally unlikely that Congress could reliably provide for adequate replacement justices without running afoul of Article III's "one supreme Court" requirement.[176] Throughout the overwhelming majority of its history, the Supreme Court has acted as a singular unit. It has not been divided into panels like the circuit courts, and although there are some instances of individual justices rendering decisions for the Court, only active justices were given that responsibility. Retired justices have been permitted to sit by designation on the lower courts, for which there is no textual mandate that there be only "one" of any particular court, but not on the Supreme Court. In short, history and practice generally support the idea that relying on retired justices to perform the same tasks as active justices runs afoul of the requirement that there be only one Supreme Court.

There has been some pushback, however, on the notion that Article III precludes the use of retired justices to substitute for their recused colleagues. Michael Dorf and Lisa McElroy, building on the work of Tracey George and Chris Guthrie, addressed the question as part of their commentary on a Senate proposal to permit retired justices to sit by designation on the Court.[177] They concluded that such a measure would be constitutional on the basis that retired justices remain Article III judges until their resignation and thus are members of the Supreme Court.[178] They concede that their argument is in tension with a formalistic conception of an "indivisible" Supreme Court—the idea that the Court is a singular entity that must act singularly—because the retired justices would participate only when an active justice was unavailable, but they offer two responses. First, they note that the text of Article III does not explicitly require that the Court be indivisible. Rearranging the composition of the Court would thus appear permissible, provided the additional members are justices who have retired, rather than resigned, from the Court.[179] They offer some historical evidence for this position but acknowledge that the evidence is far from conclusive of their point.

They then go on to argue that even a formalistic conception of indivisibility could be satisfied by allowing en banc review by the active members of the Court of any decision involving a retired justice. This would effectively make the body containing the retired justice a lower court, subject to Congress's constitutional authority to ordain and establish such courts, and would not run afoul of maintaining an indivisible Supreme Court. The problem with this argument is that it does not answer the question at hand. Requiring the possibility of en banc review merely pushes the debate about what "one supreme Court" looks like to a higher level of the judiciary. Based on the plain language of Article III, original jurisdiction cases could not be heard by retired justices without dividing the Court's membership, nor could the requirement that the Court shall have appellate jurisdiction "in all the other cases" brought before it be met where a retired justice participated in the final resolution of an appeal. An en banc panel of active justices would instead encounter precisely the same docket that the current Court faces. The only difference would be that some cases would have come to the active justices on appeal from a decision of a group of justices that includes retirees, rather than through the more traditional path of the circuit and district courts. Dorf and McElroy recognized the possibility of this redundancy but argued that Congress could use the Exceptions Clause to solve it by "'except[ing]' *all* cases from the 'real' Supreme Court's appellate jurisdiction, [or alternatively] . . . by excluding everything but . . . some . . . residual category" of cases.[180] This expansive reading of the Exceptions Clause is problematic for several reasons but, even if taken as true, still proves the relevant point that under the most creative reading of the "one supreme Court" requirement, retired justices could not take the place of active justices as the final arbiter in a case over which the Court has jurisdiction. The "real" Supreme Court would still consist exclusively of active justices. Relying on the Exceptions Clause may work to find a useful role for retired justices to play in the disposition of active cases, but it does not affect the definition of the Court under Article III.

A common response to separation-of-powers concerns about recusal has been that Congress's collective control over the size of the Court, the number of justices required to constitute a quorum, and the qualifications of the justices also translate into power over recusal.[181] This argument misses the point in terms of inherent judicial power. Neither the number of justices nor their qualifications for membership on the Court have any impact on the Court's ability to decide a case. Taking the constitutionally assigned judicial power to mean the power to decide cases properly before it, the total number of justices on the Court or their qualifications for membership are wholly beside the point. The same is true for the number of justices who must be present to render a decision in a particular case. Whether Congress sets the quorum requirement at nine or one, that fact alone does not limit the Court's or any individual justice's ability to decide a particular case. It is only when Congress becomes involved in deciding which justices may participate in a specific case that it acquires some influence over the Court's ability to exercise its constitutional authority. Only the *combination* of the power to set quorum requirements and to control the total number of available justices in a given case threatens the Court's ultimate power to decide. Because quorum alone cannot trigger complete recusal but substantive recusal standards can, the latter is constitutionally problematic in a way that the former is not. In short, because Congress's authority to control the Court's size, qualifications, and quorum requirements does not, standing alone, limit the Court's ability to decide cases, that authority cannot be used as support for the far more intrusive power to set recusal standards for the justices.

There are some extreme examples in which Congress could use its power to confirm justices or set the overall size or quorum requirements for the Court to prevent the justices from deciding a single case, but these examples are too burdened with their own constitutional infirmities to provide a persuasive analogy for the constitutionality of recusal standards. It is possible, for instance, that Congress could refuse to confirm enough presidential nominees that the Court became literally unpopulated, but that decision would almost certainly run afoul of Article III's mandate that there be "one" Supreme Court.[182] Even if allowing the Court to go unpopulated were considered a permissible use of the Senate's power to confirm, the argument could be made that the president would have an obligation to use his recess appointment power to ensure that the Court remained in existence, either in honor of Article III's one Court requirement or to avoid infringing on the Court's inherent power to decide cases.

Congress could also use its quorum power to preclude the Court from deciding cases either by raising the quorum requirement or by letting membership fall below existing quorum requirements, such that the Court would be statutorily precluded from rendering a decision. For example, if Congress allowed four of nine justices to leave the Court without confirming their replacements, the total number of sitting justices would be below the six currently required by statute to formulate a quorum.[183] Alternatively, Congress could set a quorum requirement higher than the statutory number of justices on the Court, for instance, by requiring ten justices to decide a case while setting the total number of justices at nine, making a quorum statutorily impossible to achieve. In those instances, the same Article III limits apply to issues of quorum and size of the Court as to Congress's power over recusal. The Court's Article III power to decide cases would preclude Congress from allowing quorum requirements to exceed membership—either the quorum limits would have to be reduced or more justices confirmed.[184]

Other than these extreme examples, which are really just the sum of congressional power to confirm justices and to set the Court's quorum threshold, the ability to control quorum requirements alone does not interfere with the Court's ability to decide cases *as an institution*. Without the power to mandate recusal, Congress cannot control when the Court will fail to achieve quorum. Justices can decide not to recuse themselves for the express purpose of maintaining a quorum and ensuring that a case can be decided by the Court. This is precisely what happened in *Evans* and *Will* when the Court used the rule of necessity to justify its resolution of cases involving a clear conflict of interest for all of the justices.[185] It is also what happened in *North American Company*, when Chief Justice Stone reversed his original decision to recuse after realizing his recusal could defeat a quorum.[186] When recusal is treated as part of the inherent judicial authority to decide cases under Article III, congressional power over the Court's membership and quorum is simply inapposite.

A slightly different approach to legislative control over recusal at the Court would be for Congress to require the justices to adopt their own set of recusal standards, without dictating the terms of those standards. This suggestion, while less constitutionally problematic than a substantive recusal statute, will not likely lead to its desired result. Even if the Court relented from its now centuries-old position that recusal is an exclusively internal matter for the justices, history suggests that any standards they voluntarily adopted either would explicitly grant the justices the same discretion they currently employ in their recusal decisions or would do so by omission. Without voluntary cooperation by the justices, there is no reliable way for Congress to successfully force the Court to adopt meaningful recusal standards. Leaving the Court free to craft its own standards from scratch will inevitably lead—absent an unforeseen and highly unlikely change of heart by the justices—to more of the same, and an attempt to offer minimum or threshold standards is just a version of the same complete recusal problem presented by the current recusal statute.

There is one aspect of recusal regulation that does not fall as neatly within the Court's inherent power to decide cases—procedural rules. Procedural rules for how the justices must go about making their recusal decisions do not raise the same complete recusal concerns as substantive recusal requirements. This fact does not, however, change the significance of the present inquiry or its potential impact on recusal practice. Many of the criticisms and suggestions for improvement of Supreme Court recusal jurisprudence focus on the procedures by which decisions are made and reviewed (or not) by a higher/neutral body.[187] Even if Congress would not violate the Court's inherent power to decide cases by enacting procedural rules for the justices, there may be other theories of inherent judicial power that would protect, at least in part, the Court's power to make its own procedural rules.[188]

More important, while congressional power over only the procedural aspects of Supreme Court recusal may appear important to supporters of additional regulation, it loses much of its weight in the absence of parallel substantive reforms. If the Court is unrestrained by Congress in deciding when a justice will be recused from a case, it is unlikely the procedural framework in which that decision was made will do much to improve it. For example, requirements that justices publish their reasons for failing to recuse themselves will, in the absence of defined, binding criteria for recusal decisions, do little to promote the integrity or public perception of the Court because there will be no baseline against which to measure the quality of the justices' explanations.[189] It is also difficult to imagine how, in cases where a justice would not voluntarily choose to publicly explain her decision, a reporting requirement would result in anything more than a cursory statement. This point is driven home by Justice Kennedy's 2015 testimony before a House appropriations subcommittee, in which he expressed his view that a justice's reasons for recusal "should never be discussed" because to publicly reveal his interest in a case "would almost be like lobbying."[190] A similar problem arises where the procedural requirement consists of the Court reviewing an individual decision of one of its members.[191] As evidenced by the fact that only once in its history has the Court experienced a public dispute between its members about recusal,[192] it is highly unlikely that internal Court review of recusal decisions would lead to any useful insight into either the decision under review or the Court's feelings about recusal more broadly. Chief Justice Roberts confirmed the justices' views on this matter in his 2011 Year-End Report, when he explained that "the Supreme Court does not sit in judgment of one of its own Members' decision whether to recuse . . . it would create an undesirable situation in which the Court could affect the outcome of a case by selecting who among its members may participate."[193] So while procedural reforms to Supreme Court recusal practices likely create fewer constitutional problems, the impact and effectiveness of such reforms will be severely limited by the absence of any binding substantive standards.

* * *

Where does this leave us? The broad legal conclusion to be drawn from the preceding analysis is that the justices' substantive recusal decisions may not be mandated or controlled by Congress. This is a novel and important point in its own right, but is it a good idea? It is fine to say that the Constitution demands a particular outcome, but it is arguably irresponsible to ignore the consequences of that conclusion. As President Jefferson explained in defense of his constitutionally suspect purchase of the Louisiana Territory from France in 1803: "A strict observance of the written laws is doubtless *one* of the high duties of a good citizen, but it is not *the highest*. The laws of necessity, of self-preservation, of saving our country when in danger, are of higher obligation. To lose our country by a scrupulous adherence to the written law, would be to lose the law itself."[194] Justice Jackson expressed this idea more succinctly in his dissent in *Terminiello v. Chicago*, when he famously stated that the Constitution is not "a suicide pact."[195] It would be overly dramatic to compare recusal to issues like national security or free speech, as in *Terminiello*. It is not unreasonable, however, to demand that a constitutional argument be made to account for its effects.

As luck would have it, treating Supreme Court recusal as the exclusive province of the justices offers several benefits over the current arrangement. One is to boost the perceived legitimacy of both Congress and the Court. This initially may seem counterintuitive. Much of the criticism of Supreme Court recusal practice has been based on the idea that the justices' recusal decisions need to be more consistent and transparent, and that the only way to achieve this is through stricter legislative controls. The Supreme Court Transparency and Disclosure Act of 2011 was inspired, at least in part, by a desire to "protect the integrity of the Supreme Court."[196] What has been overlooked is that this legislative command-and-control approach to recusal at the Court creates a legitimacy problem for Congress and the Court and potentially harms litigants. This is because any legislative attempt to make Supreme Court recusal decisions appear more like statutory rulings and less like the flexible and highly contextualized due process decisions they have been to date is at bottom an exercise in futility that is more likely to exacerbate concerns about the Court's integrity than resolve them.

Leaving aside the (serious) questions about the constitutionality of the procedures suggested by the act, such as its proposed use of other federal judges to review the justices' decisions not to recuse,[197] there is little reason to think that any procedural regime imposed by Congress will be enforceable against the Supreme Court. The Court has shown little regard for congressional attempts to guide its recusal decisions to date, and Congress has been unable to force the Court's hand, despite a validly enacted law requiring the justices to behave differently. The result is an impasse between the branches that can only be resolved by their collective acceptance of a solution. Due to the seemingly inevitable unenforceability of congressional mandates regarding Supreme Court recusal, the integrity and legitimacy of both branches of government are better protected by leaving Supreme Court recusal decisions where constitutional text, practice, and structure suggest they belong—with the justices alone.

There are potential institutional benefits for the Court being recognized as the sole authority over its recusal decisions. For starters, it would best describe actual constitutional practice, and as such may promote accountability and transparency in the Court's recusal jurisprudence. Removing Congress's external restraint from the Court's recusal decisions leads to greater transparency because the public is better able to evaluate the Court's decisions for what they are—judgments of how best to balance the unique role of the Court with core notions of impartiality and due process. This could in turn increase the accountability of the individual justices, who would no longer be able to justify their decisions by simply cloaking their own feelings about the case in a statutory argument that likely has little, if any, real effect on the outcome. Their decision will be attributable to their own views on recusal in that case, and as such is an easier target for public criticism, regardless of whether the justice offers any formal explanation of their decision.

The second benefit is more symbolic but not necessarily less important. Formally committing recusal decisions to the Supreme Court signals a public trust in the integrity and professionalism of the Court that Blackstone considered vital to an effective judiciary.[198] This signal is valuable because it is factually accurate, at least in the majority of cases. Although ethics and recusal at the Court have become a hotly debated issue, even the strongest critics of the Court's practices concede that the justices act responsibly in the overwhelming majority of cases involving recusal.[199] Signaling public trust in the courts also facilitates a sense of interbranch comity and respect that is essential to the integrity of a tripartite government. In a system dependent on separate but balanced power, it is imperative that the branches cooperate with one another.[200] But perhaps the greatest feature of this argument is that the symbolism it seeks comes virtually free of cost. While there may be very good grounds for taking issue with Blackstone's confidence in the judiciary, when it comes to Supreme Court recusal, we are already entirely dependent on the justices' judgment and integrity, and there are constitutional as well as prudential reasons why this should not and cannot change. An affirmative acknowledgment that the Court is the sole arbiter of its own recusal decisions would serve as a valuable endorsement of the Court's competence, which we are ultimately bound to accept in any event.

While the separation of powers provides a strong argument for limiting Congress's authority over recusal at the Court, it does nothing to limit the Court's authority over its own recusal practices. Reserving recusal issues for the Court leaves ample space and encouragement for the justices to seek their own solutions to public perceptions of bias or inappropriate conduct at the Court. Provided it did not seek to unduly interfere with legislative or executive authority or with the constitutionally protected rights of individuals—and it is hard to imagine how adopting more rigorous recusal procedures would—the Court would be free to experiment with its own processes. In addition to possibly leading to better recusal practices, the very process could create perception benefits for the Court, flipping what was a public perception challenge into an opportunity.[201] As for concerns that removing the specter of congressional oversight (however weak) will free the justices to make arbitrary recusal decisions, past and current Supreme Court practice shows little if any deference to congressional mandates, and the integrity and institutional reverence of the individual justices should function as a potent check against any digression, especially when the public accountability for the decision is placed squarely on their shoulders.

It is equally important to remember that removing statutory requirements does not deprive the Court of binding substantive standards to guide its decisions. The Due Process Clause provides a powerful and familiar framework for recusal decisions that is both binding on the justices without congressional involvement and most consistent with their historical approach to recusal at the Court. Any attempt by the legislature to mandate the substance of due process protections would be at best redundant and at worst unconstitutional.[202] Finally, the Court should have sole authority over its own recusal decisions because the Court has more expertise and experience than Congress in matters of judicial procedure, including recusal. This expertise will allow the justices to design standards that are responsive to the full range of issues associated with recusal at the Court. By removing the deniability provided by a statutory recusal standard, the Court could be incentivized to seek its own solutions and would have wider latitude to do so.

The issue of who decides recusal questions at the Court is an important and underappreciated question. It is also a complicated one. At its core, however, the outcome is relatively straightforward. Constitutional text, history, practice, and structure show that Congress may not control the substance of the justices' recusal decisions because doing so would unconstitutionally interfere with the Court's inherent power to decide cases properly before it. What's more, this realization has benefits for the Court and individual litigants. It is thus an important step in understanding recusal as a separation-of-powers problem. But it is not the last. Now that we have reached the point of, at minimum, skepticism about Congress's ability to direct the Court's recusal decisions, the next question is how to apply that knowledge to the reality of modern government, where there is an ongoing impasse between Congress and the Court over recusal. Just as this chapter committed to evaluating the proper source of federal recusal law from a constitutional vantage point, the next will seek to address the challenges created by an unconstitutional recusal statute from that same perspective.

4 | Constitutional Solutions

It is possible to imagine a scenario where the existence of an unconstitutional statute is a relatively low-profile affair. This is perhaps most likely where the statute is internal to the federal government, that is, when it directly regulates another branch of government rather than private actors. That is not to say that such statutes are acceptable or should not inspire public concern. The passage of any unconstitutional law is an issue of national importance. As Chief Justice Roberts and Justice Black have articulated, "'Slight encroachments create new boundaries from which legions of power can seek new territory to capture.'"[1] Recent history suggests, however, that legislation implicating the separation of powers without a concomitant impact on private citizens is less likely to draw significant public attention.

Some anecdotal evidence paints the relevant picture. In the 2012 term, there were an average of 14 amicus ("friend of the court") briefs filed in each case before the Court.[2] Amicus briefs are voluntary filings by interested nonparties and are one, although certainly not the only, way to gauge public interest in a given case. In 2010, the Court considered a constitutional challenge to Congress's creation of the Public Company Accounting Oversight Board (PCAOB), an independent agency designed to oversee the audits of public companies in the wake of the WorldCom and Enron accounting scandals of 2002.[3] The case raised an important constitutional question about the internal functioning of the executive branch, specifically the president's removal power.[4] There were approximately 15 amicus briefs filed in the *PCAOB* case, compared with an average of 9 per case that term.[5] In 2014, the Court considered the scope of the president's appointment power in *NLRB v. Noel Canning*.[6] *Noel Canning* involved the president's power to make recess appointments, temporary appointments that do not require Senate approval. More than 30 amicus briefs were filed in *Noel Canning*, more than twice the average from the previous term. Viewed in isolation, these numbers suggest robust public interest in separation-of-powers cases. They pale in comparison, however, to public participation in cases involving controversial issues of individual rights. In 2008, more than 70 amicus briefs were filed in a case about individuals' Second

Amendment right to possess handguns in their homes.[7] More than 100 briefs were filed in a 2013 case dealing with the federal government's definition of marriage, 136 were filed in the 2012 case challenging the Affordable Care Act's requirement that individuals buy health insurance, and a record 148 were filed in *Obergefell v. Hodges*, the 2015 case recognizing a constitutional right to marry for same-sex couples.[8] In terms of generating public frustration and skepticism about the Court, even the most high-profile cases involving internal government functions are likely to generate less negative publicity for the justices than cases involving individual liberties.

Therefore, even if we assume that the federal recusal statute is an unconstitutional infringement on the Supreme Court's judicial power, that fact does not necessarily have to cause any undue consternation between Congress and the Court. The justices could simply go about making their recusal decisions, and except for those in the legal academy and elsewhere who are content to ruminate about such things, the general public would likely never spend much time or energy thinking, let alone worrying, about the consequences for our constitutional system. The case of Supreme Court recusal, however, has not offered such a peaceful coexistence between the statute and the entity it purports to regulate. The Court has a long history of employing recusal practices that appear to be at best only partly controlled by the statutory language, and the public is growing increasingly attentive and suspicious, in the Bractonian sense, of the integrity of the justices' recusal decisions. The result is a tension between Congress and the Court over recusal that has drawn enough public attention to create ethical and legitimacy problems for both branches. The justices are content to protect the institutional interests of the Court as the independent, final arbiter of questions of federal law. They take this stance, however, in the wake of increasing public focus on them and their activities. Growing concern about the politicization of the Court encourages Congress to impose new and more restrictive recusal standards in order to protect litigants and promote the Court's integrity. This chapter addresses this impasse between Congress and the Court over recusal and, much like the previous chapter's approach to the problems with statutory recusal standards, looks to constitutional law for an answer. In light of the range of tensions and issues at stake over recusal at the Court, the question becomes how to craft a solution that is worthy of a conflict among two coequal branches of government.

The resolution of interbranch conflict necessarily evinces the separation of powers. The separation of powers envisions a constitutional arrangement in which all three branches operate independently from one another, while at the same time protecting against any one branch's ability to aggrandize power for itself or encroach on the power of a coordinate branch.[9] Chief among these checks and balances is the shared responsibility of all three branches to interpret the Constitution, especially with regard to the allocation of power among them.[10] As James Madison explained:

> I beg to know, upon which principle it can be contended, that any one department draws from the constitution greater powers than another, in marking out the limits of the powers of the several departments. The constitution is the charter of the people to the government; it specifies certain great powers as absolutely granted, and marks out the departments to exercise them. If the constitutional boundary of either be brought into question, I do not see than any one of these independent departments has more right than another to declare their sentiments on that point.[11]

Madison's view was echoed by Presidents Jefferson and Andrew Jackson. In an 1804 letter to former first lady Abigail Adams, President Jefferson defended his decision not to enforce a sedition law that had been upheld by the courts. He argued that "nothing in the Constitution has given [the judges] a right to decide for the Executive, more than to the Executive to decide for them. . . . [T]he opinion which gives to the judges the right to decide what laws are constitutional . . . for the legislature and executive . . . would make the judiciary a despotic branch."[12] President Jackson, in a message to the Senate explaining his decision to veto a bill pertaining to the Bank of the United States, explained that the "opinion of the judges has no more authority over Congress than the opinion of Congress has over the judges, and on that point the President is independent of both."[13] The Supreme Court echoed these sentiments in *United States v. Nixon*, almost 150 years after President Jackson: "In the performance of assigned constitutional duties each branch of the Government must initially interpret the Constitution, and the interpretation of its powers by any branch is due great respect by the others."[14] According to these venerable sources, each branch has a concurrent obligation to consider the constitutionality of its own conduct and to respect the views of its coordinate branches. Congress's interpretive responsibilities are the most interesting to questions of Supreme Court recusal because the executive has little if any role in recusal decisions at the Court, and the Court's own power to interpret the Constitution is well established.

The most detailed analysis of Congress's interpretive responsibilities has come from the wide-ranging and diverse scholarly literature on the topic. It raises questions about Congress's institutional competency to interpret the Constitution,[15] the role of institutional design in improving that core competency,[16] and how to balance the interpretive role of nonjudicial actors like Congress against that of the judiciary.[17] Within this broader debate, however, is a core conception of legislative constitutional interpretation that is consistent with the one articulated by the three former presidents and Court. James Bradley Thayer explained in his seminal article, "The Origin and Scope of the American Doctrine of Constitutional Law,"[18] that "it is the legislature to whom this power is given,—this power, not merely of enacting laws, but of putting an interpretation on the constitution which shall deeply affect the whole country."[19] In the more than 100 years since Thayer's pronouncement, a general consensus has emerged that the separation of powers places an obligation on Congress to consider the constitutionality of its actions vis-à-vis the other branches. Larry Alexander and Frederick Schauer put it this way: "A recurrent claim in American constitutional discourse is that judges should not be the exclusive and authoritative interpreters of the Constitution. . . . To hold otherwise, it is argued, is to fail to recognize the constitutional responsibilities of officials who happen not to be judges."[20] That is not to say that Congress is a better source of constitutional understanding than the courts, for instance, or that Congress as a descriptive matter engages in robust constitutional interpretation regularly. These far more controversial questions are beyond the scope of the present discussion. Because Supreme Court recusal has led to an impasse between Congress and the Court, we must simply acknowledge that Congress is constitutionally authorized and (at least partly) responsible for evaluating the constitutionality of its actions and, in turn, for resolving the constitutional tensions raised by the debate over recusal at the Court.

Reorienting Supreme Court recusal in a constitutional framework and acknowledging Congress's constitutional responsibilities with regard to the separation of powers highlight two significant questions about the impasse over recusal. The first, which is discussed in detail in the preceding chapter, is whether Congress has the constitutional authority to preclude a justice's participation in a specific case. Assuming that the answer to that initial question is, at minimum, debatable, a second question emerges. Which branch of government is best suited to resolve that impasse? The answer is that Congress—as a matter of both constitutional law and policy—should be responsible for finding alternative approaches to its regulation of Supreme Court recusal.

Why Congress?

Why is this Congress's problem? Why not focus on the Court's role in alleviating the impasse? The answer, like the question, lies in the separation of powers. Although the Court certainly possesses the constitutional power to facilitate a resolution, the mechanisms at the Court's disposal are potentially far more damaging to the Court as an institution and to our constitutional system in general than those available to Congress. Cooperation and comity among the coordinate branches are necessary to the effective functioning of our constitutional arrangement.[21] The branches are coequal and necessarily interactive,[22] collaborating on nearly every issue of national importance. Each branch is equipped with powerful constitutional checks designed to maintain a sense of equilibrium within the federal structure. Michael Stokes Paulsen calls this concept "coordinacy."[23] He explains that it "is a term of power-*relationship*, not of power-*scope*," and that it "fuels the system of 'checks and balances' that guards against 'a tyrannical concentration of all the powers of government in the same hands.'"[24] The use of those checks by the Court in a confrontational or unwelcome way may exchange short-term gains for long-term damage to governmental efficiency and productivity. For this reason alone, the Court should be cautious about resolving disputes in favor of one branch of government over another, and especially in favor of its own power over that of the president or Congress.[25]

The Court has at least three measures at its disposal to resolve its impasse with the legislative branch over recusal, none of which are ultimately satisfactory when considered in light of the separation of powers. One is to state openly and explicitly that it will not comply with any statutory mandates regarding recusal because of constitutional concerns, issues of judicial integrity, or some other institutional reason. This approach would bring transparency to the Court's position and would alleviate concerns that the Court is eluding statutory standards for some less compelling reason like political gain or mere convenience. But this approach also has some considerable weaknesses in the separation-of-powers context. For one, without grounding its statement in legally binding authority, the Court could be made to look more obstinate than it would in the absence of a public statement. A public statement of noncompliance may even exacerbate, rather than help resolve, the conflict. Chief Justice Roberts's 2011 Year-End Report, the closest example to date of a public explanation of the Court's views on the recusal impasse, provoked a largely negative reaction. It prompted a letter from five senators asking the Court to voluntarily adopt formal recusal standards.[26] William Yeomans and Herman Schwartz argued that "Chief Justice John Roberts's response in his year-end report to the increasing controversy over the ethics of Supreme Court justices served to drive home the need for the high court to adopt reforms immediately,"[27] and Sherrilyn Ifill characterized Roberts's statement as "far short of an adequate response," primarily because it did not increase the "transparency of [recusal] procedures that go to the very legitimacy of the Court's decisionmaking."[28] The Supreme Court Ethics Act of 2013, which was reintroduced in the House and Senate on April 23, 2015, cited the Year-End Report as evidence of the need for a code of ethics for the justices.[29] These reactions highlight the shortcomings of any mere statement by the Court explaining why it will not comply with statutory recusal standards. An explanation of the status quo, even one based on high-minded principles like the separation of powers or institutional competence, will simply not suffice.[30]

Alternatively, the Court could use its power as the final expositor of the Constitution to rule that the impasse between Congress and the Court over recusal is not legally justiciable—that the Court is without power under the constitution to resolve the dispute.[31] This relatively common approach in separation-of-powers cases can lead to positive results. The War Powers Resolution,[32] for instance, has long been a source of interbranch controversy. Members of Congress argue that presidential decisions to employ military force in contravention of the statute unconstitutionally interfere with the legislature's exclusive power to declare war under Article I.[33] Presidents have long contended that the statute is an unconstitutional limit on their authority to use military force as the nation's commander in chief under Article II.[34] In fact, several presidents have employed military force without strictly adhering to the statute. As Jeffrey Tulis explained, "In the aftermath of the Vietnam War, Congress passed a constitutionally aggressive statute, the War Powers Resolution. . . . Nevertheless, since the passage of the Resolution, the President has violated its terms repeatedly without challenge from Congress."[35] Yet despite being asked to intervene in the war powers debate, the courts have refrained from participating in any cases regarding the applicability and scope of the War Powers Resolution.[36] The result is a sort of political balancing act, where each branch seeks to persuade the other to exercise self-restraint in the interest of constitutional order. To the extent it appears as if the two branches are seeking to obtain power that the Constitution does not assign to them, there is a potential legitimacy problem. If the people believe that their governmental institutions have stopped abiding by our constitutional system, their confidence in, and in turn fidelity to, government could suffer. I would suggest that this generally has not happened in war powers disputes between Congress and the president in large part because of the presence of the federal judiciary to act as an independent mediator between the branches. The Court's presence as a neutral third party makes the lack of a clear legal resolution between the other two branches more constitutionally palatable. A decision by the Court not to intervene legitimizes the seemingly unruly process of political interchange and compromise between Congress and the president by making it part of the constitutional design, thus creating political space for the legislative and executive branches to better deal with complex questions about the use of military force on a case-by-case basis.

The conflict over Supreme Court recusal, however, would not similarly benefit from a decision by the Court that it is without constitutional power to resolve the dispute. Unlike with the War Powers Resolution, the interbranch conflict over recusal at the Court does not involve a third-party mediator. There is no formal constitutional role for the president in a dispute between Congress and the Court over recusal, and review by any court other than the Supreme Court would run afoul of Article III's established hierarchy.[37] As a result, the same type of political exchange and compromise—such as the justices citing the statute in their recusal memoranda despite not feeling bound by it and failing to apply it with the same force or rigor as they would other statutes—loses the imprimatur of legitimacy that comes from direct or indirect endorsement of the process by a coequal branch of government. Instead, the justices' failure to comply makes them appear unprincipled, regardless of the true quality of their decisions. Due to the seemingly inevitable unenforceability of congressional mandates regarding Supreme Court recusal and the absence of a constitutionally recognized third-party arbiter, a constitutional decision by the Court that the impasse is nonjusticiable is not a satisfactory resolution under the separation of powers.

The third way the Court could break the impasse over the justices' recusal practices is to use its power of judicial review to invalidate the statutory recusal standards as unconstitutional infringements of the Court's Article III judicial power. This would amount to essentially deleting the word "justices" from the existing statute and returning it to its pre-1948 status, when it purported to cover all federal judges other than members of the Supreme Court. This is perhaps the most intuitive response to the problem, as we generally think—at least since Chief Justice Marshall's famous pronouncement in *Marbury*—that matters of constitutional interpretation lie finally, and most comfortably, with the judiciary.[38] Despite its intuitive appeal, this approach is seriously flawed when viewed from a separation-of-powers perspective.

As a general matter, Supreme Court review of federal statutes is an unremarkable and fundamental feature of our constitutional existence.[39] The stakes become a bit higher, however, when the statutes under review regulate not subordinate government actors or the public at large but the highest levels of a coordinate branch. In those instances, questions of interbranch comity and cooperation are paramount to ensuring the continued functioning and legitimacy of our constitutional system. In the context of congressional regulation of Supreme Court recusal, concerns about comity and legitimacy counsel strongly against the Court invalidating the recusal statute.

Some examples illustrate the past effect of such comity concerns on the Court. In *Myers v. United States*,[40] the Court considered a question dividing the other two branches of government—whether Congress could limit the president's authority to remove an executive official from office. The conflict had all the makings of an impasse. A postmaster who had been removed from office brought suit against the United States alleging that President Wilson's decision to fire him violated a federal statute requiring the president to obtain "the advice and consent of the Senate" before removal.[41] The president did not claim that the Senate had consented to the postmaster's removal under the terms of the statute, but rather that Congress was without constitutional authority to interfere with the executive branch's prerogative to manage its own workforce. The Supreme Court took up the issue and held that the separation of powers precluded Congress from interfering with the president's decision to remove executive officers.[42] The statute was invalidated, and although it was not uncontroversial,[43] the decision brought relative clarity to both branches. Less than a decade later, the Court again addressed the removal issue, this time with regard to an employee of an independent agency.[44] It held that Congress could limit the president's power to remove members of independent agencies.[45] Again the Court's conclusion was adopted as the authoritative solution to the interbranch conflict. The Court has since addressed additional removal issues without any challenges to its institutional authority or capacity to do so.[46] These examples show that the Court can successfully resolve disputes between Congress and the executive, and in fact may be an important bulwark against undue conflict among the branches in its role as a neutral constitutional arbiter.

The circumstances change dramatically when the Court reviews statutes that are targeted at the Court itself or the justices. The most direct examples are cases under the Exceptions Clause of Article III.[47] The clause is the only constitutional provision that is aimed expressly and exclusively at the relationship between Congress and the Supreme Court. It does not empower any other government actor to influence the Court's appellate jurisdiction and does not permit Congress to do anything with respect to any other part of the judicial branch. For this reason, the Exceptions Clause is the purest analogue for the impasse between Congress and the Court over recusal. It provides useful insights into how the Court views its role as constitutional interpreter differently when the Court's own institutional interests are at stake.

The Court's Exceptions Clause jurisprudence is the subject of long-standing debate, but one feature of that jurisprudence—and the most important feature for present purposes—is clear. The Court has never invalidated a statute solely on the basis that it overstepped Congress's authority under the Exceptions Clause. The Court has upheld congressional authority in all but one case interpreting the clause, albeit often narrowly and with the implication that Congress may not remove the Court's jurisdiction entirely.[48] In the lone case where the Court did strike a statute that purported to limit its appellate jurisdiction under the Exceptions Clause, *United States v. Klein*,[49] the Court went to great lengths to offer alternative explanations for its holding. *Klein* struck down a statute that limited the Court's appellate jurisdiction. It did not, however, invalidate the statute on jurisdictional grounds. It relied on the fact that the statute impermissibly attempted to direct the outcome of specific cases in violation of the Court's power under Article III and improperly interfered with the president's Article II power to issue pardons.[50] The Court's Exceptions Clause jurisprudence demonstrates its reluctance to assert its own interests over those of Congress. It has generally affirmed Congress's authority to limit the Court's appellate jurisdiction.[51] Even when it found it necessary to invalidate a statute, it relied heavily on the countervailing interests of the executive in doing so.[52] The Exceptions Clause example supports the narrow proposition that the Court exercises its power of judicial review more cautiously when addressing conflicts, like Supreme Court recusal, that occur between itself and another branch of government. Yet while the Exceptions Clause analogy is strong, it is limited both by the relatively small number of cases interpreting it and by the fact that there are no corroborating examples, primarily because no other constitutional provisions single out the Court as the sole subject of regulation.

There are other cases in which the Court has displayed a predilection against ruling in favor of its own power (or the power of the federal courts in general) at the expense of another branch, but none of them involve as direct a conflict with Congress as the Exceptions Clause. Standing doctrine, for instance, is rife with cases in which the Court limits its power to hear cases through a narrow reading of Article III. As it explained in *Clapper v. Amnesty International USA*:[53]

> The law of Article III standing, which is built on separation-of-powers principles, serves to prevent the judicial process from being used to usurp the powers of the political branches. In keeping with the purpose of this doctrine, "[o]ur standing inquiry has been especially rigorous when reaching the merits of the dispute would force us to decide whether an action taken by one of the other two branches of the Federal Government was unconstitutional."[54]

The Court in *Clapper* denied standing, and thus its own power to resolve the case, to a plaintiff challenging the constitutionality of the National Security Agency's warrantless wiretapping of foreigners "reasonably believed to be" part of a terrorist organization.[55] In doing so, it "prevent[ed] the judicial process from being used to usurp the powers of the political branches" by espousing a very narrow understanding of the concept of future harm under Article III.[56]

In *Mistretta v. United States*,[57] the Court avoided another potential conflict with Congress when it upheld Congress's power to assign members of the judicial branch to serve, subject to appointment and removal by the president, on the U.S. Sentencing Commission. Mistretta argued that the commission was unconstitutional for several reasons, including that requiring federal judges to serve on a policy-making commission violated the separation of powers by unconstitutionally delegating the inherently legislative power to set sentencing guidelines to members of the judicial branch.[58] The Court was concerned by Mistretta's claim that federal judges' service on the commission—specifically in its legislative rule-making function—could weaken public confidence in the integrity of the federal judiciary, but it chose to avoid a confrontation with Congress by ruling in favor of the statute's constitutionality.

In *Morrison v. Olson*,[59] the Court upheld the independent counsel provisions of the Ethics in Government Act. The act allowed for the appointment of an "independent counsel" to investigate and, if appropriate, prosecute alleged violations of federal criminal law by high-ranking government officials. The act gave a specially constituted division of an Article III court (the "Special Division") certain responsibilities relating to the independent counsel, including setting the counsel's jurisdiction, performing various supervisory tasks, and termination. The Supreme Court concluded that the statute's assignment of the first two categories to the judicial branch did not violate the separation of powers because they were either permitted by the Appointments Clause or within the general range of judicial powers vested in the federal courts by Article III. When it came to termination, however, the Court became more protective of the other branches at the expense of the judiciary. Although it ultimately upheld the statute's termination provision, it was careful to read it narrowly, explaining that the power to terminate did not include the traditional power of removal vested in the executive branch by Article II:

> The termination provisions of the Act do not give the Special Division anything approaching the power to *remove* the counsel while an investigation or court proceeding is still underway—this power is vested solely in the Attorney General. As we see it, "termination" may occur only when the duties of

the counsel are truly "completed" or "so substantially completed" that there remains no need for any continuing action by the independent counsel. It is basically a device for removing from the public payroll an independent counsel who has served his or her purpose, but is unwilling to acknowledge the fact. So construed, the Special Division's power to terminate does not pose a sufficient threat of judicial intrusion into matters that are more properly within the Executive's authority to require that the Act be invalidated as inconsistent with Article III.[60]

The Court went on to stress that any expansion by the Special Division of the independent counsel's authority beyond the statutory parameters set by Congress would also present a constitutional problem: "We emphasize, nevertheless, that the Special Division has *no* authority to take any action or undertake any duties that are not specifically authorized by the Act. The gradual expansion of [its] authority . . . risks the transgression of the constitutional limitations of Article III."[61] Faced with potential conflicts between congressional authority and the independence and power of the federal courts, the Supreme Court in both *Mistretta* and *Morrison* exercised restraint. It found ways to interpret the relevant statutes such that they remained in force, often at the expense of judicial power.

Even when the Supreme Court rules in ways that favor the judiciary over the other branches of government, it is careful to acknowledge the importance of limiting judicial interference with those branches. In *Clinton v. Jones*,[62] the Court held that the president could be sued civilly while in office, provided the suit did not interfere with his performance of his duties as chief executive. The Court acknowledged that "'even when a branch does not arrogate power to itself . . . the separation-of-powers doctrine requires that a branch not impair another in the performance of its constitutional duties.'"[63] It went on to note that its ruling did not preclude Congress from enacting legislation providing the president with stronger protections from suit, revealing again the Court's willingness to defer to the powers of the other branches. Similarly, in *United States v. Nixon*,[64] the Court ordered President Richard Nixon to comply with a subpoena in a criminal case over his objections of absolute executive privilege.[65] It noted, however, that there should be a presumption of executive privilege based on the fact that "the privilege is fundamental to the operation of Government and inextricably rooted in the separation of powers."[66] Both of these landmark cases reveal the Supreme Court's willingness to protect the power of the courts in the face of possible intrusion from other branches. They also highlight the Court's cautious approach to its pro-judicial conclusions. When considered in connection with the Court's Exceptions Clause cases, it becomes increasingly clear that the Court is aware of the delicacy of its separation-of-powers decisions, particularly those that balance its own authority against those of the political branches.

The Court's approach to resolving conflicts between itself and the other branches counsels against using its power of judicial review to overturn the recusal statute. Such a self-serving use of its constitutional power could damage the interbranch comity and cooperation that are essential to the effectiveness of the separation of powers. As Bruce Peabody and John Nugent explained:

> We do not suggest that the judiciary should never intervene in separation of powers conflicts. But we do think this intervention should be infrequent [and] restrained. . . . The judiciary should, to the best of its ability, resist efforts to become embroiled in interbranch disputes while they are still unfolding. . . . [W]hen the judiciary does intervene in disagreements over the authority or powers of the different divisions of government, it should . . . address how its ruling will affect the various levels at which the separation of powers operate.[67]

Striking the recusal statute as it pertains to the justices would show a lack of restraint and concern for the other branches that could damage the reputation and legitimacy of the Court.

The remaining arguments against the Court striking the recusal statute are perfectly in line with the concerns expressed by proponents of recusal reform—protection of the Court's public reputation and, in turn, its legitimacy as the final expositor of constitutional law. Striking the portion of the recusal statute that governs members of the Court invites criticism that the Court is aggrandizing power at the expense of at least one of the political branches. This criticism, especially when combined with parallel critiques that the Court is becoming overly politicized, could seriously undermine public confidence in the institution and its fitness not only to adjudicate but also to fulfill its role as a check on the other branches. The Court's legitimacy could be similarly imperiled if its decision invalidating legislative recusal standards appeared unprincipled. In an area such as Supreme Court recusal and the separation of powers, where the constitutional text, history and judicial precedent are at best sparse, a decision in which the Court favors its own authority over that of another branch—even in the face of a written opinion explaining the decision—could easily be seen as pretextual and thus democratically illegitimate. Finally, the Court's Exceptions Clause jurisprudence provides yet another reason why the Court should refrain from using its power of review in the debate over recusal. Whereas application of the recusal statute could harm litigants by precluding them from obtaining judicial review in an individual case, the application of a jurisdiction-stripping statute is almost certainly more likely to bar review in a wider array of cases. Nevertheless, despite their potential for harm, the Court has been extremely reluctant to strike jurisdiction-stripping statutes under the Exceptions Clause. To the extent a jurisdiction-stripping statute is more harmful to litigants than a recusal statute, there is even less reason for the Court to overturn the recusal statute.

The Court cannot remedy its impasse with Congress without doing precisely the damage to its institutional reputation that proponents of recusal reform seek to avoid. The task, therefore, lies with Congress. Congress's assumption of responsibility for alleviating the impasse over recusal helps avoid the legitimacy problems for the Court that come from both an irresolvable dispute with Congress and an attempt by the Court to resolve such a dispute in its own favor. Congress must amend the recusal statute to exclude the justices and rely on its remaining constitutional tools to alleviate the interbranch tension over recusal.

Congress as an Effective Constitutional Actor

Just because Congress cannot set substantive recusal standards for the justices does not mean it is without potentially effective methods to remedy its impasse with the Court over recusal. By viewing the question of Supreme Court recusal as a matter of constitutional structure, we can more clearly identify ways that Congress may exercise its nonregulatory authority—what David Pozen calls constitutional "self-help"[68]—to address concerns over the justices' recusal practices without harming judicial and congressional legitimacy. There are at least five such indirect constitutional approaches for Congress to use in influencing Supreme Court recusal practice: impeachment, procedural reform, judicial confirmation, appropriations, and investigation/political discourse.

Impeachment

Congress's impeachment power is its most dramatic means of curtailing recurring recusal abuses by the justices. We discussed the difference between impeachment and recusal in chapter 3 by demonstrating how Congress's power over impeachment did not include the power to set substantive recusal standards for the justices. That is a very different analysis than the one undertaken here. The fact that the Constitution's impeachment provisions cannot be read to include the power to directly regulate recusal is very different from saying the remedy of impeachment itself is irrelevant to issues relating to recusal. The impeachment clauses do not give Congress the power to enact a federal tax fraud statute, yet that does not mean that impeachment is not a relevant remedy for a government official suspected of tax fraud.[69] Where Congress can demonstrate that a justice's recusal practices rise to the level of a high crime or misdemeanor, it is not logically inconsistent to subject that justice to impeachment, even if the impeachment power does not provide Congress with the authority to police the justice's recusal practices in the first instance. So even though it may apply only in the most extreme circumstances, impeachment can still be a useful tool for Congress to influence recusal at the Court.

The primary benefits of impeachment are its clear constitutionality as a legislative check on the judiciary and its effectiveness, both as a response to past recusal misconduct and as a powerful deterrent against future misconduct by the justices. Impeachment is a valuable tool for Congress in the recusal context because it is clear as a constitutional matter. Impeachment is best understood as an inherent legislative power, dedicated exclusively to Congress via Article I.[70] Unlike direct regulatory limits on Supreme Court recusal, impeachment is not a separation-of-powers problem but rather an anticipated and explicitly prescribed solution. Impeachment is also attractive because of the nature of the remedy. Removing a justice from office alleviates any future problems with that justice's recusal practices. It likewise stands to reason that the specter of impeachment will work as a deterrent, encouraging the justices to conform their decision making to Congress's standards. As Michael Gerhardt explained:

> Removal authority is a critical element to the separation of powers. Whoever exercises the power to remove may also be able to control the actions

of the officials subject to it. . . . This power is particularly intimidating to federal judges, because they have been the targets of its exercise more than any other class of impeachable officials, they do not have any comparable power over members of Congress, and they lack the means available to the president . . . to ward off an impeachment, such as the bully pulpit or the granting of political favors.[71]

Finally, the fact that Article III's good behavior requirement is aimed at protecting judicial independence as well as setting the standard for impeachment makes impeachment even better suited to serve as a check against recusal-based offenses. Maintaining the integrity and legitimacy of the judicial branch through impartial judging is a key responsibility of an independent judiciary. An impeachment standard that includes conduct impugning that integrity aligns the purposes of impeachment and recusal closely enough that they can be seen as related, if far from identical, remedies to a similar problem.

Impeachment's primary shortcoming in the recusal context is its lack of constitutionally mandated criteria. The converse of impeachment's strong pedigree as a legislative check on the judiciary is the potential legitimacy problem arising from the specific exercise of impeaching an individual justice. Article III guarantees the justices life tenure during "good behavior," but that term is otherwise undefined in the constitutional text. Article I provides little or no guidance as to how and when impeachment proceedings are to be instituted other than that they must originate in the House.[72] The historical evidence shows that impeachment was intended to apply to "political crimes"—offenses against the public interest.[73] Gerhardt explains that the good behavior standard applied to judges under Article III was not meant to be "looser" than that applied to the president or other officials, but instead to "take[] into account [judges'] special duties or functions," such as appearing neutral on matters of public import.[74] This vague standard welcomes both overuse and abuse of impeachment by Congress as a constitutional check against the judiciary.

These dangers, while significant, are neither unique to Congress's exercise of the impeachment power nor fatal to impeachment's potential usefulness for recusal. Arbitrariness and overuse are no more of a threat in impeachment than in any other largely discretionary exercise of authority under the Constitution. The power to declare war, for example, does not come with any easily cognizable objective legal standards—it is a political decision by a political branch that is checked only by electoral and political processes.[75] The president's veto power is a similarly discretionary act that is checked not by constitutional restraints but by political and electoral checks on the president.[76] Impeachment enjoys similar political limitations, as well as the additional constraint of requiring two separate and coordinated efforts by both houses of Congress.[77] The bicameral process of adopting articles of impeachment in the House and then trying and convicting a justice pursuant to those articles in the Senate ensures a level of commitment and deliberation on behalf of Congress that protects members of the Court from frivolous or cavalier impeachment. In addition to large investments of time and money, impeachment also comes with potentially high political costs for the legislature. The severity of removing a Supreme Court justice from office requires significant explanation by Congress, if for no other reason than to avoid charges of overreaching. History confirms the limited reach of judicial impeachment. Federal judicial impeachment has rarely been used by past legislatures,[78] suggesting that Congress understands both the severity of the remedy and the dangers of an overly aggressive approach to its use.

Another possible objection to using impeachment to shape the justices' recusal practices is that eliminating Congress's power to regulate recusal directly will make it politically easier for Congress to be more aggressive in its use of impeachment, thereby simply trading one constitutional problem for another. There are at least three reasons why this will not likely be the case. The first is that the power to impeach for what could be called recusal-related violations ostensibly already exists. The fact that there is a recusal statute on the books does not give Congress any greater power to impeach on recusal grounds than it would in the absence of such a statute. This is especially true in light of the understanding of good behavior that includes conduct supporting the integrity of the judiciary, the fact that failure to recuse has never been a criminal offense, and the reality that recusal is effectively unenforceable against the justices as a statutory matter. Second, the political costs to Congress of impeachment are the same regardless of whether there is a recusal statute on the books. There may be some additional room to pursue impeachment if the public sees the disappearance of the recusal statute as simply a shift in congressional options to control the members of the Court, but the severity of the remedy when compared with recusal as well as the large amount of time and resources needed to impeach a justice suggest that impeachment will not become a far more frequent exercise simply because a recusal statute is deemed constitutionally invalid. To the extent that other less noble reasons for impeachment are present, such as the ability to change the outcome in a specific case or to influence the composition of the Court, a shift in congressional focus from recusal to impeachment is at best helpful and at worst inapposite. Impeachment is far less attractive than recusal for those seeking to affect a single case. Where impeachment is sought to influence the composition of the Court, those motivations exist independent of a recusal statute. Third, at least in the context of the Supreme Court, there is reason to believe that a shift from statutory recusal standards to impeachment would not meaningfully change the actual level of congressional control over the justices' recusal practices. As discussed earlier, the federal recusal statute is effectively unenforceable against the justices, such that repealing it would not significantly weaken the present ability of Congress to affect recusal at the Court. Without a significant power gap to fill, there is no reason to think that Congress would turn frequently to impeachment as a means of inserting itself into Supreme Court recusal, especially when the attendant political and procedural costs are taken into account. In short, because impeachment is constitutionally dedicated to Congress and could be an effective (albeit rarely used) remedy, it remains a viable tool for congressional involvement in the debate over Supreme Court recusal.

Procedural Reform

Congress can also use its power to promulgate procedural requirements for the federal courts as a way of exerting some control over the justices' recusal practices. The operative word in this category is "procedural" due to the working assumption that the separation of powers precludes direct congressional regulation of the justices' substantive recusal decisions. With that caveat in mind, there are several ways in which Congress could seek to regulate Supreme Court procedure. One is through the Exceptions Clause of Article III. The Exceptions Clause could be used by Congress to regulate or "strip" appellate jurisdiction from the Court in cases where a certain number of recusals occurred, or conversely where a certain number of recusal motions were denied. As explained in chapter 3, use of the Exceptions Clause is controversial.

It has the potential, as in the recusal examples mentioned earlier, to effectively eviscerate the Court's otherwise valid appellate jurisdiction or incentivize meritless recusal motions by litigants who were successful below. Moreover, the Court is the final word on the Exceptions Clause, so Congress's authority to limit the Court's appellate jurisdiction would remain dependent on the Court's own reading of the clause. Even without any narrowing construction by the justices, the Exceptions Clause is underinclusive in the recusal context because it cannot reach cases involving the Court's original jurisdiction. At most, then, the Exceptions Clause could serve as an incentive to encourage or discourage recusals, as justices would presumptively be less likely to recuse where doing so would imperil the Court's jurisdiction over a case, and more likely to do so where it would not.[79] This does not seem like enough of a benefit to merit the rather extreme approach of stripping the Court of jurisdiction.

One alternative to the Exceptions Clause as a vehicle for procedural reform is Congress's power over the Court's quorum requirements. Quorum standards apply to all cases before the Court and do not necessarily pose a separation-of-powers problem.[80] Quorum values could be used to either encourage or discourage recusals—a high quorum requirement would likely encourage participation, and a lower number could lower the perceived cost of a justice's decision to recuse. Quorum's influence will be limited by the fact that the substantive decision to recuse is ultimately left to the justices themselves. This permits easy circumvention of any quorum requirements,[81] but in the absence of regulatory recusal standards it at least makes the justices accountable for a decision to circumvent quorum in a way they were not under a regulatory recusal regime.

Finally and likely most important, Congress could require that the justices follow specific procedural steps in making and issuing their recusal decisions under its traditional power to regulate the procedures of the federal courts.[82] Procedural reforms, such as a requirement that the justices publish explanations of their recusal decisions or that those decisions be subject to review by the entire Court, are popular among reformers concerned about the public perception and legitimacy of the Court. They are also less susceptible to separation-of-powers arguments than substantive recusal requirements.[83] This does not mean that procedural requirements are without their shortcomings. The suggested procedural reforms are unenforceable against the justices and are unlikely to be effective in the absence of parallel substantive reforms. Any potentially symbolic or persuasive effects of procedural change are arguably outweighed by the costs of creating irresolvable conflict between two branches of government. Nevertheless, even if procedural reforms do not drastically change the outcome of individual recusal decisions, they can serve to increase the transparency of the process either by increasing the amount of substantive information provided by the justices in their recusal decisions or at minimum by shifting responsibility for providing that information (and thus blame for not providing it) from Congress to the Court. Procedural reform is an example of an indirect constitutional tool that is collectively far greater than the sum of its parts. Despite the limitations of each of the proposed reforms, the overall impact of procedural reform offers potential benefits in terms of transparency and accountability, both of which enhance the Court's public perception and legitimacy without the constitutional impasse created by substantive regulation of the justices' recusal practices.

Judicial Confirmation

The Senate can further influence Supreme Court recusal through its power over judicial confirmations. The Senate's power to confirm judges is seemingly unconstrained as a constitutional matter.[84] Moreover, Supreme Court confirmation hearings have become increasingly detailed and substantive. As Lori Ringhand and Paul Collins demonstrated in their exhaustive empirical study of the past seven decades of Supreme Court confirmation hearings, "It is evident there was a steady increase in the amount of dialogue that transpires at the hearings" since 1939, and "substantive issues . . . have long dominated the hearings."[85] It is true that senators' inquiries about specific and controversial areas of the law are often met with generic, noncommittal responses by nominees in order to avoid appearing as if they have prejudged issues that could come before the Court. There is no reason to believe that senators' questions regarding a nominee's views on recusal would not be answered, however, because a potential justice's views on judicial recusal would be largely immune from such an objection. Recusal questions are technically not the subject of cases before the Court, as they are committed entirely to the judgment of an individual justice. They are more akin to questions about judicial philosophy, which is a popular topic at confirmation hearings. According to Ringhand and Collins, "Judicial philosophy is the third most frequently occurring issue following chatter and civil rights. Comments about judicial philosophy, which include such things as discussions of constitutional interpretation, stare decisis and judicial activism, constitute 12.4% of the comments in the dataset."[86] More important, questions about judicial philosophy have not been treated as objectionable by the nominees. In fact, Chief Justice Roberts's most memorable statement from his own confirmation hearing explained his jurisprudential philosophy by analogizing judges to baseball umpires.[87] In light of the chief justice's Year-End Report, it is clear that the Court is equivocal about which, if any, specific standards govern its recusal decisions. Without attempting to impose binding legal requirements on those decisions, the Senate could exercise its unbounded discretion over judicial confirmations to screen Supreme Court candidates based on their views of Supreme Court ethics and recusal. This approach is admittedly limited, as confirmations are based on a wide range of political and legal factors. A candidate's views on recusal may not be sufficient to deny her confirmation, and questioning a nominee about recusal would not have any legal effect on a justice after confirmation. Yet by focusing at least in part on recusal at a nominee's confirmation hearing, the Senate could encourage the nominees to take a public position on recusal that could influence the new justice's views once on the bench. This is consistent with at least one commentator's view that "the most important recusal related jurisprudential changes are not actually changes to recusal rules at all. Rather, they are changes to other rules regulating judges—rules of judicial conduct and judicial selection—that explicitly consider how certain judicial behavior may influence the perception of judicial impartiality."[88]

Appropriations

Congress's power of the purse is another potentially useful, indirect means of legislative influence over the Court's recusal practices. Like many of the other indirect methods, Congress's appropriations power has the benefit of a clear constitutional pedigree. There is no question that the ultimate power to provide funding for the coordinate branches lies squarely and solely with Congress.[89] Appropriations are also a powerful source of leverage over the other branches. Because appropriations are inherently focused on the Court as an institution, rather than the individual justices, Congress's power of the purse could be an effective way to encourage the Court to adopt its own recusal reforms. This would be perhaps the best of all possible outcomes, as a decision by the justices to voluntarily adopt clearer and more transparent recusal practices could promote the legitimacy of the Court without disrupting the balance of power between it and Congress.

There are, however, limits on any congressional attempt to influence Supreme Court recusal through appropriations. Although the institutional focus of appropriations may serve as a benefit in attempting to change the recusal practices of the Court as a whole, it does not make appropriations a good way for Congress to address an individual justice's recusal practices. Appropriations are also limited by the fact that they do not address the Court's recusal practices directly. They are a source of pressure designed to incentivize the justices to change their behavior in exchange for funding that likely has little or nothing to do with recusal. While this is not a weakness in terms of the relevance or availability of congressional influence over recusal, it does render appropriations inferior to other approaches such as procedural reforms and even investigations that are able to target and potentially change specific justices' recusal practices directly. In the event Congress chose to rely heavily on its appropriations power to influence the justices' recusal practices, additional problems could arise. A decision to withhold funding in order to affect recusal could have serious consequences for the Court's ability to perform its constitutionally assigned judicial function. At the extreme, a deprivation of funding could impair the Court so severely as to threaten the Article III requirement that there be "one supreme Court."[90] It could also backfire politically by making it appear as if Congress is holding the Court hostage by withholding critical funding, especially since the judicial branch is generally (and correctly) perceived as the most frugal of the three branches. This sort of interbranch conflict could have delegitimizing effects greater than any presented by a conflict over recusal at the Court. Notwithstanding these limits, Congress's power of the purse is another constitutionally recognized tool by which Congress may influence the justices' conduct, and as such is a potentially useful feature in the process of reformulating the balance of power between Congress and the Court over recusal.

Investigation and Political Discourse

Finally, Congress can use its general investigatory power—as distinct from its power to investigate in connection with impeachment proceedings—in connection with its inherent political platform to conduct public hearings and debates on issues of national importance. Although the Constitution does not explicitly grant Congress the power to investigate, there is a long and uninterrupted tradition of investigations by the legislative branch.[91] Louis Fisher, a well-known constitutional scholar specializing in the separation of powers, described Congress's investigative power as useful to, among other things, "inform the public, and to protect its integrity, dignity, reputation, and privileges."[92] In light of the constitutional and practical realities of Supreme Court recusal, any lasting, effective institution-wide reform will ultimately be up to the justices themselves. One way for Congress to instigate such reform is to bring additional public awareness and pressure to bear on the justices so they are driven to reevaluate their own recusal practices. Congress should stop short of employing the full weight of its investigatory authority—such as its subpoena power—as this would implement questions of interbranch coordination and comity that may themselves be inconsistent with the separation of powers. In the recusal context, Congress's use of its political and investigatory power should be akin to an ongoing confirmation hearing, whereby Congress may enhance the public's awareness and knowledge of the Supreme Court's recusal practices as a way of encouraging the justices to remain vigilant in thinking about and evaluating those practices. This not only is within the scope of Congress's authority but also may help promote better dialogue and cooperation between the branches.[93] Congress began to explore this approach in 2011, as justices were asked to testify before Congress on two separate occasions about ethical and recusal practices at the Court.[94] Following those public appearances, and in conjunction with public pressure from academics and the media to consider reform, Chief Justice Roberts dedicated his 2011 Year-End Report to explaining the Court's obligations regarding ethics and recusal issues. Although it is impossible to draw a definite causal link between the increased public and congressional attention on the justices' recusal practices and the chief justice's decision to publicly address those practices in his annual report, at least some connection between the two is easy to imagine.

More important, it is rational to assume that the Court would take the feelings of a coordinate branch seriously, especially when those feelings are corroborated by public opinion. The Court's first public statement regarding recusal since 1993 occurred in the wake of just this type of congressional and public pressure.

Treating Supreme Court recusal as a matter of constitutional law raises the question of how the separation of powers can help us reach a constitutionally acceptable and effective resolution to the ongoing impasse between Congress and the Court over recusal. The answer lies at the intersection of Congress's status as a constitutional interpreter and the branches' shared responsibility to cooperate with one another in a tripartite constitutional regime. Where the Supreme Court is at odds with a coequal branch of government, the separation of powers suggests that the Court should not take it upon itself to resolve the dispute, especially where the better constitutional argument favors the justices. Congress must take up the interpretive mantle and correct the constitutional impasse in a way that best promotes effective government. In the recusal context, this means repealing that part of the recusal statute that purports to govern the justices and relying on less direct methods of influencing the Court's recusal decisions. Congress may exercise its largely unfettered constitutional discretion to impeach, fashion procedural standards, confirm judicial nominees, appropriate funds, and apply political pressure in order to protect against recusal decisions that imperil the public's perception of the Court and its institutional legitimacy. Collectively these methods offer benefits that are potentially lost in the current impasse over recusal. Congress's pursuit of indirect constitutional mechanisms represents a more effective and cooperative use of our constitutional structure to resolve difficult problems. It offers the public an example of its federal government at work that makes sense within the constitutional framework. More specifically, it can raise public awareness about recusal and promote greater transparency and accountability among the justices by subjecting their recusal decisions to public scrutiny. It also has the potential to improve the justices' decision making by incentivizing them to reconsider their own recusal practices and to incorporate standards that meet public expectations.

Despite these advantages, Congress's indirect means of promoting better recusal practices at the Court may still seem, taken alone, like cold comfort to proponents of serious reform. Each of Congress's indirect approaches comes with a built-in weakness. Even the most committed adherent to the idea that Congress can use its power of the purse, for instance, to affect the justices' recusal decisions should feel uneasy about the prospect of spending manipulations resulting in widespread changes at the Court. This is because while withholding funding may incentivize the justices to change their own approach to recusal, there will also be the potential political costs of using funding as a sword against the Court and the collateral damage of weakening the Court's ability to perform its constitutionally required duties. The other indirect approaches mentioned here all come with inherent limitations based on some combination of their potential ineffectiveness, the possibility of unintended consequences, or their high political costs.

* * *

So now what? If the recusal statute is unconstitutional as applied to the justices, and our constitutional arrangement suggests that Congress is left with potentially useful, but limited, tools with which to shape recusal at the Court, how do we address ongoing concerns about the Court's recusal practices? Absent direct congressional control, there must be some other limiting principle to prevent the justices from issuing recusal decisions that appear arbitrary or, even worse, as the product of some ulterior motive. Keeping with our theme of taking a constitutional approach to Supreme Court recusal, we begin our search in the Constitution itself. The limiting principle must come free of the separation-of-powers problems associated with direct congressional regulation and must be within the competence of the judicial branch to administer. The Due Process Clause meets both of these criteria.

5 | Due Process and the First Amendment

Due process has been a consistent presence in judicial recusal. The two clearly overlap, as both due process and recusal stress the right of litigants to a fair proceeding by an impartial arbiter.[1] The Court has developed a doctrine of due process recusal through a line of cases stretching back nearly a century, but all of those cases involve state or lower federal court judges. None of them directly address recusal at the Supreme Court. It is also far more common for recusal standards at both the state and federal level to be set through statutes and ethical standards that go well beyond the limits of due process. The Supreme Court has repeatedly stated that "all questions of judicial qualification may not involve constitutional validity," and several circuit courts have interpreted the federal recusal statute as applying more broadly than the Due Process Clause.[2] This presumption in favor of statutory recusal remedies and the lack of Supreme Court review of its own recusal practices under the Due Process Clause tell us very little about how and when members of the Court should recuse themselves. The constitutional issues surrounding Supreme Court recusal force us to look directly to the Constitution to find a template for the justices' recusal decisions.

The movement toward recusal as a purely constitutional question for the justices has several advantages over the existing (and, I contend, unconstitutional) statutory model. First, even if one is not fully persuaded by the foregoing arguments, any doubts about the recusal statute's constitutionality make the Due Process Clause a preferable source of recusal guidelines for the Court. There is no separation-of-powers problem with the justices' recusal practices being regulated by the Due Process Clause. The clause governs all government actors explicitly and supremely, including the justices, and it is not subject to dilution or the creation of exceptions by either Congress or the president.[3] Shifting from statutory to due process–based recusal standards solves any potential separation-of-powers problems raised by Congress's regulation of the justices' recusal practices.

Second, a constitutional focus on recusal standards for the Court creates the necessary space for the justices to consider prudential and institutional factors in their recusal decisions. As the entity with the final authority to interpret the Constitution, the Court can employ a holistic approach to its application of the Due Process Clause to recusal. There is an argument (pursued in greater detail later in this chapter) that constitutional structure supports applying the clause differently to the Supreme Court than to state or lower federal courts. It suggests a more pliable standard for the justices that takes into account many of the issues that have driven recusal at the Court since the Founding but that have been neither prevalent in recusal decisions regarding the lower courts nor memorialized in constitutional or statutory text. But even if the Supreme Court is not treated as inherently different from other courts, the fact that due process has long been recognized as an inexact constitutional science invites the justices to think broadly in setting guidelines for their recusal decisions.[4] The Court's due process jurisprudence is consistent with this view. It has moved beyond Blackstone's limited common law standard toward the wider view advocated by Bracton and embraced in modern recusal statutes. Access to a broader range of considerations is important for recusal at the Court because it permits the justices to fashion standards that promote fair and impartial judging while continuing to protect the Court's place in our constitutional structure.

Third, a recusal regime based on due process accurately describes current Supreme Court practice. Chapter 2 discussed the justices' long history of relying on nonstatutory justifications for their recusal decisions. Their approach to recusal has consistently been closer to a due process analysis than an application of common law or statutory standards. In their memoranda describing their decisions not to recuse, Justices Rehnquist and Scalia each relied on factors like the prior decisions of other justices, the unique role of the Court within our constitutional system, and the possibility that more rigid recusal standards would incentivize the strategic use of recusal to sway the outcome of controversial cases.[5] Shifting the focus of recusal to the Due Process Clause allows the justices to explain their conclusions on the same grounds as they were formulated—as complex considerations of the justices' impact on the fairness of an individual case and on the Court's ability to fulfill its constitutional duty—without the need to retrofit those conclusions into any statutory regime.

A clearer sense of the guiding principles behind the justices' recusal decisions can also lead to a more consistent and effective set of decisional rules for recusal cases. Current examples of the justices' recusal decisions cite a wide range of legal sources, including the prior decisions of other justices, the federal recusal statute, and the justices' individual sense of fairness and impartiality. Some of those decisions occurred before the statute was amended to include members of the Court. The Court's 1993 policy statement focused on cases involving the justices' relatives, and the chief justice's 2011 Year-End Report spoke more broadly about the high degree of deference due, and the wide range of information brought to bear by, each justice in deciding whether to recuse.[6] Viewing Supreme Court recusal as a constitutional issue with a constitutional solution provides the justices with an opportunity to normalize the legal framework for their decisions around the concept of due process without unduly limiting the individual discretion that the members of the Court clearly value and believe is due to them under Article III. Departing from the statutory framework also offers opportunities for increased transparency and accountability. Observers will have an accurate account of the standard being employed by the justices, and the justices themselves may feel more inclined to explain their decisions once they are the product of a judicially managed constitutional doctrine.

Due process further offers some valuable guiding principles for the justices. The Court has spent the last century formulating a set of rules for applying due process to judicial recusal cases. Although none of these cases involve the justices themselves, they offer a doctrinal framework that sets thoughtful limits on a justice's ability to participate in specific cases. The price of flexibility in Supreme Court recusal under the Due Process Clause is not, therefore, recusal itself. The Due Process Clause addresses core situations in which recusal is mandatory, and those core principles closely map some of the most durable aspects of the common law. Given that recusal law is virtually unenforceable against the Court by anyone other than the justices themselves, due process offers a unifying doctrinal approach that provides enough reasoned limitations and flexibility to mirror the best practices of recusal at the Court.

Fourth, connecting the justices' recusal decisions with due process reveals the wider panoply of constitutional issues implicated by recusal and puts the actual decision to recuse on the same legal footing as those other issues. The separation-of-powers issues surrounding recusal have been well documented here. The question of who decides whether recusal is appropriate is a matter of constitutional text, history, and structure. Supreme Court practice tells us that whether an individual justice should recuse herself from a given case is also a matter of constitutional structure and institutional responsibility. Once we recognize the constitutional ramifications of Supreme Court recusal, it will not do to rely on any subconstitutional legal authorities to guide (let alone legally bind) the justices. Statutory recusal standards for the Court are, as a matter of constitutional supremacy, trumped by separation-of-powers concerns.[7] The same is true for other constitutional principles that may affect recusal, such as the justices' First Amendment rights. The substance of those rights in the recusal context is taken up later in this chapter, but suffice it to say that any decision to recuse based on judicial speech at minimum implicates the First Amendment. A purely statutory recusal standard would thus find itself routinely subordinated to separate constitutional concerns. Only a constitutional approach to Supreme Court recusal can accommodate the full range of forces at play in a justice's recusal decision.

A Due Process Standard for Recusal at the Court

What that constitutional approach should look like, however, is an altogether different matter. The Court has never considered how due process affects its own recusal decisions. The justices' decisions are made individually and are not subject to review by their peers, so there has not been any occasion for members of the Court to weigh in on their colleagues' decisions. The most public recusal debate within the Court took place between Justices Black and Jackson over Justice Black's decision to participate in the *Jewell Ridge* case.[8] The fight over *Jewell Ridge* created significant personal and professional tension between the justices, but it never rose to the level of a constitutional dispute. Justice Jackson's opinion implied that Justice Black should have recused himself from the case but conceded that there was little in the way of binding standards for the justices' conduct:

> The Court itself has never undertaken . . . to formulate any uniform practice on the subject. Because of this lack of authoritative standards it appears always to have been considered the responsibility of each Justice to

determine for himself the propriety of withdrawing in any particular circumstances. Practice of the Justices over the years has not been uniform, and the diversity of attitudes to the question doubtless leads to some confusion as to what the bar may expect and as to whether the action in any case is a matter of individual or collective responsibility. There is no authority known to me under which a majority of this Court has power under any circumstances to exclude one of its duly commissioned Justices from sitting or voting in any case.[9]

Justice Jackson never mentioned the Due Process Clause, even though the Court had applied the clause to a recusal case two decades earlier in *Tumey v. Ohio.*[10] This omission is consistent with the Court's consistent refusal to treat its own recusal practices as part of a clearly defined legal framework. Even on the rare occasions where justices have explained their own recusal decisions, they have stopped far short of constitutionalizing their recusal obligations. The Court's reluctance to construct a relevant framework leaves us with the task of determining the appropriate due process standard for Supreme Court recusal, as well as how we should go about deriving that standard.

Identifying the appropriate standard raises the same questions of constitutional theory and interpretation that applied to the evaluation of Article III's effect on who decides recusal questions at the Court. The Article III analysis was truly an issue of first impression—the Court provided absolutely no guidance on the matter—and presented the basically binary question of the constitutionality of a federal recusal statute that purported to regulate the justices. I say "basically" because there is the lingering question of Congress's authority to prescribe procedural rules for the justices in recusal cases. Overall, however, the constitutional question under Article III was an all-or-nothing proposition about the facial constitutionality of legislative recusal standards for the Court. Such a fundamental and novel question about government power demanded a wide range of interpretive techniques. The original history of the relevant provisions, Congress's and the Court's historic recusal practices, and constitutional structure all offered useful—and corroborating—evidence of the irreconcilable conflict between the Article III judicial power and the federal recusal statute.

The due process question does not present quite the same blank slate or binary choice. There is no doubt that due process is a legitimate limit on federal power, including that of the federal courts. The question here is one of degree: How much should the clause impact the justices' recusal decisions? Like the Article III question, the due process analysis is largely one of first impression and is thus open to a wide range of interpretive approaches. Choosing among them invites a host of methodological objections that would unnecessarily complicate and distract from the conclusions drawn. Rather than advocate for a particular school of constitutional thought, it is best to employ the same varied tools of constitutional construction that were applied to Article III to understand how due process affects recusal—Founding-era historical evidence, long-standing government practice, including Supreme Court precedent, and constitutional structure.

Due Process and Recusal at the Founding

The evidence from the Founding is sparse. It does not appear as if recusal was discussed at the adoption of the Due Process Clause.[11] The Court in *Tumey v. Ohio* explained that "in determining what due process of law is, under the Fifth or Fourteenth Amendment, the court must look to those settled usages and modes of proceeding existing in the common and statute law of England before the emigration of our ancestors."[12] The common law standard at the Founding mandated recusal only in cases of pecuniary interest, so on that view due process requires recusal only in cases where the judge has a personal monetary interest in the outcome. It is at best unclear whether the original understanding included members of the Court. There are no statements by any of the justices acknowledging that they were constrained by due process principles in their recusal decisions. Chief Justice Marshall recused himself in *Martin* from a case in which he had a pecuniary interest,[13] but he also recused himself in *Stuart* from a case he had helped decide in the court below, a scenario that did not require recusal under the common law.[14]

Congress's activities around the time of the Founding only confuse matters more. Its most powerful statement, the first recusal statute, closely followed the common law standard but did not regulate the justices. This may be more reflective of Congress's views of its own lack of legislative authority than of substantive recusal law, but it is at least some evidence that the common law standards for recusal may not have originally applied to the Supreme Court in the same way they applied to the lower courts. In sum, the relationship between due process and Supreme Court recusal at the Founding was unclear. While there was a relatively straightforward understanding of when recusal was required at common law, that standard was not explicitly applied by the members of the Court in their own practices, nor was it applied to them by Congress. What is clear, however, is that the law of recusal did not remain static over time. The historic practices of the Court and Congress tell a much broader story about how due process and recusal interact. They tell a story of increasing skepticism about judicial integrity and a perceived need to provide litigants—and perhaps the judicial system as a whole—with more stringent recusal standards.

Our History with Due Process Recusal

Both Congress and the courts have a history of making decisions that are relevant to the Due Process Clause's effect on recusal. In the case of the courts—more specifically the Supreme Court—those decisions take the form of judicial opinions applying due process principles to recusal questions. Congress's historical practices have been less direct, coming mostly in the form of legislation that regulates recusal without explicitly relying on due process. Taken together, however, judicial and legislative history offer valuable insight into the interaction of due process and recusal. The Supreme Court has developed a dynamic approach to due process that is instructive in terms of both the appropriate interpretive approach to due process questions and the substantive impact of due process on recusal. The fact that the Court's evolution tracks Congress's development of statutory recusal standards gives additional force to the notion that recusal under the Due Process Clause is a dynamic concept that is moving toward stricter limits on judicial participation in close cases.

The Court's historical practice is, like evidence from the Founding, incomplete. Much like Chief Justice Marshall's decisions in *Stuart* and *Martin*, it is often unclear what legal framework the justices are relying on to determine their recusal status. This uncertainty is exacerbated by the fact that the justices' recusal decisions are unreviewable. Without the need to defend their decisions, there is virtually no incentive for the justices to make a detailed legal argument, and even less incentive to subject their recusal practices to constitutional scrutiny. Literally speaking, it is difficult to identify any historical practice by the members of the Court in applying the Due Process Clause to their own recusal decisions. There is thus no basis on which to draw conclusions about the meaning of the clause from the Court's own historical experience with recusal.

There is, however, a line of due process precedent from the Court regarding state and lower court recusal. This line of precedent is a form of historical practice, and even though it does not expressly implicate the justices, it is at least as revealing as the limited Founding-era evidence regarding due process and recusal. The Court's first significant treatment of due process recusal occurred in *Tumey v. Ohio*.[15] An Ohio statute empowered mayors to act as local judges in cases alleging violations of the Ohio Prohibition Act.[16] Penalties under the act were monetary fines for the first two offenses, with a fine and possible prison sentence for third and later offenses. The mayor was permitted to sit as a judge only in cases occurring within his jurisdiction that did not involve a possible prison sentence. In cases where the defendant was found guilty, half of the fine paid went to the state treasury, and the remaining half went to the municipality "'where the prosecution is held.'"[17] Municipalities were given discretion to spend their half of any fines collected to aid in prosecution of the law. The mayor was empowered to order that any defendant who was sentenced to pay a fine be imprisoned until his fine had been paid.[18]

Ed Tumey was arrested for possession of intoxicating liquor in North College Hill, Ohio, in violation of the Prohibition Act. He was brought before Mayor Pugh of North College Hill and convicted. Mayor Pugh sentenced Tumey to pay a fine of $100 and ordered him imprisoned until the fine was paid. Under Ohio law, half of that fine would be given to the village of North College Hill. A North College Hill ordinance designated its share of any fines under the Prohibition Act the "secret service fund" and explained how the contents of that fund were to be allocated.[19] In addition to providing funding to "deputy marshals . . . the [prosecuting] attorney . . . [and] detectives and secret service officers" involved in the case, the ordinance provided Mayor Pugh with "the amount of his costs in each case, in addition to his regular salary" from the secret service fund.[20] None of the local officials, including Mayor Pugh as the acting judge, received any compensation for their services if the defendant was not convicted. Mayor Pugh received $12 in compensation due to Tumey's conviction. Tumey challenged the mayor's qualifications to participate in the case under the Due Process Clause, arguing that his due process rights to a fair and impartial trial were infringed because the judge had a personal financial interest in the outcome of the case. The case ultimately reached the Supreme Court, where the justices found in favor of Tumey, holding that it did indeed offend due process for the judge to have a direct financial interest in a case over which he was presiding.[21]

The Court began its due process analysis by distinguishing between legislative and constitutional recusal standards. It explained that "all questions of judicial qualification may not involve constitutional validity. Thus matters of kinship, personal bias, state policy, remoteness of interest would seem generally to be matters merely of legislative discretion."[22] In terms of the due process limits placed on recusal, the Court looked to precolonial English law for guidance. It relied on the fundamental maxim of common law recusal that no person should be a judge in her own case and cited the practices of fourteenth-century English courts and iconic common law decisions such as *Dr. Bonham's Case* in support of that proposition.[23] It concluded that although due process does not reach all manner of recusal questions, the history of common law recusal requires removal of a judge with "a direct, personal, substantial pecuniary interest" in the outcome of the case.[24] Because Mayor Pugh had such an interest in Tumey's conviction, due process forbade the mayor from presiding over Tumey's prosecution. All in all, *Tumey* can be read as a relatively easy case decided on clear, long-established common law rules.

The majority opinion in *Tumey* includes language, however, that forecasts a willingness to go beyond such a narrow view of due process and recusal. The Court hinted at a view of due process based not only on Founding-era evidence but also on American custom. In response to arguments that the mayor's compensation in Tumey's case was too small to compromise the mayor's impartiality, the Court explained that payment for convictions cannot "be regarded as due process of law" because it "has not become so embedded by custom in the general practice, either at common law or in this country."[25] It acknowledged that there are likely some mayors who would not be persuaded to act partially in exchange for $12 but reminded us that:

> the requirement of due process of law in judicial procedure is not satisfied by the argument that men of the highest honor and the greatest self-sacrifice could carry it on without danger of injustice. Every procedure which would offer a possible temptation to the average man as a judge to forget the burden of proof required to convict the defendant, or which might lead

him not to hold the balance nice, clear, and true between the state and the accused denies the latter due process of law.[26]

While it is important not to overstate the breadth of the Court's intent in *Tumey*, it is also important not to ignore it. Rather than focus on the pecuniary interest standard that for centuries had represented the common law of recusal, the Court at least implied that a more complex set of inquiries may be relevant. The presence of a "possible temptation to the average man" that would prevent him from "hold[ing] the balance nice, clear, and true between the state and the accused" potentially includes a range of removable conduct well beyond a direct pecuniary interest. It could include personal animus, for example, a criterion that the Court earlier stated was the exclusive province of the legislature.[27] The fact that it is an objective standard also distinguishes it from the common law, as the pecuniary interest standard focused on the specific interests of the presiding judge, not the likely reaction of a reasonable judge confronted with similar circumstances. Later cases continued this expansion of constitutional recusal standards beyond those set at common law.

Roughly thirty years after *Tumey*, the Court returned to due process and recusal in *In re Murchison*.[28] Under Michigan law, judges could serve as a "one-man grand jury."[29] In *Murchison*, a Michigan judge serving as a one-person grand jury commanded two witnesses to testify as part of the proceeding. Suspecting both of the witnesses of perjuring themselves, the judge charged and tried both of them for contempt. He convicted and sentenced them both. The witnesses objected to their convictions on due process grounds, claiming that the judge who charged them with perjury could not also try and convict them of the same charge. The Court held that it was indeed a violation of the defendants' due process rights to have the same judge charge, try, and convict them.[30] *Murchison* is an important development in the Court's due process jurisprudence because it is a clear departure from the strict common law rule that only a direct pecuniary interest in a case requires recusal. The judge in *Murchison* did not have any pecuniary interest in the outcome. What he did have was a reason to be biased against the witnesses he eventually tried. Under Blackstone's view of recusal, this would not merit removal because "the law will not suppose a possibility of bias or favour in a judge, who is already sworn to administer impartial justice."[31] The Supreme Court in *Murchison* did, however, suppose objective bias in a judge set to try individuals that he had brought charges against. It did not cite any common law cases for this proposition, relying instead on its own recent precedents.

Murchison is also significant because the Court used language that seems broader than the narrow path to recusal articulated by Blackstone and, for the most part, the Court in *Tumey*. It began with the uncontroversial statement that due process requires a fair trial, including a trial conducted by a judge without an interest in the outcome.[32] In unpacking the term "interest," however, the *Murchison* Court noted that "interest cannot be defined with precision. Circumstances and relationships must be considered."[33] Citing the "possible temptation" language from *Tumey*, it went on to explain that due process "may sometimes bar trial by judges who have no actual bias and who would do their very best to weigh the scales of justice equally between contending parties. But to perform its high function in the best way *'justice must satisfy the appearance of justice.'*"[34] The distinction between actual and potential bias is not necessarily a strong departure from the common law pecuniary interest standard, as a pecuniary interest does not, as the *Tumey* Court pointed out, equate directly to actual bias.[35] It is potentially significant, however, that the *Murchison* Court explicitly mentioned the "appearance of justice" in its due process analysis.[36] Especially in a case like *Murchison* that did not involve any monetary questions, consideration of the "appearance" of a judge's conduct could open up the due process inquiry to require recusal in cases that are outside the common law standard and do not involve a possibility of actual bias against the litigant.

The Supreme Court invoked the appearance of justice concept in its next major pronouncement on due process and recusal, *Mayberry v. Pennsylvania*.[37] Like *Murchison*, *Mayberry* involved a contempt proceeding. The criminal defendant, Mayberry, represented himself at trial and repeatedly "vilified" the judge in open court, including calling the judge a "hatchet man for the State," a "dirty sonofabitch," and a "stumbling dog."[38] He told the judge to "Go to hell" and asked him, "What are you working for? The prison authorities, you bum?"[39] When the same judge charged and found Mayberry guilty of contempt, with a sentence of between eleven and twenty-two years in prison, Mayberry objected on due process grounds. He argued that the judge could not be impartial in his contempt proceeding in light of their previous interactions. The Court held that due process required that a new judge oversee Mayberry's contempt proceeding. It articulated the applicable due process standard as follows: "At times a judge has not been the image of 'the impersonal authority of law' but has become so 'personally embroiled' with a lawyer in the trial as to make the judge unfit to sit in judgment on the contempt charge. . . . 'These are subtle matters, for they concern the ingredients of what constitutes justice. Therefore, justice must satisfy the appearance of justice.'"[40]

The Court then concluded that "insults of that kind are apt to strike 'at the most vulnerable and human qualities of a judge's temperament.'"[41] The Court's opinion focused on a nonfinancial interest of the judge and on the probability of bias. Neither of these features was unique; both were also part of the majority's reasoning in *Murchison*. What *Mayberry* added to the due process calculus was a larger role for the appearance of justice. By admitting that the line drawing required to determine when a judge is too personally embroiled with a defendant will be "subtle," the Court brought additional attention to the appearance of a judge's decision. There has been a fair amount of academic debate and commentary over whether the probability of bias and the appearance of justice standards are truly distinct concepts.[42] Whatever the specific contours of the Court's stated approach, it has drifted further from the Founding-era pecuniary interest standard toward a more dynamic and flexible understanding of the Due Process Clause.

This dynamic approach could be seen again the following year in *Ward v. Village of Monroeville*.[43] *Ward* marked a return both to Ohio and to the pecuniary interest line of due process reasoning in *Tumey*. An Ohio statute authorized mayors "to sit as judges in cases of ordinance violations and certain traffic offenses."[44] The due process problem arose because "a major part of village income [was] derived from the fines, forfeitures, costs, and fees imposed by . . . [the] mayor's court."[45] *Ward* involved a due process objection to fines levied by the mayor, on the basis that he could not be impartial when a conviction led to a direct monetary benefit to his municipality. This is notably different from the direct and personal financial interest enjoyed by the mayor in *Tumey*, but it was nonetheless sufficiently problematic for the Court in *Ward* to conclude that due process required the mayor's recusal. Citing *Tumey*'s reliance on "whether the mayor's situation is one 'which would offer a possible temptation to the average man as a judge,'" the *Ward* Court explained that a "'possible temptation' may also exist when the mayor's executive responsibilities for village finances may make him partisan to maintain the high level of contribution from the mayor's court."[46]

Ward represents a different type of movement off the traditional common law standard. Rather than relax the necessary causal connection between the facts of the case and the judge's reaction to them, as the possible temptation standard arguably does, *Ward* adds a new category of relevant facts to the equation. *Ward* looked for possible bias based on an indirect financial interest in the case. This is neither the standard relied on at common law nor an inquiry into the personal relationship between litigant and judge. Instead, the Court in *Ward* acknowledged that due process prohibits judges from participating in cases where they have no more than an indirect financial interest in the outcome. Without belaboring the range of unforeseen consequences that could come from such a ruling, *Ward* offers another dimension in which to view the Court's consistent expansion of its due process jurisprudence regarding recusal.

Aetna Life Insurance Company v. Lavoie[47] helped define the parameters of the indirect financial interest identified in *Ward*. Margaret Lavoie brought a bad-faith refusal to pay claim against her insurance company, Aetna, for refusing to pay more than $1,000 of her costs for a twenty-three-day hospital stay that Aetna concluded was unnecessary. Twice the lower courts ruled in Aetna's favor, and twice the Alabama Supreme Court reversed under Alabama law. A jury ultimately awarded Lavoie $3.5 million in punitive damages. The Alabama Supreme Court affirmed the award in an unsigned 5–4 opinion. The opinion clarified Alabama law in several ways that proved favorable to plaintiffs seeking bad-faith claims against their insurers. After the decision, Aetna learned that Justice T. Eric Embry, the author of the opinion affirming the damage award, had two suits pending in lower courts in Alabama against insurance companies, both of which included bad-faith claims and requests for punitive damages. One of the suits was an individual suit by Justice Embry. The other was a class action on behalf of all Alabama state employees insured under a particular insurance plan, which happened to include every member of the Alabama Supreme Court. Aetna moved to recuse Justice Embry on the basis of his involvement in these related lawsuits, and to recuse the entire Alabama Supreme Court based on its justices' potential inclusion in the class action suit.[48]

The Supreme Court concluded that Justice Embry's participation

violated the Due Process Clause, but that the participation of the remainder of his colleagues on the Alabama Supreme Court did not. In
the process, the U.S. Supreme Court articulated a useful distinction regarding the types of indirect financial interests that seriously threaten
due process. The Court relied on its formulations in *Ward* and *Murchison* to set the standard for recusal under the Due Process Clause.
It reiterated that most of the criteria for disqualification, like personal
bias, are not constitutionally mandated and that there is no precise way
to define the level of personal interest necessary to trigger recusal.[49] It
then cited the "possible temptation" and "appearance of justice" standards as the governing tests under the Due Process Clause.[50] The Court
concluded that a "general hostility toward insurance companies" was
not enough of an interest in the case to require Justice Embry's recusal,
but that because his opinion had the "clear and immediate effect of en-
hancing both the legal status and the settlement value of his own case,"
his interest was sufficiently "direct, personal, substantial, [and] pecuniary" to merit recusal on those grounds.[51] Finally, the Court held that the
remaining members of the Alabama Supreme Court in Justice Embry's
class action suit did not need to recuse because their potential interest
was at best slight and there was no evidence that they were even aware
of the class action suit while the *Aetna* case was before them. The Court
also cited the "rule of necessity," noting that if recusal were required,
the Alabama Supreme Court would be unable to resolve the important
issues of state tort law presented in the case.[52]

Aetna aids in the necessary line-drawing process required to determine when a judge's interest in a case causes her participation to run
afoul of the Constitution. The Court's decision is consistent with the
idea that the Due Process Clause creates a floor, rather than a ceiling,
for recusal standards by holding that general hostility toward an indus-
try does not rise to the level of a constitutional issue. At the same time,
the opinion exhibits a willingness to go beyond both the traditional
common law threshold and the Court's previous decision in *Ward* to
hold that an even more attenuated, nonpecuniary interest may trigger
due process recusal. In *Ward*, the mayor-judge was able to guarantee
the direct influx of money into his village's coffers through his decisions. By contrast, Justice Embry's decision created a more favorable
legal environment for his pending lawsuits but did not directly result in
a favorable verdict or any monetary gain. Under the most generous application of his ruling, it appears as if a jury would still have to find that

Justice Embry's insurers did in fact act in bad faith before he would enjoy any monetary benefit. Moreover, the majority in *Aetna* did not rely solely on the prospect of Justice Embry accruing monetary benefits. It also referred to improvements in the legal status of Justice Embry's case as a factor supporting recusal, leaving open the question whether, if the suit were for nonmonetary relief, the recusal analysis would have come out the same way. According to Justice William Brennan, who authored a concurring opinion in *Aetna*, the answer appears to be yes:

> I do not understand that by this language the Court states that only an interest that satisfies this test will taint the judge's participation as a due process violation. Nonpecuniary interests, for example, have been found to require recusal as a matter of due process. Moreover, as this case demonstrates, an interest is sufficiently "direct" if the outcome of the challenged proceeding substantially advances the judge's opportunity to attain some desired goal even if that goal is not actually attained in that proceeding.[53]

Aetna advances our understanding of recusal and due process by closing some doors to recusal while opening others. A judge's generic bias remained inadequate to trigger constitutional protections (statutory requirements may still be used in such cases),[54] but it appears increasingly likely after *Aetna* that a judge's interest in a case that is neither clearly direct nor monetary may nonetheless create a constitutional bar to her participation in that case.[55] In the continuing search to identify the appropriate standard to apply to Supreme Court recusal, *Aetna*'s additional move away from the traditional common law standard and its broader understanding of what merits disqualification provide a more detailed legal framework within which to think about the justices' recusal practices.

Just four years after *Aetna*, the Court declined to hear the direct appeal of a case involving a trial judge who sentenced a defendant to death after having prosecuted that same defendant for murder roughly twenty years earlier.[56] Justice Marshall (joined by Justice Brennan) dissented from the Court's decision not to hear *DelVecchio v. Illinois* on the grounds that "the trial judge's participation in this case, given his involvement in the prosecution of a 1965 murder charge against the defendant, presented an unacceptable appearance of partiality."[57] This is significant because two members of the Court used the "appearance of partiality" standard, which is more lenient than the Court's approach in earlier cases and also is the standard applied by the federal recusal statute since 1974. While a dissent from a denial of certiorari is certainly not precedent setting, it is nonetheless relevant to the question of how much of an impact the judge's interest in the case must have to violate the Due Process Clause. Through his willingness to use the broader appearance-of-partiality standard, Justice Marshall implied a closer relationship than has been generally understood between the recusal requirements under the Due Process Clause and those in the federal recusal statute.

The next step in the development of the Court's due process doctrine was *Caperton v. A. T. Massey Coal Company, Inc.*[58] In *Caperton*, a West Virginia jury awarded $50 million to petitioners for claims that respondent coal company Massey had engaged in fraudulent misrepresentation, concealment, and tortious interference with contractual relationships. Soon after the jury award against it, Massey's president and CEO Don Blankenship contributed $3 million to Brent Benjamin's campaign for state supreme court justice in West Virginia. Blankenship's contribution was more than the combined contributions of all other donors to Benjamin's campaign, including Benjamin's own committee. Benjamin defeated the incumbent justice by fewer than 50,000 votes. Just before Massey appealed its case against Caperton to the state supreme court, Caperton filed a motion seeking to recuse Justice Benjamin under the Due Process Clause. It argued that Justice Benjamin was unfit to participate in a case involving his largest campaign supporter. Justice Benjamin denied the motion to recuse. The West Virginia Supreme Court reversed the jury verdict against Massey by a vote of 3 to 2 and denied Caperton's request for rehearing by the same margin. Justice Benjamin was in the majority for both decisions.[59]

The U.S. Supreme Court reversed, holding that Justice Benjamin was indeed required to recuse himself under the Due Process Clause. In doing so, the Court articulated a potentially broader, but controversial, account of the Due Process Clause's recusal requirements. Writing for the Court, Justice Kennedy restated the Court's consistent refrain that most recusal cases do not rise to the level of a constitutional issue.[60] He then went on, however, to explain as follows:

> The *Tumey* Court concluded that the Due Process Clause incorporated the common-law rule that a judge must recuse himself when he has "a direct, personal, substantial, pecuniary interest" in a case. . . . As new problems have emerged that were not discussed at common law, however, the Court

has identified additional instances which, as an objective matter, require recusal. These are circumstances "in which experience teaches that the probability of actual bias on the part of the judge or decisionmaker is too high to be constitutionally tolerable."[61]

Justice Kennedy's description of the Court's evolving understanding of the Due Process Clause suggests a broader set of constitutional recusal standards. In addition to explicitly acknowledging the expansion of recusal standards in response to changing circumstances, he noted the objective nature of modern recusal standards and the "probability of actual bias" standard, both of which had been part of the Court's slow march from the narrow recusal standards of the common law toward the reasonable appearance standard of section 455. This message was clouded, however, by Justice Kennedy's warnings against reading *Caperton* too broadly. He described the facts in *Caperton* as "extreme by any measure" and even cast the Court's other recusal decisions as involving "extreme cases."[62] *Caperton* thus remains somewhat of an enigma. On the one hand, it seems to favor more wide-ranging due process standards for recusal. On the other, it contains caveats and qualifications that appear to limit it to its "extreme" facts, or at minimum to cases the Court views as similarly unusual. Whether viewed as a generally applicable expansion or a targeted treatment of difficult facts, *Caperton* is consistent with the Court's ongoing trend of more aggressively using the Due Process Clause to promote recusal.

In 2015, the Court granted certiorari in a case that is factually similar to *DelVecchio*, the due process recusal case it had declined to review in 1990. In *Williams v. Pennsylvania*, the Court will decide whether the chief justice of the Pennsylvania Supreme Court, Ronald Castille, was required to recuse himself from a capital case against the defendant, Terrance Williams.[63] Chief Justice Castille "personally authorized the pursuit of [Williams's] death sentence" while serving as the Philadelphia district attorney.[64] He cited this decision as evidence of his support of the death penalty while running for election to the Pennsylvania Supreme Court. After ascending to the bench, he participated in a case reviewing the conduct of his own district attorney's office in its prosecution of Williams. The majority in that case, which included Castille but did not depend on him for the deciding vote, overturned a lower court decision staying Williams's execution based on the prosecution's refusal to turn over exculpatory evidence in its possession.

Williams does not seem poised to significantly alter the Court's expanded view of due process recusal. For one thing, the petition for certiorari that was granted by the Court cites *Caperton*'s "objective" inquiry into judicial bias and asks whether the Constitution is violated by Castille's actual bias, probability of bias, or appearance of bias.[65] The Court's reference to apparent or potential bias is consistent with the standards it articulated in *Aetna* and *Caperton*. Second, the facts of *Williams* are such that it is likely to be a rather narrow decision, at least as it pertains to the state of due process recusal doctrine. Chief Justice Castille's prior involvement with the case is so extensive that it would be easy to characterize *Williams* as one of the "extreme cases" Justice Kennedy referred to in *Caperton*. The other question on certiorari, whether due process is violated when the allegedly unfit judge is not the deciding vote on a multimember tribunal, is also a specific factual inquiry that is not likely to require the Court to revisit its standards for recusal under the Due Process Clause. In sum, the questions presented in *Williams*, along with the unique facts of that case, suggest that it will serve as merely the most recent example of the Court's expansive and flexible approach to due process recusal.

The Supreme Court's due process cases involving recusal reflect the Court's dynamic view of due process. This is no small development, as the interpretive approach to a novel constitutional question can have powerful consequences for the results. Fortunately, the Court has so far only opened additional avenues for exploration. It has expanded the definition of judicial interest from a purely monetary investment in a case to nonfinancial factors that present a judge with more attenuated benefits, like an improved litigation position. It has employed an objective consideration of whether a reasonable judge would likely feel biased, or in some cases whether the appearance of justice would be jeopardized in determining if recusal is warranted. Yet in doing so, the Court retained the common law view that a direct pecuniary interest is grounds for recusal, thus leaving both the common law and Supreme Court precedent as guides.

The movement in the Court's due process jurisprudence has been mirrored by Congress's legislative choices over the same period. In the first 120 years after the Founding, federal law went from requiring recusal only when a judge had a direct pecuniary interest in the case at hand—the traditional common law standard—to mandating recusal when a judge had served as counsel for either party in the same case, when a relative appeared before her as a party, when she was asked to decide an appeal from a case she had presided over below, or when she was a material witness in the case before her. The requirement that a judge recuse herself from hearing an appeal of a case she participated in below is reminiscent of Chief Justice Marshall's decision to recuse himself from *Stuart v. Laird*. Even more interesting is that the chief justice's decision in *Stuart* predated the statutory requirement, such that we can see a sort of reflexive relationship between Congress's and the Court's views on proper recusal protocol. Just as the Court may rely on congressional standards to inform its decisions, so too may Congress look to the Court's practices. To the extent this reciprocity is real, it supports the present argument that congressional practice can tell us something about how the Due Process Clause pertains to recusal at the Court. If Congress and the Court are indeed cognizant of the other's positions on recusal, then legislative recusal practice, even if it does not mention due process explicitly, can help explain the justices' views on the matter and, in turn, how due process affects their recusal decisions.

An active correlation is not necessary, however, for legislative recusal practices to be relevant to the relationship between due process and recusal at the Court. The simple fact that the Court's due process jurisprudence tracks the legislative developments in American recusal law can be helpful in understanding the constitutional limits of the justices' recusal practices. Starting in 1948, Congress, following the lead of the American Bar Association, expanded its recusal standards first to include members of the Supreme Court and then, in 1974, to require recusal of judges who conveyed a reasonable appearance of partiality.[66] This latter move was consistent with many of the Court's due process cases at the time. In *Murchison*, some twenty years before the 1974 amendment to section 455, the Court famously stated that "justice must satisfy the appearance of justice."[67] In *Mayberry*, only one year before the ABA introduced the reasonable appearance standard in its Model Code, the Court reiterated the appearance of justice language from *Murchison*, with Chief Justice Burger adding in his concurrence that protecting the integrity of the judicial process—a core principle behind the 1974 amendment to section 455—is also a valid concern in constitutional cases.[68] The Court's trend toward expanding due process recusal protections continued over the following decades in cases like *Ward*, *Aetna*, and *Caperton*, with the ultimate result being a "probability of bias" test that has much in common with section 455's reasonable appearance standard. It is possible that the apparent alignment of Congress's and the Court's views on recusal is a coincidence, but it is also possible that the two appear in tandem due to growing public interest in, and concern over, the integrity and politicization of the judiciary. Although the Court never explicitly described its due process approach as depending upon the evolution of public opinion, its expansion of the constitutional bounds of recusal occurred in parallel with Congress's amendments to the federal recusal statute. This relationship is at minimum strong circumstantial evidence that the Court's understanding of due process and recusal has some positive relationship to Congress's views on recusal in the federal courts, including the Supreme Court.

The converse is also true. On its face, it is impossible to connect legislative changes in federal recusal law with constitutional issues of due process without putting words in Congress's mouth. Congress has not explicitly connected its regulation of recusal to due process, and the Supreme Court has clearly stated that legislative recusal standards are distinct from those mandated by the Due Process Clause.[69] Nevertheless, to the extent that Congress's recusal reforms have paralleled the Court's due process jurisprudence, legislative practice is at least consistent with that jurisprudence. This consistency offers at worst no challenge to, and at best some support for, the idea that the Due Process Clause mandates a broader approach to recusal than was present at the Founding.

In sum, judicial and legislative practice regarding due process and recusal are substantively consistent. Both branches expanded their view of recusal, even though the Supreme Court never took up the question with regard to its own practices and Congress never expressly identified the Due Process Clause as the driving force behind its position. The Court adopted broader definitions of judicial interest and entertained objective arguments about potential bias in setting recusal standards for state and lower court judges under the Due Process Cause. Congress moved from a narrow view of individual interest to requiring recusal in cases with a reasonable appearance of partiality. This substantial overlap provides common ground between the public's interest in more stringent recusal standards for all federal judges and the Due Process Clause's expanding role in providing those standards. Taken together, the judicial and legislative practices surrounding recusal and due process reveal an increasingly prominent role for constitutional standards in judicial recusal, including recusal at the Court. The remaining interpretive question is how this view comports with other constitutional provisions.

Constitutional Structure and the Limits of Due Process Recusal

The Constitution's structure offers perhaps the most valuable insight into the Due Process Clause's impact on Supreme Court recusal. There are two dimensions in which constitutional structure can be brought to bear. One is internal to the judiciary and addresses how (if at all) the Supreme Court's status at the top of the judicial branch changes the way that due process principles impact the justices' recusal decisions. The second involves the interaction of the Due Process Clause with other constitutional provisions, specifically the First Amendment. The First Amendment would ostensibly prohibit recusals that were otherwise required under the Due Process Clause if those recusals were based on a justice's constitutionally protected speech. This potential conflict must be incorporated into any coherent view of due process recusal at the Court.

WHY DUE PROCESS RECUSAL IS DIFFERENT AT THE SUPREME COURT
AND THE LOWER FEDERAL COURTS

The Supreme Court's unique place atop the judicial branch makes it a better candidate for due process recusal standards than the lower courts, for which statutory restrictions raise far fewer constitutional objections.[70] There are advantages to preserving recusal as a legislative question. Statutory recusal standards are more easily adaptable and thus responsive to public feelings about the integrity of the judiciary than a constitutional doctrine that can only be changed by the courts or constitutional amendment. Because legislation is the province of the political branches, there is also a potential legitimacy benefit for lower federal courts in having Congress prescribe their recusal standards. A purely constitutional standard will be under the ultimate control of the very branch it purports to regulate and thus raises at least the specter of self-dealing by judges empowered to shape the boundaries of their own recusal doctrine. Perhaps for this reason, the Supreme Court has consistently stated that Congress may prescribe broader recusal protections than the Due Process Clause requires. In a well-known passage from his concurrence in *Republican Party of Minnesota v. White*, Justice Kennedy explained that the state "may adopt recusal standards more rigorous than due process requires, and censure judges who violate these standards."[71] In a case on remand from the Supreme Court, Judge Frank Easterbrook of the Seventh Circuit noted that "disqualification for 'appearance of impropriety' is a subject for statutes, codes of ethics, and common law, rather than a constitutional command."[72]

The Court's position seems clear enough. Whatever the prevailing standard under the Due Process Clause, it presents a narrower set of restrictions than those available to the legislative branch. But what about distinctions within the judicial branch? Is there reason to treat due process recusal differently when applied to the Supreme Court as opposed to state or lower federal courts? Should due process principles provide a stricter or more lenient recusal regime for the justices than for other judges? The answer to all of these questions is, paradoxically, yes. The Court's unique place in our constitutional structure suggests a range of additional considerations that support at times a more watchful and, for different reasons, a more forgiving set of constitutional boundaries for its recusal practices.

Stricter due process requirements for the Court could help protect its democratic legitimacy. The Supreme Court's legitimacy is of critical importance to the structure and function of our federal government. Its ability to issue final, binding decisions on matters of federal law provides uniformity that is essential to a cohesive national government. It is equally important that the Court be able to bind the country without its own threat of force, that is, without the ability to execute its own judgments. The separation of powers depends on the division of authority (overlapping as it may be) among the three branches. To empower the courts to enforce their own judgments by force would be a dangerous consolidation of executive and judicial power in a single branch. The courts' legitimacy thus depends on public confidence.[73] As Chief Justice Roberts explained in *Williams-Yulee v. The Florida Bar*: "The importance of public confidence in the integrity of judges stems from the place of the judiciary in the government. Unlike the executive or the legislature, the judiciary 'has no influence over either the sword or the purse; . . . neither force nor will but merely judgment.' The judiciary's authority therefore depends in large measure on the public's willingness to respect and follow its decisions."[74]

While the legitimacy of all federal courts is critical to an effective separation of powers, Supreme Court legitimacy is arguably even more significant. The Supreme Court is the only federal court that is mandated by the Constitution.[75] It is also the only federal court whose decisions are unreviewable. It is permanent and very difficult to rehabilitate in the event it began to lose popular support or respect. One way that public confidence in the Court and its members could erode is through perceived abuses of the justices' recusal power.[76] More stringent due process recusal standards for the Court could help alleviate those perceptions. The fact that the justices would be setting their own recusal standards promotes a sense of transparency and accountability in the Court's recusal practices. Increasing the protections for litigants against its own potential biases would bolster public confidence in the integrity and fairness of the Court's decisions and, in turn, its legitimacy.

The Court's finality is an independent reason to treat Supreme Court recusal questions more strictly. The Court's decisions are final because they are unreviewable; rulings can only be revised by the Court itself at a later date. The problem of unreviewable decisions is compounded in the recusal context. Imagine a lower court judge who wrongly fails to recuse herself and then issues a decision tainted by her failure to recuse. Both of those problems can be addressed on appeal. The case can be either remanded to a new judge based on the original judge's flawed recusal decision or simply reversed on the merits to the extent the decision was tainted to the point of reversible error. By contrast, a flawed recusal decision by a Supreme Court justice is not subject to either remedy because it is unreviewable. The otherwise removable justice will remain on the case, and any harm done to the decision-making process or integrity of the Court's decision will go unaddressed. Errors in the Court's ultimate determination based on that justice's participation are similarly unlikely to be reversed, except in the extremely rare instance where the Court grants a motion to revisit its own decision or it reverses its previous holding in a later case. The relative permanence of the justices' decisions thus counsels for heightened due process protections against unqualified or potentially biased judges.

An additional basis for more searching due process scrutiny of Supreme Court recusal is that the Court is subject to fewer legislative controls than the lower courts. Independent of whether federal recusal legislation is constitutional, the simple fact that Article III mandates the existence of the Supreme Court and leaves the question of whether to create lower federal courts solely to congressional discretion means that the Supreme Court is more insulated from legislative management than the inferior courts. The Constitution permits Congress to eradicate the federal judiciary with a single statute.[77] This is not true for the Supreme Court, and this structural phenomenon suggests that other constitutional limitations on the Court—like the Due Process Clause—must be read more strictly in order to maintain the appropriate bounds on the Supreme Court's authority where Congress lacks the power to do so.

A final, related, reason to consider harsher due process limits on the justices is the position advanced here that Congress is constitutionally precluded from regulating the justices' substantive recusal decisions. Under this theory, because lower courts are subject to additional legislative restrictions on their recusal practices, the sheer optics of the situation suggest that it makes sense to apply a harsher constitutional standard to the unregulated entity, the Supreme Court, than to the regulated ones, the lower courts. Public perception is likely to be skewed against the Court if it is subjected to only the constitutional limits placed on the lower courts but not the statutory ones. This is more of a prudential argument than a legal one. The mere existence of a recusal statute for the lower courts should not affect the scope of constitutional protections for recusal. Legislation can be repealed as easily as it was enacted, and it seems strange to say that repeal of a statute requiring recusal in the lower courts would decrease constitutional protections against the Court. So without overstating the importance of this argument, suffice it to say that, assuming the other arguments for treating the Court differently are at least somewhat persuasive, the realities of congressional involvement with lower court recusal may serve as an additional policy reason to subject the justices' recusal practices to heightened due process scrutiny.

The arguments for heightened review of recusal at the Court are not, however, the only way of looking at how the justices should apply due process principles to their recusal decisions. The Court's finality, for instance, can also be used to argue for lesser due process restrictions on the justices. Consider Chief Justice Stone's decision to unrecuse himself in order to preserve a quorum of the Court in *North American Company v. SEC*.[78] Regardless of whether Chief Justice Stone made the correct decision (recall that there was no federal statute purporting to govern his conduct at this time), his decision was based on an important principle. Although he reversed his decision to recuse without any apparent change in the relevant facts, the reversal had the effect of keeping the Court open for business in that case. Without Chief Justice Stone's decision, the parties would have been unable to take advantage of the Court's jurisdiction. A similar concern was raised in Justice Rehnquist's memorandum in *Tatum*[79] and in Justice Scalia's memorandum in *Cheney*.[80] Both justices argued that recusal was not prudent in their cases because it could result in the Court being unable to resolve an important legal issue.[81] The justices were referring primarily to the effect of a tie vote, which is made more likely by an odd number of recusals from a nine-member Court, but their concern is just as relevant in the context of complete recusal or recusals that cause the Court to lose a quorum. The idea that the concept of finality supports a less stringent due process regime for recusal at the Court is not limited to cases where recusal renders the Court unable to perform its duties. The loss of a single justice may not threaten quorum requirements, but it could change the complexion (or even the outcome) of a decision. None of these consequences attach to recusal in the lower courts because of the practice of assigning judges to fill vacancies on other courts.[82]

Chief Justice Stone's decision makes even more sense in controversial cases or in cases where there is a split among the lower courts. A justice is forced to decide between protecting the litigants from whatever conflicts that justice may experience, and increasing the risk either that the case will not be resolved at all or that the outcome will be affected by changing the composition of the Court. When a decision to recuse leaves in place competing views among the circuit courts, it makes it very difficult for federal law to perform its function of providing uniform standards for the entire country. When it changes the outcome of federal law based on the absence of one or more justices from that decision, it begs the question whether a full-fledged treatment of the issue is of greater import than an unbiased treatment of the case by a subset of the justices. Without answering this difficult question, its very existence is grounds for seeking less stringent due process requirements on justices' recusal decisions than those applied to the lower courts.

Focusing on recusal's consequences also creates a conflict between recusal and the appellant's right to appeal. Where the justice who is eligible for recusal would have sided with the respondent, no harm is done because the appellant's right to appeal is not harmed by the removal of an unsympathetic justice. Where the potential recusant is sympathetic to the appellant's views, that justice must decide whether the appellant's opportunity to vindicate her position, either through being granted review or by succeeding on the merits of the appeal, is more important than the need to present an objectively unbiased Court. This is not to say that a justice's disposition in a given case should affect her decision to recuse, but only to point out that when recusal could foreclose the Court's ability to fulfill its role as the final and impartial arbiter of federal law, the appellant's right to seek review should be considered in balance with the principles supporting recusal. Once we recognize that this balancing exists and merits the justices' attention, it becomes clear that only a more flexible due process standard will enable the Court to fulfill its constitutional duty as the nation's highest court while also making responsible recusal decisions.

Like finality, the Court's legitimacy can also be a double-edged sword when thinking about whether Supreme Court recusal should be treated differently from recusal in the lower courts. As discussed earlier, one conception of legitimacy—the promotion of public confidence in, and compliance with, the Court's decisions—is served by more rigorous due process protections. But there is a subset of this conception of legitimacy, the power of the Court to garner acceptance of its most controversial decisions, that may be better achieved through more permissive recusal standards. This subset is admittedly narrow. It applies only to those cases that are so potentially divisive that compliance could be threatened by the appearance of sharp divisions among the justices. The most obvious example of such a case is *Brown v. Board of Education*,[83] in which the justices affirmatively sought unanimity in order to lend additional force to, and hopefully prevent any violent public response to, their decision.[84] If the Court in *Brown* was correct in finding value in unanimity, then strict recusal standards under the Due Process Clause could interfere with that mission. Especially in a case where the outcome is not in doubt, should a justice who may have grounds to recuse herself under the Due Process Clause be permitted to remain in the case in order to join her colleagues in a statement of solidarity designed to promote public confidence in a critical decision and, in extreme cases, deter violent opposition to that decision? Any answer short of a clear no suggests that flexibility within the Court's due process standards is at least valuable enough to be part of a broader conversation about those standards.

So what to make of the interaction between Supreme Court recusal and the Due Process Clause? At first glance, it seems like a stalemate has emerged, whereby the reasons for ratcheting due process protections for the justices up or down generally cancel each other out. This is partly true. The Court's singular and complex role in our constitutional structure makes it an entity simultaneously worth constraining and liberating. Like any complex and important question, arguments can and should be made for both sides in hopes of discovering the better approach. That task is taken up later in this chapter. Regardless of how that exercise turns out, the threshold point is made that we should treat the Supreme Court differently from state and lower federal courts when it comes to due process and recusal. The arguments for greater and lesser due process restrictions share a common theme. The Court's responsibilities as the final arbiter of federal law trigger questions that are unique to the Court and that impact the constitutional boundaries of the justices' recusal practices. How those considerations ultimately affect the constitutional analysis, however, is a potentially even more controversial and difficult question. To answer it, we must first account for other constitutional provisions, like the First Amendment, that could also impact recusal standards for the Court.

SUPREME COURT RECUSAL AND THE FIRST AMENDMENT

Unlike the Court's unique place within the structure of government, First Amendment issues are not relevant to all of the justices' recusal decisions. Whether the First Amendment protects a justice from recusal only comes up when the potentially disqualifying conduct is protected speech. That said, recusals that are based on judicial speech quite clearly implicate the First Amendment. A requirement that a judge or justice remove herself from a case based on something she said or wrote is, on its face, a restriction on her free speech rights.[85] There is an ongoing scholarly debate, however, about whether recusal requirements are enough of a burden on speech either to merit First Amendment protection at all or to justify the strict judicial scrutiny afforded to content-based speech restrictions.[86] The Supreme Court has previously addressed the issue with respect to limits on judicial campaign speech. Justice Kennedy's concurring opinion in *White* indicated that recusals could be a useful way to limit judicial participation in cases where judges' campaign speech may have created a conflict of interest.[87] Because recusal based on campaign speech would not directly prohibit any speech, the argument goes, recusal may not create enough of a burden to rise to the level of a First Amendment violation. This puts recusal in the category of what Michael Dorf describes as an "incidental" infringement on a protected right.[88] Even when recusal does create a real burden on judicial speech, some argue that it still should not be viewed as a First Amendment issue because it is less intrusive than other forms of disciplinary action.[89] This is an implication of Justice Kennedy's concurrence in *White*, where he suggested recusal as a potential alternative to prohibiting protected campaign speech.[90] Neither of these arguments is persuasive, however, when we talk about federal recusal, including recusal at the Court.

As an initial matter, federal judges are not elected, so arguments from campaign speech cases are, at least on one level, inapposite. The Court in *White* treated campaign speech as core political speech under the First Amendment, meaning it received the highest level of constitutional protection.[91] A far wider range of judicial speech, including nonpolitical speech, can trigger recusal. More important, the two arguments for treating recusal requirements as less of a threat to free speech fail on their merits when applied to federal recusal. Incidental burdens on speech are generally defined as those arising from content-neutral provisions.[92] Under this definition, recusal does not amount to an incidental burden on judicial speech. A motion to recuse a judge or justice based on what she has said in the past is not content-neutral. It depends heavily on the specific content of the judge or justice's speech and whether it meets the recusal threshold provided by, in the case of the Supreme Court, the Due Process Clause. As for the severity of recusal versus other forms of discipline, that may affect whether the consequence is permissible under the applicable First Amendment doctrine but not whether the First Amendment applies in the first instance. A less drastic result like recusal may be easier to justify under the applicable First Amendment test than, for example, public censure or suspension, but that does not tell us whether First Amendment protections are triggered by the recusal requirement or what test applies to them. The important point at this stage is that recusals based on judicial speech are direct infringements on speech that, at least to some degree, generate First Amendment protections.

Such situations are also not uncommon. In 2014, Justice Ginsburg's qualifications to participate in a controversial abortion case were drawn into question due to comments she made in an interview about the case while it was still pending in the lower court.[93] Justice Kagan's fitness to review the Affordable Care Act was challenged, at least in part, because of an e-mail she wrote while solicitor general to her friend and former

colleague Laurence Tribe celebrating the passage of the act.[94] Justices
Alito, Scalia, Breyer, and others have been criticized for speaking before interest groups that could potentially come before the Court as
litigants. In all of these cases, questions arose as to whether the justices
should recuse themselves based on their speech. If statutory recusal
standards carried the day, the relevant inquiry would be whether the
federal recusal statute is constitutional when applied to cases involving
judicial speech. Because we have determined that the recusal statute
is unconstitutional as applied to the Court, we are able to more easily identify a previously neglected issue in recusal law—how the First
Amendment and Due Process Clause interact to shield litigants from
rulings by unqualified justices while simultaneously protecting the justices' right to freedom of speech under the First Amendment.

As with many novel issues, the answer is not readily apparent. The
Supreme Court has never directly addressed whether the First Amendment limits recusals based on judicial speech. There are, however, three
existing First Amendment doctrines that can serve as useful analogues
for judicial speech limitations in the recusal context—the content-
based speech doctrine, the public employee speech doctrine, and the
attorney speech doctrine.[95] To determine how each of these doctrines
may affect recusal at the Court, we must find a consistent way to test
them against the prevailing due process standards. Under the Court's
due process jurisprudence, recusals may be required when there is a
reasonable probability of judicial bias.[96] It is not clear precisely how this
standard relates to the reasonable appearance standard featured in the
federal recusal statute, but it is safe to say that the statutory standard
marks the outer bounds of American recusal law.[97] No other recusal
standards implicate as wide a range of judicial conduct as the reasonable appearance standard. It is also easy to interpret the probability-of-
bias test more narrowly than the appearance-of-impartiality standard.
As some commentators have noted, a literal comparison of the two standards suggests that the probability-of-bias test is focused on the degree
of actual bias likely to be felt by a reasonable judge or justice, whereas
the reasonable appearance standard looks to whether the public will
perceive a lack of impartiality in a judge.[98] Without leaning too heavily
on the merits of this distinction, it becomes evident that the probability-
of-bias and appearance-of-impartiality standards are at minimum theoretically distinguishable from one another. This theoretical distinction
makes the two tests separate templates against which we can compare

the relevant First Amendment doctrines impacting recusal, and in turn test the constitutional boundaries between First Amendment protections of judicial speech and recusal requirements under the Due Process Clause.

The Court has divided government restrictions on private speech into two categories. Content-based restrictions, which "distinguish favored speech from disfavored speech on the basis of the ideas or views expressed," are subject to strict judicial scrutiny.[99] Under the strict scrutiny standard, a restriction on speech must be "'narrowly tailored to serve a compelling state interest.'"[100] Content-neutral restrictions, which "confer benefits or impose burdens on speech without reference to the ideas or views expressed," are subject to more permissive, intermediate scrutiny.[101] The Supreme Court applied the content-based speech doctrine to judicial speech in *White* when it struck down Canon 5(A)(3)(d)(i) of the Minnesota Code of Judicial Conduct, which prohibited a candidate for judicial office from "announc[ing] his or her views on disputed legal or political issues."[102] The Court concluded that the canon was a content-based speech restriction—and thus should be subject to strict judicial scrutiny[103]—because it prevented judicial candidates from publicly discussing their opinions on almost all specific legal questions.[104]

Addressing the state's purported interest in ensuring the actual and apparent impartiality of its judges, Justice Scalia, writing for the Court, identified two kinds of impartiality at issue—impartiality toward parties and impartiality toward legal issues. He concluded that the government has a compelling interest in preserving judicial impartiality toward the *parties* to legal proceedings but held that the canon was not narrowly tailored to achieve that impartiality because it merely restricted speech that would indicate a judicial bent on legal subject matter, a "bias" that could be applied equally to all parties.[105] Justice Scalia then explained that judicial impartiality toward legal *issues* was not itself a compelling state interest, largely because it is neither possible nor desirable to find judges with no preconceived legal ideas.[106] Therefore, because the canon was unable to satisfy strict scrutiny in preventing bias against the parties or the issues in a particular proceeding, the Court held that it violated the First Amendment.[107]

The Court revisited the intersection of the content-based speech doctrine and judicial speech in 2015. In *Williams-Yulee*,[108] it upheld Canon 7C(1) of the Florida Code of Judicial Conduct, which prohibited judicial candidates from personally soliciting campaign contributions. The Court held that campaign solicitations by judicial candidates are the type of informative, politically relevant speech that is entitled to the highest level of First Amendment protection—strict scrutiny—and that this was the "rare case" in which a restriction on speech could meet that high standard.[109] Distinguishing judges from other politicians, the Court concluded that Canon 7C(1) served the compelling government interest of "'protecting the integrity of the judiciary' and 'maintaining the public's confidence in an independent judiciary'" by preventing judges from "asking for favors" from the very public they are charged with serving impartially.[110] It went on to explain that Canon 7C(1)'s prohibition was narrowly tailored to the asserted government interest because it targeted all campaign solicitations by judicial candidates equally and prohibited a specific category of speech that was especially likely to affect that interest.[111] Interestingly, the Court rejected Williams-Yulee's argument that recusal rules could solve the Florida Bar's concerns. It concluded instead that such rules could result in so many postelection recusal motions as to "disable many jurisdictions" or "'erode public confidence in judicial impartiality,'" not to mention creating a "perverse incentive for litigants to make campaign contributions to judges solely as a means to trigger their later recusal."[112] It did not comment on how, if at all, the proposed recusal rules would impact the judges' First Amendment rights.

Williams-Yulee featured the opposite result from *White*, but otherwise the two cases have much in common. Both cases treated judicial campaign restrictions as content-based limits on speech, and both applied strict scrutiny to determine if their respective restrictions satisfied the First Amendment. They both involved the speech of judicial candidates, rather than sitting judges, and did not address the free speech implications of judicial recusal, let alone of recusal at the Court. Their content-based speech analysis is nonetheless relevant to the justices' recusal practices because it can help identify the appropriate boundaries between free speech and the due process principles served by recusal. The reasonable appearance standard is the most logical starting point because it is the most aggressive possible approach to due process recusal. The broadest possible reading of the Court's due process recusal standards requires at least a reasonable appearance of partiality, and more likely a showing of a probability of actual bias. Even peremptory recusals under section 144 function more narrowly than the reasonable appearance test because they require a finding of actual bias and give judges broad discretion in determining whether the supporting affidavits merit such a finding.[113] As an initial step, then, it is worth asking whether the content-based speech test would protect speech that creates a reasonable appearance of partiality. If the answer is no, then the First Amendment and Due Process Clauses do not overlap with respect to recusals based on the reasonable appearance standard, and that standard may be applied to recusal at the Court. If the answer is yes, then we must look for a different due process recusal standard that does not penalize justices for engaging in constitutionally protected judicial speech. Based on the Court's due process jurisprudence, the most logical alternative is the probability of bias test.

Content-based speech restrictions are unconstitutional unless they serve a compelling government interest in a way that is narrowly tailored to the achievement of that interest.[114] The primary interest served by the reasonable appearance standard is to protect the integrity of the judiciary. Because it is not necessarily limited to cases where actual bias exists or is even likely, the appearance standard does not necessarily improve the quality of judging for the litigants in the case. It is best understood as a defense against weakening the prestige and legitimacy of the judiciary in the eyes of the observing public, including the litigants, by excluding a judge who may appear partial even if that appearance is misleading. This satisfies the compelling government interest test as articulated in both *White* and *Williams-Yulee*. As in those cases, however, the question of whether the reasonable appearance standard is narrowly tailored to the task of protecting the integrity of the Supreme Court is a far closer call. The campaign restrictions in *White* and *Williams-Yulee* are by definition inapposite to the case of federal recusal because federal judges never campaign for their offices. As a remedy, recusal is likely more narrowly tailored than prohibiting an entire category of judicial campaign speech because recusal applies only to a sitting justice's participation in a single case and imposes consequences for speaking without cutting off the speech altogether. On the other hand, recusal is a significant intrusion into a justice's ability to decide a case under Article III.[115] Most important to the application of First Amendment doctrine, there are alternative ways to promote judicial integrity without requiring recusal. Requiring a justice to publicly explain her recusal decision could help alleviate any misunderstandings about her qualifications without interfering with her ability to decide the case before her. This less restrictive means of promoting judicial integrity makes it more likely that the reasonable appearance standard will fail the content-based speech test.

A reasonable probability of actual bias triggers a different analysis. The government has the additional interest of ensuring a fair trial on top of its concern for safeguarding judicial integrity. This interest in a fair trial is without question a compelling government interest—it is a foundational feature of constitutional due process and was described as compelling by the majority in *White*.[116] Recusal is also far more likely to be narrowly tailored in this circumstance, as removal of a judge from a case in the face of a probability of actual bias is perhaps the only way to ensure an impartial forum.

The content-based speech test offers some useful insight into the limits of due process protections in recusal cases based on judicial speech. Where recusal is based on a reasonable appearance of partiality, it is more likely to run afoul of the First Amendment on the grounds that it is not narrowly tailored to protecting the integrity of the Court. Where recusal is based on a possibility of bias, it is more likely to survive First Amendment scrutiny because it is narrowly tailored to the compelling interest of preserving a fair tribunal for the parties.

The content-based speech doctrine is not, however, the only possible fit for Supreme Court recusal. In his concurring opinion in *White*, Justice Kennedy provided some insight into how the justices may treat a First Amendment challenge to recusal standards. He expressly distinguished recusal from judicial campaign speech and suggested that the law regarding public employee speech could be useful in evaluating judicial speech and recusal.[117] Justice Kennedy's statement is not enough to definitively conclude that judicial recusal is governed by the public employee speech doctrine, and in fact there are several reasons why his analogy seems particularly flawed. It is enough, however, to further investigate the relationship between public employee speech and the relevant due process recusal standards facing the Court.

Public employees receive less First Amendment protection than other citizens. Prior to the Court's 1968 decision in *Pickering v. Board of Education*,[118] public employees enjoyed few, if any, First Amendment protections. The Court reasoned that public employment could be conditioned on restrictions of employees' rights because the employee did not have a right to that employment.[119] In *Pickering*, the Court slightly altered its stance by holding that the speech of government employees is protected by the First Amendment, subject to a balancing test weighing the interests of the employer "in promoting the efficiency of the public services it performs through its employees" against the interests of the employee "in commenting upon matters of public concern."[120] Marvin Pickering, a public school teacher, was fired by the school board for sending a letter to the editor of a local newspaper.[121] Pickering wrote the letter in opposition to a proposed district-wide tax increase for educational funding. He objected to the new taxes based on what he believed was the board's mishandling of funds from a similar tax increase three years earlier. In particular, he criticized the board's "allocation of financial resources between the schools' educational and athletic programs."[122] Reasoning that Pickering's criticism of the school's use of funds was a matter of public concern that was not harmful to the local schools or to the teacher's performance, the Court held that Pickering's speech was protected by the First Amendment.[123]

Pickering marked a high point in public employees' First Amendment rights. In three cases since *Pickering*, the Court has established and clarified a pair of threshold questions that limit First Amendment claims by public employees. In *Connick v. Myers*,[124] Assistant District Attorney Sheila Myers was faced with a transfer that she opposed. She responded by circulating an intraoffice questionnaire pertaining to "office transfer policy, office morale, the need for a grievance committee, the level of confidence in supervisors, and whether employees felt pressured to work in political campaigns."[125] Myers was terminated because of her refusal to accept the transfer and because her circulation of the questionnaire amounted to an act of insubordination. Myers objected to the termination on the grounds that the questionnaire was protected speech under the First Amendment, and the district and circuit courts agreed.[126] The Supreme Court held that the speech of public employees must relate to a matter of public concern in order to be protected under the First Amendment.[127] It explained that matters of public concern are judged by "content, form, and context"[128] and concluded that Myers's distribution of the questionnaire was not constitutionally protected because the speech was merely "an employee grievance concerning internal office policy"[129] and did not address a matter of public concern.[130]

In *Garcetti v. Ceballos*[131] and *Lane v. Franks*,[132] the Court required yet another finding before applying the *Pickering* balancing test to employee speech. In addition to requiring that the speech at issue involve a matter of public concern, the Court in *Garcetti* required that the speech be pursuant to the employee's status as an ordinary citizen in order to be protected, rather than part of her official government duties.[133] The speech at issue in *Lane* was a public employee's subpoenaed testimony in a criminal trial, which the Court concluded was not part of the employee's professional duties as director of a community college's program for underprivileged youth.[134] *Lane* clarified *Garcetti*'s general rule protecting only non-work-related speech by stating that "the critical question under *Garcetti* is whether the speech at issue is itself ordinarily within the scope of an employee's duties, not whether it merely concerns those duties."[135] Taken together, the public employee speech doctrine protects only speech made by public employees in their capacity as ordinary citizens about matters of public concern. Such speech may nevertheless still be restricted under the *Pickering* balancing test if the employer's interests in efficient government operation outweigh the employee's interest in the speech.

In light of Justice Kennedy's suggestion in *White* that the appropriate First Amendment doctrine to apply in recusal cases is the public employee speech doctrine,[136] the inevitable next question is what the doctrine would mean for Supreme Court recusal or, more specifically, how it would interact with the Due Process Clause to set boundaries for the justices' recusal decisions. First, it is worth noting that the semantics of the public employee doctrine seem to make it inapposite to judicial recusal, and especially to recusal at the Court. It is awkward, for example, to think of federal judges as public "employees." They seem like public employees because they are paid from the public fisc and are clearly associated with the federal government. Unlike most public employees, however, federal judges, including members of the Court, are appointed to their positions by the president with the advice and consent of the Senate.[137] It is difficult, moreover, to characterize someone with life tenure as anyone's "employee." The only entity with the power to terminate federal judges is Congress via impeachment, and the impeachment process is entirely distinct from recusal. Appellate courts retain significant authority over lower courts, but not as much as an employer over an employee, as evidenced by the fact that appellate courts are highly deferential to lower court recusal decisions.[138] Supreme Court justices are even further removed from being public employees, as their recusal decisions are not subject to appellate review.[139] Because their professional experience more closely resembles that of Congress and the president than a traditional government employee, federal judges, and especially the members of the Court, do not seem like proper subjects of the public employee speech doctrine.[140]

Second, the public employee speech doctrine looks like a bad fit with judicial recusal because its failure to protect speech within a judge's official duties is inconsistent with our concept of judicial independence. There is a strong argument that with the security of independence comes both the constitutionally protected freedom to speak without fear of reprisal and a corresponding duty to engage in public discourse and education about the law.[141] If recusal can be justified simply on the basis of a judge making a speech to law students about a current constitutional issue—an activity that is arguably within the judge's professional responsibilities, yet could very plausibly create enough of a reasonable appearance of partiality to merit recusal—then a serious question exists as to whether the current recusal standards are even theoretically compatible with the public employee speech doctrine.

These threshold issues aside, we must apply the public employee speech doctrine at different points along the potential spectrum of due process recusal standards to determine if the two doctrines can interact successfully with one another. Beginning with the most expansive view of due process, we see that the requirement that a justice remove herself from a case under the reasonable appearance standard does not square with the *Pickering* balancing test or the related tests in *Connick* and *Garcetti*. The recusal standard comports nicely with the government's interest in promoting the judiciary's obligation to provide adjudication that not only is unbiased but also appears so to a reasonable observer. The reasonable appearance standard does not, however, work well with *Pickering*'s protection of the employee's interest in public discourse or with the fact that speech that is outside the official's professional duties and on a matter of public concern is protected under the First Amendment. Recusal is required under the reasonable appearance standard as soon as a judge's speech puts her impartiality reasonably in question. There is no consideration of the speech's public import or its relationship to her position as a judge. As a result, the reasonable appearance test will run into significant constitutional problems as it seeks to force recusals based on judicial speech that the public employee doctrine considers constitutionally protected.

The probability of bias test may be more compatible with *Pickering*'s protection of employee speech. Provided we read the probability test as requiring some concern about actual bias, rather than merely its appearance, recusal based on judicial speech is less likely to conflict with First Amendment protections of public employee speech. Even where a judge or justice is speaking in her capacity as an ordinary citizen on a matter of public concern, a statement that increases the probability of actual bias against one of the parties in the case before her threatens "the efficiency of the public services it performs through its employees" more than conduct that creates only an appearance of partiality.[142] Actual bias is the death knell of a fair and impartial judicial system, which is at the core of our collective understanding of due process.[143] It is thus easy to imagine that a probability of actual bias could be seen as outweighing a judge's personal interests "in commenting upon matters of public concern."[144] If we understand such commentary to be part of the official judicial role, then not only may the threat of actual bias be too much to overcome, but also the public employee doctrine may cease to protect such speech altogether, as it would be speech in the judge's official capacity as a public employee and thus unprotected under *Garcetti* and *Lane*.[145]

As with the content-based test, the First Amendment protections for public employee speech seem primed to conflict with the most stringent due process recusal requirement, the reasonable appearance standard, yet may fit within the probability of bias standard. This correlation is helpful because it reinforces the idea developed under the content-based speech doctrine that the probability-of-bias test is compatible with the First Amendment.

Like public employees, attorneys also enjoy fewer First Amendment protections than other citizens. Justice Kennedy's concurrence in *White* was silent about using the Court's attorney speech precedent to assess the constitutionality of judicial speech restrictions, but Erwin Chemerinsky has observed that "there is a logic to holding attorneys and judges to the same standard."[146] The critical case governing attorneys' First Amendment rights is *Gentile v. State Bar of Nevada*,[147] which involved an attorney who was reprimanded for violating a state ethical rule during a press conference.[148] The attorney, Gentile, held a press conference just a few hours after his client was indicted on criminal charges of removing money and drugs from a safe deposit box rented by undercover police officers.[149] At the press conference, Gentile claimed that the state was using his client as a "scapegoat" when the real culprit was "'the police department, crooked cops.'"[150] Gentile's client was acquitted by a jury roughly six months later, at which time the state bar reprimanded Gentile for violating Nevada Supreme Court Rule 177, which prohibited attorneys from making "extrajudicial statements" with "a substantial likelihood of materially prejudicing an adjudicative proceeding."[151] The Nevada Supreme Court upheld the bar's decision and summarily dismissed Gentile's constitutional challenges "as lacking merit under either the federal or Nevada constitutions."[152] Gentile appealed the Nevada Supreme Court's constitutional decision to the U.S. Supreme Court. In reviewing Gentile's constitutional claims, the Court explained that attorneys' First Amendment rights in court are "extremely circumscribed."[153] Moreover, lawyers' "extrajudicial statements pose a threat to the fairness of a pending proceeding since lawyers' statements are likely to be received as especially authoritative."[154] The Court held that Nevada's "substantial likelihood of material prejudice" test struck the appropriate balance between attorneys' First Amendment rights and the state's interest in a fair judicial system.[155] Therefore, states may limit attorney speech when it is substantially likely to materially prejudice an adjudicative proceeding.

The Court's material prejudice test does not seem compatible with the reasonable appearance standard for recusal. It is easy to imagine a statement by a judge or justice that could create a reasonable appearance of partiality but that may not create the "substantial likelihood of material prejudice" needed to sanction that speech under the Court's holding in *Gentile*. Picture a scenario in which a sitting Supreme Court justice referred to a lawyer practicing before the Court as "simply one of the very best and most persuasive advocates in America." That same justice's decision to participate in a case argued by that lawyer may very well create a reasonable appearance of partiality but may not cause a reasonable person to believe that the justice was likely to be materially prejudiced in her judgment of the case. At minimum, enough of a theoretical distinction exists between a reasonable appearance of something and the substantial likelihood that the same thing will have a material impact on the outcome of a case to justify treating the two differently.

Gentile's material prejudice test seems much closer to the Court's probability of bias standard. Both focus on an objective measure of the bias reflected in certain speech. The fact that the attorney speech doctrine focuses on speech related to an ongoing proceeding does not distinguish it from recusal cases because recusal is a case-specific remedy.[156] Recusal asks if a judge will be prejudiced in the case before her, and recusal based on the judge's speech asks if the speech at issue created sufficient prejudice to merit removal of that judge from the case at hand. Unlike disciplinary actions or other sanctions, recusal is necessarily intertwined with an ongoing proceeding, such that the attorney speech doctrine's focus on the relationship between attorney speech and an active proceeding is a natural feature of recusal-for-speech cases. The material prejudice test is potentially narrower than the probability-of-bias test, but if that is true, the worst-case scenario is that the recusal standard would have to be dialed back slightly to accommodate the slice of cases in which material prejudice does not quite result from the judge or justice's speech, but a sufficient probability of bias is there to merit recusal. This does not seem like a large group of cases, but regardless of its size the remedy is the same—to tweak the recusal standard to ensure that only unprotected speech, namely, speech that creates a substantial likelihood of material prejudice, can trigger recusal under the Due Process Clause.

That worst-case scenario is likely irrelevant, however, because the probability of bias test can survive strict scrutiny under the content-based speech doctrine. In cases where a statute required recusal for speech that did not materially prejudice the case at hand, the next step would be to see if there is some other justification for regulating that speech. The attorney speech doctrine allows for additional limits on attorneys' speech due to their unique role in society. It does not simply replace more generally applicable doctrines like the content-based speech test. Because the probability-of-bias standard satisfies strict scrutiny under the content-based speech doctrine, any restrictions beyond those allowed by the attorney speech doctrine may still be permissible under the First Amendment.

After weighing the possible effects of all three of the applicable First Amendment doctrines, some important commonalities emerge with regard to judicial recusal. All three doctrines pose problems for the reasonable appearance standard. The content-based speech test presents the fewest problems, which is somewhat ironic considering it offers the broadest speech protections. By focusing on a wider range of possible government interests, the content-based analysis best accommodates the goals and purposes of judicial recusal. The reasonable appearance standard still cannot coexist easily with the content-based speech test because recusal is potentially too drastic a remedy for problems of judicial integrity. By contrast, the Supreme Court's probability-of-bias standard finds common ground with all three First Amendment doctrines. This is primarily because of the theoretical differences between the probability and appearance standards. It is generally easier to justify restrictions on speech that create a reasonable probability of actual judicial bias in a given case than those that create only an appearance of such bias. Whatever doctrine is applied, the probability-of-bias approach to recusal under the Due Process Clause appears compatible with the First Amendment.

So what does this analysis of the First Amendment's intersection with due process recusal standards tell us about recusal at the Court? As a reminder, we are trying to define how and when constitutional due process requires recusal at the Court. The First Amendment offers a structural limitation on the scope of the Due Process Clause. The Due Process Clause cannot mandate recusals that would otherwise violate a justice's First Amendment rights to free speech. There are, however, some limitations to the First Amendment analysis. First, it applies only to cases in which recusals are based on judicial speech.[157] Without embarking on a long and complex discussion of what does and does not constitute speech under the First Amendment, it is clear that recusal can be triggered by nonspeech events. A judge's prior work experience, personal relationships, or financial holdings can require recusal under a range of applicable standards, and none of these events are likely to meet the constitutional definition of speech. Any argument for limiting recusals based on the First Amendment must therefore keep in mind that the amendment cannot be a blanket limitation.

The preceding analysis is also constrained by the fact that it treats the First Amendment as an amalgamation of three distinct doctrines. The result is that the most restrictive doctrine must prevail, or else we risk advocating for a due process standard that is doomed from the start because it conflicts with at least one reading of the First Amendment. The more precise approach would be to make a detailed, normative argument for the best way to treat judicial recusal under the First Amendment and then compare that favored doctrine against the available due process formulations. This greater precision is fraught with its own perils. It risks hijacking the desired conversation about recusal at the Court in favor of a complex, novel interpretation of the First Amendment. This unwanted foray into First Amendment law can be avoided because the three doctrines interact with due process recusal in similar ways.

The outer limit of due process recusal is the probability-of-bias test because it accommodates the entire range of potential First Amendment concerns that could attach to judicial recusals. Because this is also the recusal standard most frequently cited by the Court, it is a safe starting point for our development of due process recusal standards for the justices.

When Due Process Requires Recusal

Evidence from the Founding, from judicial precedent and legislative practice, and from structural considerations points to a due process recusal standard for the Court that looks far more like the present statutory standard than Blackstone's common law requirement. The Supreme Court has historically employed a range of factors in its own recusal practices, and in the past century it expanded the Due Process Clause to require recusal in a wider array of cases than ever before. In virtual parallel with the Court's constitutional expansion of recusal law, Congress has engaged in its own persistent extension of the federal recusal statute to cover more and more judicial conduct, including activities that create a reasonable appearance of judicial bias. The generalized endgame is a national view of recusal that has evolved from a largely financial inquiry into one that looks much more like a Bractonian standard of suspicion about judicial fitness.

Merely concluding that recusal under the Due Process Clause is more expansive than the common law standard in place at the Founding does not tell us enough, however, about what the specific terms of recusal are under the Constitution and how, if at all, they should differ for members of the Court as opposed to lower court judges. The answer to the second question helps simplify the first. A structural analysis reveals that the Supreme Court operates under constitutionally different conditions than the lower federal courts, and as such it must approach recusal questions with an institutional perspective that is largely unnecessary for those courts. Concerns about the Court's legitimacy, finality, and independence raise constitutional issues that, despite not being part of the Court's existing due process jurisprudence (because that jurisprudence has yet to address recusal at the Court), are nevertheless critical to establishing the appropriate due process recusal threshold for the justices.

After two centuries of slow expansion, it appears that the Due Process Clause requires recusal when a judge exhibits a reasonable probability of bias. The matter becomes more complicated, though, when structural considerations are taken into account. This is why it is so important when dealing with a novel constitutional issue like recusal at the Court to employ a wide range of analytical tools. Although developed through legislative and judicial practice, the probability-of-bias standard has never been applied to the Court itself, so it has by definition never been tested for its fit within the broader constitutional design. A structural analysis offers perspective on how the probability-of-bias standard can be adjusted to meet the specific, and often unique, needs of the justices. The two primary structural issues facing due process recusal are the First Amendment and the institutional duties and prerogatives of the Court under Article III.

The First Amendment has the more clearly defined role. In cases involving recusal based on judicial speech, all three of the potentially relevant doctrines—the content-based, public employee, and attorney speech doctrines—tolerate the probability of bias standard. By contrast, none of them coexist easily with the reasonable appearance standard. That is why the probability-of-bias standard is the preferable approach to due process recusal. It is the standard most clearly articulated by the Court's due process jurisprudence and is the one that fits most easily within the First Amendment framework for judicial speech. But while constitutional limitations like the First Amendment are important factors to consider in crafting a due process standard, they do not necessarily drive the analysis.

The other structural question is how to deal with the Court's unique status at the top of the federal judiciary. Concerns about the Court's legitimacy counsel in favor of adopting due process recusal standards above and beyond the probability-of-bias standard. The same concerns also suggest limiting due process requirements in favor of giving members of the Court more discretion in their recusal decisions. Heightened recusal standards further protect the public's confidence in the judiciary and the integrity of its final pronouncements on matters of federal law. They also help compensate for the fact that Congress has far less authority over the justices than it does over other federal judges. A more relaxed recusal standard would permit the justices to participate in cases in which they deem it important to protect the Court's ability to decide, to display a unified front for a particularly controversial decision, or to ensure that an important or controversial legal question receives the justices' full consideration.

Due to the high variability of these factors, it is nearly impossible to reach a blanket conclusion as to how institutional features of the Court affect recusal decisions under the Due Process Clause. As luck would have it, such a blanket conclusion is neither necessary nor advisable. The value of bringing institutional concerns to light is so the justices' decisions can be evaluated in the proper context. Chief Justice Stone may have been correct in *North American Company* that the Court's institutional interest in achieving a quorum trumped competing concerns about the potentially negative public image of a justice participating in a case from which he had previously recused himself.[158] By contrast, Justice Black's decision to protect the Fair Labor Standards Act from constitutional attack in *Jewell Ridge* may not have been justified when compared with the cost of his participating in a case argued by his former law partner and involving a statute he helped enact while in the Senate.[159] It may be that neither of these examples is persuasive, such that Chief Justice Stone was wrong to participate in his case and Justice Black was entirely justified in doing so in his. Those conclusions are immaterial. What matters here is that the various institutional questions surrounding recusal at the Court are not, nor should they be, static factors in a rigid test. They are, at their base, prudential questions about how to make recusal decisions in a way that honors both the constitutional requirements of due process and the responsibilities of the Court as the head of the judicial branch. Combining all the relevant sources of constitutional meaning, the standard for Supreme Court recusal should be the probability-of-bias test, as informed and modified by institutional factors such as the legitimacy and effective functioning of the Court. Recusal under this regime is a case-by-case inquiry that contextualizes, but does not supplant, the core constitutional standard under the Due Process Clause.

Starting from that premise, the value of this interpretive exercise comes into full relief. Because previous considerations of Supreme Court recusal failed to think of it in constitutional terms, several important aspects of the justices' practices were also overlooked. The most poignant of these is the realization that legislative recusal mandates unduly interfere with the Court's authority under Article III. This necessarily leads to the equally important, but also previously unappreciated, question of where else to look for recusal standards to guide the Court. The answer, not surprisingly, is the Constitution. But when we look to the various constitutional provisions that could bear on a justice's decision to recuse, several candidates emerge. The Due Process Clause is the driving force, but its influence is shaped by the Court's constitutional responsibilities under Article III and the protections of the First Amendment. The result is a case-by-case balancing act that pits structural concerns and the individual rights of the justices against the undisputed mandate that every litigant be given access to a fair hearing. Without first casting recusal at the Court as a constitutional issue, and then embarking on the full-throated evaluation of how due process and recusal interact at the Court, these constitutional issues may well have continued to be overlooked, and the justices' recusal practices misunderstood.

But does it really matter? What are the actual costs of failing to see the Court's recusal practices as rooted in constitutional due process? There are at least three answers. One is that treating recusal at the Court as a matter of constitutional law best describes the justices' actual recusal practices. This claim cannot be empirical, due to the justices' reluctance to explain their recusal decisions, but it is consistent with virtually all the internal accounts of how recusal works at the Court. In an era when Supreme Court recusal has begun to garner so much national attention, it is helpful to have an accurate framework within which to describe what the justices are actually doing when they make recusal decisions. A second reason to consider the constitutional issues affecting Supreme Court recusal is that it helps the public to better understand the substantive reasons for the justices' recusal decisions. This is important to Supreme Court transparency and accountability because it empowers commentators to address recusal decisions on their own terms. Whether this leads to wider acceptance of, or frustration with, the Court's practices, setting the appropriate terms for the debate allows a more truthful and, in turn, more productive dialogue about the proper role of recusal at the Court. Lastly, recognition of the full range of constitutional factors at play in Supreme Court recusal will help litigants to better frame their own recusal arguments and to more easily understand the likelihood of success of those arguments. Rather than relying on statutory standards that are ineffective and incomplete, litigants seeking to challenge a justice's fitness to participate in a given case can now offer a more persuasive account of their position by incorporating due process principles and institutional factors into their presentation. Even if this does not change the outcome in many (or any) cases, it further increases judicial transparency and accountability by refining litigants' exchange with members of the Court over recusal. It may even pressure individual justices into offering more detailed explanations of their decisions or, in controversial cases, reconsidering their position altogether.

* * *

The process of recasting Supreme Court recusal as a matter of constitutional law has involved several iterations. The first was to examine what the separation of powers can tell us about where recusal standards for the justices come from. The second was to determine, given the constitutional problems with congressional control of recusal at the Court, how to alleviate the ongoing impasse between Congress and the Court over recusal. The third was to establish how the justices' recusal practices may be constrained in the absence of binding legislation. The ultimate answer is that Supreme Court recusal is a constitutional question that, like many issues of governmental power, cannot be easily articulated in a rigid test. It requires an amalgamation of constitutional provisions and principles that, taken together, reveal a full view of the constitutional ramifications of recusal at the Court.

But that is not all we stand to gain from thinking of Supreme Court recusal in constitutional terms. Constitutionalizing recusal at the Supreme Court also offers a new and valuable perspective on recusal in other venues, particularly state and lower federal courts.

6 | Beyond the High Court

Recusal and the Constitution in the Lower Federal Courts

Recusal triggers different constitutional questions for the lower federal courts than it does for the Supreme Court.[1] Supreme Court recusal comes with an underappreciated but real legacy of tension between Congress and the Court. There is no such historical tension in the lower courts. In fact, on its face there does not seem to be any problem at all with Congress exercising complete control over lower court recusal. Congress has a wider array of constitutional tools at its disposal to regulate the lower federal courts than it does to regulate the justices, including the power to create (and by extension destroy) the lower courts and to define their jurisdiction. Considering how little attention has been paid to the constitutional issues surrounding Supreme Court recusal, it comes as even less of a surprise that Congress is widely assumed to have virtually unlimited power to regulate recusal in the lower courts. But as the preceding analysis of Supreme Court recusal suggests, that is not necessarily true. Article III directly vests all federal courts, supreme and otherwise, with some degree of inherent judicial power. This inherent power cannot, as a matter of constitutional law, be interfered with by Congress. A recusal statute that unduly limits the inherent power of the lower courts is, just as it is with the Supreme Court, unconstitutional.

It is thus a mistake to simply assume that Congress's authority over lower court recusal is as obvious or complete as is commonly believed. The argument for congressional control of lower court recusal must be tested—as we did with the Supreme Court—against any competing constitutional limits on that control. To fully understand the constitutional features of recusal in the lower courts, we must address the intersection of their Article III power with Congress's wide range of authority over them. Congress's greater legislative authority over the lower federal courts makes the constitutional analysis different, but not completely dissimilar, from our preceding treatment of recusal at the Supreme Court.

Article III vests the judicial power in both the Supreme Court and any "inferior Courts as the Congress may from time to time ordain and establish." Article I empowers Congress "to constitute Tribunals inferior to the supreme Court."[2] These provisions were the product of a compromise at the Constitutional Convention between those who thought the Constitution should affirmatively and permanently establish a system of federal courts and those who thought the state courts should decide all manner of cases in the first instance, subject only to federal review by the Supreme Court.[3] The final language of Article III took the creation of lower federal courts out of the constitutional debates and left it to the policy judgment of Congress. Making the lower courts' very existence a matter of public policy greatly enhanced Congress's power over them. In one of its first official acts, Congress accepted Article III's invitation by enacting the Judiciary Act of 1789, which established a system of lower courts and bestowed upon them the power to decide certain categories of cases.[4]

Congress's broad authority over the lower courts has created the strong presumption that it may regulate the recusal decisions of federal trial and appellate judges. The overwhelming (to put it lightly) assumption has been that Congress's power to create, and in turn destroy, the lower federal courts gives it unilateral power over the recusal practices in those courts. The strength of this argument is the unbroken historical trend of Congress setting, and the courts enforcing, binding recusal standards for lower court judges. Congress has consistently exercised control over the recusal practices of the lower federal courts since 1789 and has done so without serious resistance from judges or commentators.[5] The result is a presumption of legislative control over lower court recusal that does not apply to the Supreme Court, which was not subject to a federal recusal statute until 1948. Lower court judges also have not historically strayed from the applicable recusal statute to make their recusal decisions, and even if they did, the situation could be corrected on appeal. Unlike Supreme Court recusal decisions, those of the lower courts are reviewable by at least one layer of appellate court, making them judicially enforceable in ways that the justices' decisions are not. Yet despite its grounding in both constitutional text and history, legislative control over lower court recusal cannot be taken strictly at face value. Now that we have lifted the veil, so to speak, on the constitutional features of recusal law, there are unanswered questions about how the separation of powers affects the interaction between Congress and the lower federal courts over recusal.

The Inherent Power of Lower Federal Courts

The first of these questions is, what constitutional powers do the lower courts possess that could offset Congress's authority over them? The response is that Article III vests the lower courts with the same "judicial power" it grants to the Supreme Court. That judicial power must have some inherent, inviolate content or else the independence of the federal judiciary would be a myth—Congress could use its power to establish the lower courts to control every aspect of their function, making them subservient to the legislative branch in a way that would violate virtually any conception of the separation of powers or constitutional checks and balances. Therefore, if we can define what the judicial power of the lower courts consists of, we can determine whether federal recusal standards infringe on that power in violation of Article III.

The very nature of the question about the inherent power of the lower courts is different, however, from that regarding the Supreme Court because of the circumstances under which they were created. More to the point, the idea of an inviolate judicial power for the Supreme Court is easier to understand within the Constitution's text and structure than a similar power for the lower courts. The Supreme Court is, after all, created by the Constitution itself and cannot be extinguished without a constitutional amendment. The lower federal courts exist at the pleasure of Congress.[6] Even a cursory glance at this difference suggests that Congress should have greater leeway in its regulation of the lower courts for the simple reason that the greater includes the lesser—the power to "constitute" must also include the power to limit the lower courts far more than a body like the Supreme Court that is Congress's constitutional peer. This intuition about Congress's oversight of the lower courts has fueled a body of scholarship about the inherent power of Article III courts that is instructive to our inquiry about how (if at all) the Constitution's grant of judicial power protects lower court judges from legislative recusal requirements. The literature reveals that, no matter the precise characterization of judicial power, recusal legislation could indeed interfere with an inherent power of the lower federal courts. Put another way, there are at least some constitutional limits on Congress's power to set recusal standards for those courts.

Two of the most revered scholars to tackle the inherent power of the lower federal courts were Felix Frankfurter, at the time a Harvard law professor and later a Supreme Court justice, and one of his most well-known students and protégés (and later also a Harvard law professor), James Landis. In 1924, the two coauthored an article on the power of Congress to require jury trials in certain contempt proceedings.[7] The overarching issue was whether the power to hold parties in contempt was "inherent" in the identity of the federal courts. If yes, then Congress would be precluded from interfering with the courts' exercise of their inherent contempt power by requiring that juries be involved in contempt rulings. If no, then Congress would be permitted to regulate the contempt proceedings. The article concluded that although the general power to hold parties in contempt was an inherent feature of all courts, requiring juries for contempt proceedings did not, for largely historical reasons, unduly interfere with the courts' core powers under Article III.[8] The most important feature of the article for present purposes is its recognition of a narrow set of inherent powers of the federal courts that must be protected from congressional interference. In the words of the authors: "Are there, then, any limitations upon Congress? Of course there are. . . . these limitations have their source in the fact that the 'Tribunals inferior to the Supreme Court' which Congress is authorized to 'constitute' must be 'Courts.'"[9] By that logic, anything fundamental, or "inherent," to the existence of a court must also be fundamental to the exercise of the Article III judicial power, and thus is immune from congressional regulation. All that remained was to identify the fundamental features of courts. Frankfurter and Landis gave four inherent features, the first two of which are most relevant to the topic of recusal. The first was that courts "decide and not merely . . . advise. . . . They are an independent organ of government with finality of judgment within their domain."[10] The second was that "independence of judgment must be left to the court in cases where it may decide."[11] Putting these together, the power to finally and independently decide cases over which they have jurisdiction is a fundamental feature of courts. Much like the rest of Frankfurter's and Landis's work, this contention proved to be highly influential, even prophetic.

Decades later, commentators taking up the inherent powers question offered varied formulations for determining which judicial powers fit within the indispensable core of Article III. James Liebman and William Ryan concluded that the essential feature of judicial power—that which is immune from congressional interference—is judges' ability to decide cases properly before them finally and independently, in a way that gives effect to the entire spectrum of supreme (federal) law.[12] This feature of judicial power is virtually indistinguishable from the one put forth by Frankfurter and Landis and continues to garner support.

One example is in the work of Robert Pushaw, whose wide-ranging examination of the constitutional power of the federal courts identified three main categories of judicial power: "pure," "implied indispensable," and "beneficial" power.[13] He argued that the first category, pure judicial power, "is immune from political-branch control" because the "separation of powers dictates that neither Congress nor the president can interfere with this power."[14] He defined pure judicial power as "the issuance of a final judgment after finding the facts and expounding the law as necessary to decide a case."[15] The second category, implied indispensable powers, included only those powers that were necessary to allow courts "to perform their express constitutional functions."[16] These functions included exercising "the core 'judicial power' of deciding cases" and the power to "protect the court's integrity" by allowing judges to "maintain their authority, regulate their internal administrative affairs, and supervise the judicial process."[17] Pushaw defined the third category, beneficial powers, as those that are "helpful, useful, or convenient in implementing Article III" but are not constitutionally protected from congressional interference.[18] He maintained that "the Necessary and Proper Clause entrusts Congress with all policy determinations concerning the existence and extent of the beneficial powers."[19]

Building on the work of Frankfurter and Landis and Liebman and Ryan, Pushaw identified a potentially broader set of indispensable judicial powers. In addition to the act of finally deciding cases, he argued that any function necessary to allow a court to decide cases is also indispensable and therefore cannot be limited by Congress. Pushaw's beneficial powers show us the boundaries of inherent judicial power by identifying a category of judicial authority that is not inherent and that Congress may therefore regulate.

Pushaw's characterization of the judicial power is consistent with that of Evan Caminker, who just prior to Pushaw's article produced his own taxonomy of judicial power, but in a different dimension. Rather than characterize different levels of judicial power based on the nature of the power itself, Caminker sought to allocate judicial power to different actors within the judicial branch. He separated the judicial power structure into three categories: intrinsic, hierarchical, and systemic attributes. He identified "'intrinsic' attributes of the judicial power" as "those which must be exercised by each and every discrete court adjudicating a case."[20] These powers are, according to Caminker, so fundamental as to be necessary to every level of the judiciary. They are "indefeasible by Congress" and include the by now familiar "authority to decide a case" over which a court has jurisdiction.[21]

Hierarchical and systemic powers may be regulated by Congress as long as they are still available at some level of the judiciary. The power to unify federal law and supervise lower courts can be thought of as hierarchical, Caminker explained, because while they are critical to the functioning of the Supreme Court, those powers are not necessary to the mission of the lower courts, which are neither supervisory over other courts nor unifying in any comprehensive sense. In the systemic context, Congress may interfere with the power of some courts, as long as that power remains somewhere within the federal judicial system. Finality is the most obvious example of a systemic attribute. Each and every federal court cannot, by definition, be the final word on a given legal question. Courts can be bound by the decisions of earlier courts, and Congress can allocate certain legal questions to different courts within the system (and prevent other courts from addressing those issues), provided all of the relevant federal law was ultimately addressed by a federal judge.[22]

Taking each of these formulations of the judicial power, where does lower court recusal fit? Every conception of inherent judicial power includes the power of a court to decide cases properly before it. This inherent power is relevant to lower court recusal for the same reasons it is relevant to recusal at the Supreme Court. If a recusal statute requires the complete recusal of a court, then that court is effectively stripped of its inherent power to decide a case properly before it, in violation of its Article III judicial power. A recusal statute for the lower courts could also interfere with their "implied indispensable" power under Pushaw's theory. The power to decide recusal matters is necessary to protect the court's exercise of its constitutional function of deciding a case properly before it. To the extent the power of an individual court to decide a case was considered a beneficial power under Pushaw's theory or a hierarchical or systemic attribute within Caminker's approach, then any interference with that power by a recusal statute would not necessarily create a constitutional problem. The statute would be part of Congress's power to influence the functioning of the lower federal courts and would not be prohibited by any inherent judicial power to the contrary. Both Pushaw and Caminker, however, describe the power to fully and finally decide cases properly before them as inherent or intrinsic to the courts, rather than beneficial, hierarchical, or systemic.

According to the relevant literature on the inherent power of lower federal courts, Congress's setting substantive recusal standards for the lower courts threatens the courts' inherent power to decide cases properly before them. Substantive recusal standards could threaten—as I argued earlier in connection to the Supreme Court—the complete recusal of a district or circuit court. This in turn would unconstitutionally interfere with that court's inherent power to decide that case. Whereas complete recusal may seem less likely in the lower courts than in the Supreme Court due to assumptions about the numbers of lower court judges, this assumption is simply wrong with respect to many of our lower federal courts.

Some of the more populous courts like the Eastern District of Pennsylvania and the Ninth Circuit may be numerically and geographically diverse enough to be generally immune from the effects of widespread recusal,[23] but other courts are not. As of March 2015, the U.S. Court of Appeals for the First Circuit consisted of ten judges (only one more than the Supreme Court), four of whom had obtained senior status and thus do not necessarily participate in the full range of cases before the court.[24] These numbers are even more telling when we remember that the circuit courts require three-judge panels to decide most cases. The district courts are no safer. Just as an example, during the same period in 2015, the District of Wyoming had three judges and the District of Rhode Island had four, one of whom was a senior judge.[25] The Southern District of Alabama had four total judges, three active and one senior, and the Southern District of Illinois had five sitting judges, one of whom is senior.[26] For all these courts, it is entirely possible—even probable in some circumstances—that mandatory recusal statutes could deprive the entire court of the ability to decide a case properly before it. This is true under the current standards in section 455, and could become even more likely in the event Congress chose to adopt stricter standards, something that it would be permitted to do if it has the constitutional authority to regulate recusal, and that it has shown interest in pursuing, as indicated by bills introduced in 2011, 2013, and 2015 seeking to impose stricter ethical and recusal standards on the Supreme Court.[27]

Much like the Supreme Court, the judges of a particular district have something in common. They are all geographically connected and almost always have a track record of distinguished service within their state and/or district. They are all also, inevitably, familiar with state politics, as they frequently arrive at their positions on the bench through a recommendation by a U.S. senator from their state to the president.[28] In the process of becoming a leader among the local legal community and developing the political connections necessary to be nominated to the bench, district and circuit court judges become part of an increasingly elite and exclusive group within their communities. As with Supreme Court justices, it is simply unrealistic to assume that a mutual friend would not appear as counsel before them or that they would not have relationships with the most influential people and organizations within their districts and states. This is not an indictment of the judges or their behavior but rather a statement about the unacknowledged reality of judicial recusal, namely, that there is at least as good a reason to believe that complete recusal is rare because judges make it so (by interpreting recusal statutes loosely or not at all to protect their ability to participate in cases) as because the statute never requires it. The fact that federal recusal statutes make complete recusal a real possibility raises constitutional questions about the validity of those statutes regardless of whether complete recusal actually occurs.

It is no answer, moreover, to argue that only courts serving smaller populations are in serious danger of widespread recusal. Each of the aforementioned courts is an Article III court, with all the constitutional prerogatives and powers that accompany that distinction. Their decisions carry all the weight and binding effect of any other federal court, and litigants expect and are entitled to the same adjudicative services and constitutional protections available in more metropolitan settings. It is likewise inadequate to argue that Congress could simply enlarge each of the district and circuit courts beyond the point where complete recusal is a realistic possibility. In addition to being highly unlikely, especially in light of the high vacancy rates that persisted in the federal courts from 2009 to 2014,[29] increasing the number of sitting judges rises to the level of a constitutional solution only if the presence of those judges is constitutionally guaranteed. As long as Congress retains control over the size and occupancy of the federal courts—a power clearly assigned to Congress by Article I and something I do not propose changing—complete recusal and the constitutional problems it creates remain a possibility. In light of the lower courts' inherent constitutional authority to decide cases properly before them, and the real possibility that mandatory recusal could deprive them of that prerogative, we must reconsider the constitutional dynamics of federal recusal to protect lower court judges from infringement by Congress.

There are three categorical objections to this concern about lower court recusal that merit more detailed treatment. One is that Congress has already solved the problem by allowing for the assignment of judges from one court to temporarily fill vacancies on another. Under this rationale, even courts with relatively small numbers of judges are effectively immune from the possibility of complete recusal because of the ability of federal judges from other districts and circuits to "fill in" for their recused colleagues on another court. If complete recusal never happens, then there is no interference with the lower courts' authority under Article III because the power to decide cases lies with the courts, not the individual judges or a specific district. The second is that Congress has the power to cause complete recusal within a court based on its sweeping authority to control the jurisdiction of the lower courts. If Congress can remove a lower court's jurisdiction in its entirety, the argument goes, then it should be able to do so in an individual case by triggering complete recusal. Third, the complete recusal argument is better addressed through constitutional structure, in particular its potential redundancy with the Due Process Clause. While all these positions have some intuitive appeal, they are ultimately inadequate to fully address the constitutional issues raised by recusal statutes for the lower courts.

Judicial Assignment as a (Possible) Solution

Judicial assignment—the process of temporarily sending judges to sit on different courts—has a long pedigree in America. As early as 1850, the Supreme Court justice responsible for a given circuit could reassign a district judge to serve in place of another district judge within that circuit. The same authority was granted to circuit judges in 1869. The chief justice could also reassign district judges to sit in a contiguous circuit.[30] In 1907, Congress empowered the chief justice to reassign "disabled" district judges from any circuit.[31] In 1922, Congress created the Conference of Senior Circuit Judges and allowed a senior circuit judge to designate and assign a district judge "whenever any district judge by reason of any disability or necessary absence from his district or the accumulation or urgency of business is unable to perform speedily the work of his district."[32] The current state of the law for judicial designations permits designation of judges to other courts both in- and outside the designated judge's home circuit. The chief circuit judge may designate active or senior judges (but only with the consent of the senior judge) to serve in other districts within a circuit.[33] Assignments outside of a circuit may be made only by the chief justice, and only after a specific court requests such assistance from the Judicial Conference Committee on Intercircuit Assignments.[34] Senior judges must consent to intercircuit assignments, but active judges may be (although rarely are) assigned without their consent.[35] The common theme throughout the history of judicial assignments is that the ultimate decision to designate or assign Article III judges has consistently been made, via delegation from Congress, by other Article III judges.

This approach to the problem—allowing other Article III judges to determine which of their colleagues will be designated, presumably with the designated judge's consent, to other courts for particular cases—is constitutionally preferable because it keeps the assignment question within the judicial branch. The decision to recuse has been, since Blackstone's time, consistently reserved for the judge whose participation is in question and any judges empowered to review that decision on appeal. The process of deciding whether to recuse is thus part of the judicial power under Article III, at least according to the original meaning of the term and the unbroken historic recusal practices of the federal courts.[36] Congress's choice to empower the courts to designate judges for assignment without requiring them to do so leaves the decision of how to avoid complete recusal with the branch of government that will feel the negative effects of it. This avoids many of the separation-of-powers concerns attending recusal in the lower courts because it prevents Congress from causing complete recusal and in turn interfering with a court's inherent power to decide cases properly before it. With the possibility of complete recusal effectively removed, the potential infringement on the constitutional authority of lower court judges is similarly removed, and Congress can feel confident in relying on its Article I powers, specifically the Inferior Tribunals Clause and the Necessary and Proper Clause, to regulate recusal in the lower courts.

The problem with relying on judicial assignment is that it responds to a constitutional problem with a statutory remedy. Allowing judges to sit by designation does expand the pool of available judges dramatically enough to render the possibility of complete recusal extremely unlikely, but there are no legal guarantees that this remedy will remain in place. If Congress chose to repeal or amend the designation statutes, for example, by limiting designations to judges within the same state, the constitutional problem of complete recusal could become far more serious. The only way to satisfactorily cure the constitutional infirmity of complete recusal is with a constitutional solution. In this case, that leaves two options. One is to constitutionally prohibit Congress from repealing or significantly amending the designation statutes, but that would require a pretty drastic overcorrection and infringement on Congress's authority to pass legislation. The other, far less intrusive, way would be to interpret the judicial power of Article III to include the power to assign judges in order to avoid complete recusal. This approach treats the judicial assignment statutes as legislative contributions to an area ultimately reserved to federal judges, such that the statutes could remain binding (as exercises of Congress's necessary and proper power, for instance) because they properly respect the judicial power to remedy vacancies by granting the judiciary broad discretion in its assignment decisions. It would also reserve some of Congress's power over judicial assignment. The need for judicial power to remedy vacancies is driven by the need to avoid complete recusals. Assignments that are not directed at complete recusal are not constitutionally reserved to the courts, so Congress may still regulate in that area, if it so chooses. Imagine a statute that permits judicial assignment to avoid overburdening an understaffed, but not completely recused, court. Under the suggested approach to assignment, Congress would retain its Article I authority over that issue because alleviating judicial burdens does not implicate the same constitutional issue as providing for judges to decide cases where none currently exist.

Jurisdiction versus Recusal in the Lower Courts

Locating the power to remedy lower court vacancies in the courts so as to avoid complete recusal is not likely, however, to be an uncontroversial position. Skeptics may rely on the fact that Congress has greater control over the jurisdiction of the lower courts than of the Supreme Court to argue that it has a correspondingly greater power over recusal in the lower courts than in the Supreme Court.

Article III outlines nine categories of cases that fall within the jurisdiction of the federal courts.[37] Yet starting with the Judiciary Act of 1789, Congress has only granted the lower courts jurisdiction over a much smaller subset of cases.[38] This legislative control over federal jurisdiction has been widely accepted by Congress and the courts since the Founding but has been a frequent subject of debate in the scholarly literature. Renowned constitutional scholars have taken up the question of exactly how much of the federal courts' jurisdiction comes directly from Article III and how much of it depends on congressional authorization. The contours of this debate are useful because they orient congressional power over federal court jurisdiction in a set of theoretical frameworks that can then be applied to recusal. Each of these jurisdictional frameworks seeks to accommodate the countervailing force of Article III. They incorporate Article III's vesting of the judicial power and of jurisdiction over certain categories of cases in the federal courts in order to determine the scope of Congress's power over lower court jurisdiction. Applying these models of constitutional jurisdiction to questions of lower court recusal confirms that Congress's power over the jurisdiction of the lower courts does not also include power over recusal in those courts.

Before applying jurisdictional models to recusal, there are some important threshold issues, most of which revolve around the well-received idea that jurisdiction is not synonymous with either judicial power or recusal. There is strong affirmative evidence—some of which was also taken up in connection with the Exceptions Clause analysis in chapter 3—that jurisdiction and judicial power are different concepts. Liebman and Ryan's historical analysis of Article III led to the clear conclusion that "when Article III says 'judicial Power,' its drafters meant just that and not, e.g., 'jurisdiction.'"[39] John Harrison likewise distinguished between judicial power and jurisdiction:

> Judicial power and jurisdiction are obviously closely related concepts, but, just as obviously, they are not the same concept. According to the Constitution's usage, the Supreme Court and the inferior federal courts have the same judicial power—they are vested with the judicial power of the United States—even though they have different jurisdictions. The judicial power is thus less specific than a particular court's jurisdiction, as the potential is less specific than the actual.[40]

Beyond having the power of Harrison's convictions, this distinction also has logical force. Jurisdiction is the power of courts to exercise the remainder of their judicial powers in particular cases. These judicial powers, however, extend far beyond the jurisdictional, including the power to issue comprehensive, independent decisions in cases properly before them and to manage cases through the power to hold parties in contempt. If we read jurisdiction broadly enough to include the entire range of judicial powers understood to be inherent in the functioning of the federal courts, then congressional control over a court's jurisdiction could easily threaten that court's independence writ large. Assuming that our system's tolerance of legislative control over lower court jurisdiction was not meant as an implicit rebuke of judicial independence, jurisdiction must be only one aspect of judicial power.

In addition to the conceptual gap between jurisdiction and judicial power, a similar gap exists between jurisdiction and judicial recusal. Jurisdictional questions operate on the institutional level of courts, whereas recusal questions are specific to individual judges. To combine the two would conflate Congress's control over which institutions can decide cases with the power to deselect individual members of that court. This is potentially important because it has serious implications for Congress's overall authority to regulate the coordinate branches. It is one thing to claim that the power to create a system of courts includes the power to limit that system's power over certain categories of cases. It is quite another to argue that the power over a system of courts leads directly to the power to prevent individual, life-tenured, presumably independent judges from participating in a specific case.

Moreover, the fact that complete recusal can begin to look like a jurisdictional rule by effectively denying a court the power to decide a case does not make the two concepts identical. Jurisdiction determines a court's ability to hear certain categories of cases, most often defined by the nature of the subject matter or parties before the court. Recusal focuses on a judge's ability to deal impartially with the facts and other circumstances in the case before her. It is very difficult, if not impossible, to preemptively identify a category of cases that will require recusal in every instance without making the argument circular. Even the most promising example of denying jurisdiction over cases in which federal judges have a personal interest in the outcome is overbroad, as it requires judges to determine their personal interest in the case, making the jurisdictional statute function like a recusal statute, not a jurisdictional one. It does not make jurisdiction and recusal the same to say that jurisdiction is lacking in every case in which a certain number of recusals are warranted. That merely uses recusal as the basis for jurisdiction; it does not make them synonymous. In short, because jurisdiction is only a subset of the judicial power vested in the federal courts by Article III, and because it is an institutional, rather than an individual, concept, it is sufficiently distinct from both judicial power and recusal to make any comparison between them unproductive.

Even if these threshold issues are not persuasive, Congress's power over lower court jurisdiction still cannot justify widespread recusal legislation. Taken on its own terms, the jurisdiction analogy does not lead to the conclusion that Congress has broad control over recusal in the lower courts. There are four prominent theories of legislative control over federal court jurisdiction. Each of them supports the general conclusion that recusal decisions properly reside—to some degree, at least—within the judicial, rather than the legislative, branch.

The first "theory" is more of a default position, but it is the one largely reflected in practice. It is similar to the judicial power argument presented earlier, namely, that the "greater" power to create (and destroy) the lower courts comes with the "lesser" power to control their jurisdiction. This argument runs into textual difficulties, however, as section 1 of Article III vests the judicial power in all federal courts without qualification, and section 2 then extends that same judicial power to nine categories of cases. This makes it difficult to argue that Congress has total dominion over the jurisdiction of the courts when Article III explicitly outlines the power that all federal courts are able to exercise simply by virtue of their existence. If this drastic approach were adopted and Congress tried to strip all manner of jurisdiction from the lower courts without abolishing them (something it has never done), it would still confront the textual argument that if federal courts exist, they must retain at least some measure of the power explicitly granted to them by the jurisdictional provisions of Article III. It would also force a version of the inherent powers argument, under which federal judges are entitled to employ their inherent authority (like the power to decide cases) independently and free from legislative interference. If Congress cannot eradicate lower court jurisdiction directly, then it cannot use recusal to do so indirectly.

The second theory is the logical opposite of the first. It contends that the text of Article III, which vests the judicial power in any lower court that Congress may "ordain or establish," necessarily imbues each and every lower federal court with the full measure of the "judicial power," such that Congress cannot in any way limit federal court jurisdiction over the cases described in section 2 of Article III. Once the lower courts have been granted that power, the theory goes, Congress may not legislate any of it away. A. Benjamin Spencer described this viewpoint as the "constitutional vesting thesis" and explained its deviation from long-standing precedent regarding lower court jurisdiction by noting that "the Supreme Court's embrace of the idea that Congress may manipulate the jurisdiction of the inferior federal courts is a position arrived at without thorough examination of its constitutionality."[41] The constitutional vesting thesis thus rejects the idea that Congress can interfere with the jurisdiction of a lower court any more than it can the Supreme Court. If the constitutional vesting thesis is correct, and Congress does not have authority to limit the jurisdiction of the federal courts, then it cannot rely on that power to regulate recusal. Congress cannot use a power it does not have to justify recusal or any other form of legislation. The constitutional vesting thesis has the appeal of being relatively straightforward and consistent with the text of Article III, but it is burdened, independent of Spencer's explanation, by the fact that it is at odds with long-standing legislative and judicial practice.

The third theory is the two-tiered theory of jurisdiction famously put forth by Akhil Amar.[42] Amar argued for two levels of federal jurisdiction, one of which was beyond Congress's control to regulate, and another that was a matter of legislative discretion. He based his theory on the text of Article III, section 2, which states that the judicial power shall extend to "all" cases arising under federal law ("federal question" cases), cases involving ambassadors, and admiralty cases. According to Amar, by vesting the judicial power in "all" of these cases, section 2 excludes Congress from interfering in the federal courts' jurisdiction over them.[43] By contrast, the second tier of cases, those falling within the remaining six categories, may be restricted by Congress because section 2 does not use the word "all" when describing its grant of jurisdiction over them.[44] Amar's theory is controversial, but for present purposes it is enough to note that even under his two-tiered theory of legislative power over lower court jurisdiction, recusal remains largely protected from legislative interference. As an initial matter, the two-tiered theory excludes Congress from interfering in perhaps the most critical aspect of federal court jurisdiction, cases arising under federal law. Amar's construct prohibits Congress from limiting the lower courts' jurisdiction in so-called federal question cases, so by analogy Congress would be excluded from regulating recusal in those cases as well. This alone significantly discredits any jurisdiction-based argument for recusal legislation, as the federal question portion of the lower courts' docket implicates the broadest range of inherent judicial power, including finality, and was considered by the Framers to be critical to the preservation of constitutional liberty.[45]

Turning to the remaining six categories, which Amar claims fall under federal jurisdiction only at Congress's discretion, four of them are so narrow or come with so many caveats that congressional control over them is a near nullity. Three of those four categories involve cases where a state is a party. Section 3 of Article III makes clear that such cases are also subject to the original jurisdiction of the Supreme Court, so that there will always be some federal forum to resolve such disputes.[46] When paired with a state's right to sovereign immunity from suit in state courts, the only cases involving a state as a party that are assured to be heard outside of the federal courts are cases in which a state chose to sue a private entity in its own courts.[47] Because that suit is highly likely to be in state court anyway, congressional discretion over lower court jurisdiction involving cases where a state is a party proves to be at most minimal, and more likely illusory.

The other category of cases in which Amar's claimed congressional discretion is largely inconsequential is those involving the United States as a party. Because such cases will almost always involve a question of federal law, they can be largely rolled up into the set of federal question cases that Amar concedes are entitled to mandatory federal jurisdiction. For those rare cases in which the United States is a party to a state law claim, the United States will be immune from state court jurisdiction on sovereign immunity grounds.[48] The result is a strong incentive to include federal claims in every case against the United States, thus making the case arise under federal law and subjecting it to mandatory federal court jurisdiction. Even in cases arising under federal law, the United States is generally immune from suit. For tort claims against the United States, the Federal Tort Claims Act (FTCA) provides the only cause of action.[49] Because FTCA claims unquestionably arise under federal law for jurisdictional purposes, they would receive mandatory federal jurisdiction under Amar's two-tiered theory. This leaves cases where the United States is a plaintiff and asserts only state law claims as the remaining sliver of cases involving the United States as a party that may be susceptible to congressional control. This is likely to be at best an extremely narrow set of cases, as the United States is likely to have some federal recourse for its claims against a private citizen. It is also a brand of jurisdiction that Congress is unlikely to limit. Limiting the United States' ability to sue a private citizen in federal court would seriously burden a coordinate branch by restricting its choice to litigate in its own courts. While this is not an impossible policy choice in some circumstances, we have now reached such a small core of cases involving the United States as a plaintiff that the analogy to recusal becomes almost uninteresting. Conceding that if we get past the threshold problems of analogizing jurisdiction to recusal we can find a basis for Congress to regulate recusal in cases in which the United States sues a private citizen on a purely state law claim in fact concedes very little at all. In total, the four second-tier categories of cases that involve either a state or the United States as a party offer very little real opportunity for Congress to regulate federal court jurisdiction over those cases and, in turn, little basis for it to fashion recusal standards for those cases.

The bulk of the work of Amar's two-tiered jurisdictional theory is done in the final two categories of cases in section 2 of Article III— cases involving citizens of different states and cases involving citizens of the same state "claiming Lands under Grants of different States."[50] The second of these, cases involving land grants of different states, is by comparison so narrow as to fall into the same category as cases involving the United States as a state court plaintiff. The first of these categories, however, is not at all trivial in terms of its impact on federal court jurisdiction. Traditionally known as "diversity jurisdiction," it occupies a significant amount of the federal courts' docket, so Congress's ability to limit it represents a significant amount of legislative authority. Like the other categories in Amar's second tier, however, diversity cases that also involve claims arising under federal law would be effectively subject to mandatory jurisdiction. Purely state law cases between citizens of different states could, however, be stripped from the lower federal courts under Amar's theory. In those cases, if the jurisdiction-recusal analogy holds (which I earlier contended it does not for various threshold reasons), then Congress would be able to regulate recusal in diversity cases. This makes some intuitive sense, as diversity cases are the most maligned examples of federal jurisdiction, with critics arguing that the reason for allowing such jurisdiction in the first place—state bias against out-of-state litigants—is a remnant of a bygone age, and that in a country with an expanding federal presence and an increasingly national perspective, congressional banishment of such cases to state courts would be a welcome arrangement.[51] In any event, if we apply Amar's two-tiered jurisdictional framework to recusal, we find that in general, only diversity cases would be subject to meaningful congressional action. This seems exceedingly unlikely, as regulating recusal in only a subset of cases would arguably impair, rather than promote, the integrity of the courts. Forcing judges to remove themselves only in diversity cases creates an appearance of arbitrariness (or at least incompleteness) in the judges' decisions that is not likely to engender public confidence. Taking into account the assumptions made to get to this point of the analysis, including the fact that the two-tiered theory of jurisdiction is a minority view that is inconsistent with the historical practices of both Congress and the courts, the conclusion that Congress's jurisdictional authority over diversity cases may open those cases to additional recusal regulations seems relatively insignificant.

The final theory of judicial power is referred to as the "systemic view." Its roots are traceable back to Justice Joseph Story's famous opinion in *Martin v. Hunter's Lessee,* and it stands for the proposition that Article III commits federal jurisdiction over every category of cases in section 2 to at least one entity in the judicial branch. In Justice Story's words:

> It would seem, therefore, to follow, that congress are bound to create some inferior courts, in which to vest all that jurisdiction which, under the constitution, is *exclusively* vested in the United States, and of which the supreme court cannot take original cognizance. They might establish one or more inferior courts; they might parcel out the jurisdiction among such courts, from time to time, at their own pleasure. But the whole judicial power of the United States should be, at all times, vested either in an original or appellate form, in some courts created under its authority.[52]

Under this systemic view, the opportunity to appeal state court decisions analyzing federal questions to the Supreme Court satisfies the constitutional requirement that "the judicial Power shall extend to all Cases . . . arising under" federal law.[53] Congress retains significant authority over federal jurisdiction under this approach but is ultimately limited by the fact that each category of case or controversy listed in section 2 of Article III must at some point in its lifetime be cognizable in a federal court. This is very different, of course, from the constitutional vesting thesis, which requires the full measure of judicial power to rest equally in every Article III court. From the point of view of analogizing jurisdiction to recusal, however, the two approaches are not that far apart. The constitutional vesting thesis, by ensuring that the federal courts have the full scope of jurisdictional authority provided by Article III, likewise ensures that cases involving recusal issues will remain in the hands of federal judges. The systemic thesis, by ensuring that the cases described by Article III land in some federal court, also guarantees that recusal cases will ultimately be matters for federal judges. Combined with an understanding of the Court's Article III judicial power that includes judges making their own recusal decisions in the first instance, this means that a systemic approach would abhor complete recusal and will be of a piece with the current judicial assignment system, where members of the judicial branch are empowered to make decisions to protect the exercise of their own power.

Analogizing lower court recusal to theories of federal jurisdiction is useful because it allows us to test constitutional questions about recusal against cutting-edge theories of judicial power. As discussed earlier, however, it is at best an imperfect analogy, as jurisdiction and recusal differ from one another in some critical ways. Even accepting the analogy at face value, we see that the prevailing theories of judicial power in the jurisdictional context tell a pretty consistent story about recusal. The "greater includes the lesser" argument falls short of permitting complete recusal because of the text of Article III and the inherent power of the courts to decide cases properly before them. The constitutional vesting thesis excludes congressional interference with jurisdiction at any level of the judiciary and thus provides recusal with the same protection against congressional interference. The two-tiered theory is both controversial and unrepresentative of actual practice, but it offers broad protection against legislative tinkering. There is an exception for diversity cases, but not for the core of the federal courts' responsibilities—cases dealing with issues of federal law. Finally, the systemic approach is the one that most closely models actual practice, and it, like the constitutional vesting thesis, protects against complete legislative regulation of both jurisdiction and recusal. Just as the systemic approach requires that some federal adjudicator have the power to exercise the jurisdiction granted in Article III, by analogy to recusal it would guarantee that the final decision regarding recusal remains in judicial hands.

Constitutional Structure and Lower Court Recusal

A last objection to leaving federal courts responsible for alleviating complete recusal problems is constitutional structure—the presence of other constitutional limitations on Congress that make tinkering with judicial assignment standards unnecessary. One possible source of such a limitation is the Due Process Clause, which guarantees at least some judicial forum for viable legal claims. Recusal standards are generally seen (and designed) to promote due process protections by excluding potentially biased judges from specific cases. Even recusal statutes that wrongly exclude qualified judges would not present due process problems, as litigants do not have a constitutional right to any specific judge in a given case. Complete recusal, however, could deprive litigants of a federal forum for their case, implicating a different set of due process concerns about access to the courts.[54] For the overwhelming majority of lower court cases, this concern is unfounded, as state tribunals have concurrent jurisdiction over those cases and are empowered to render the same binding judgments as federal courts. For cases such as patent or admiralty disputes that fall under the exclusive jurisdiction of the federal courts, however, complete recusal does create an access problem for litigants that threatens their due process rights. In those instances, the constitutionally suspect outcome is the statutory preclusion of a federal court from exercising its jurisdiction to decide a case before it. In other words, the due process threat of recusal statutes in the lower courts is identical to the concerns over recusal's threat to the courts' inherent power under Article III. The remedy is also the same—to eliminate mandatory recusal statutes for the lower courts or, more plausibly, to ensure that the judicial branch retains control over judicial assignments so that complete recusal can be reliably avoided. Treating complete recusal as a due process problem is thus incomplete. It addresses only cases that may not be heard by state courts. It could still leave a wide range of lower federal courts vulnerable to having their Article III power to decide cases violated by complete recusal.

The First Amendment is likewise no help. It applies only to cases where recusals are based on judicial speech, so in all other cases of recusal, the First Amendment has no impact whatsoever, let alone one that could alleviate concerns about complete recusal. When it does apply, the First Amendment can only help push us toward a particular recusal standard (the probability-of-bias test, for instance). It cannot solve the dilemma of complete recusal. Complete recusal is just as much of a threat to the lower courts under either the probability of bias or reasonable appearance standards.

In terms of finding a substantive recusal standard for the lower courts, the First Amendment provides a service beyond the scope of the current project. Supreme Court recusal more easily conflates the issues of who decides recusal questions and what those recusal standards should look like because all the responses are constitutional. Because Congress cannot set substantive recusal standards for the justices, we are free to divine one from constitutional history, practice, and structure. The First Amendment can help in that analysis because it sets boundaries around the relevant due process principles. That is different from using the First Amendment to evaluate the constitutionality of an existing recusal statute, like the one for the lower federal courts. That analysis requires a determination of which First Amendment test applies to the recusal statute. That question, as I explained in chapter 5, is too ambitious for the present discussion. We have, though, unearthed some useful guidelines for thinking about the First Amendment ramifications of lower court recusal.

The potential bias standard for recusal is currently featured in the Court's due process jurisprudence and satisfies all three of the relevant tests under the First Amendment, including the one most easily analogized to judicial speech, the content-based doctrine. It is therefore a viable choice for regulating lower court recusal. The content-based doctrine may also tolerate the reasonable appearance standard for judicial recusal, but that is a far closer question. The statute must survive the narrowly tailored prong of the content-based speech test, which will be difficult in light of the fact that public perception of judicial integrity may be advanced as much by judicial transparency and disclosure regarding recusal as by recusal itself. That said, the Court's decision to uphold the prohibitions on judicial campaign solicitations in *Williams-Yulee* may offer some hope. The *Williams-Yulee* Court held that an outright ban on judicial campaign solicitations was narrowly tailored to promote public confidence in the judiciary because it left judicial candidates with other avenues of political speech, including other avenues to solicit campaign contributions.[55] Recusal could encounter a similar fate. By not expressly prohibiting judicial expression, recusal is arguably less of a burden on speech than the provision in *Williams-Yulee*, and is thus more likely to be seen as narrowly tailored to promote public confidence in the courts. The reasonable appearance standard could also benefit from the justices' reluctance to trigger the likely political fallout from invalidating a popular recusal statute in a way that augments the power of the judiciary at Congress's expense. If the courts evaluate the reasonable appearance standard by comparing it with other speech restrictions that have survived First Amendment review, then it too is likely to survive. If they compare it with some of the legislature's other choices in promoting public confidence in the courts, it has less of a chance to satisfy the content-based speech doctrine.

In the event the reasonable appearance standard from section 455 fails the content-based speech test, it would not be the end of legislative recusal standards for the lower courts. Possible solutions could include seeking to more closely tailor the recusal standard toward the appearance of judicial integrity, maybe through a combination of disclosure and recusal, or by moving the substantive threshold from the reasonable appearance of partiality test toward the probability-of-bias standard. Regardless of how this ultimately plays out, the primary lesson of our constitutional treatment of lower court recusal holds true. Any legislative recusal standard for the lower courts is constitutionally suspect under Article III unless the judicial branch retains the power to prevent complete recusal through judicial assignments.

* * *

Embracing judicial recusal as a constitutional matter has serious consequences for the Supreme Court but may be most surprising for its application to the lower federal courts. Congressional authority to create those courts, as well as to do whatever is "necessary and proper for carrying into Execution" their power, seems to open the door wide to something as seemingly benign as legislative recusal standards.[56] When we look more closely, however, we see similar separation-of-powers problems at all levels of the judiciary. The overwhelming consensus among the Court and commentators is that the power to decide a case properly before it is an inherent, indefeasible power of all federal courts. Legislative recusal standards unconstitutionally deprive lower courts of that power when they require complete recusal. That is generally true whether we view Congress's power over the lower courts as derived from its power to create the courts, to regulate their jurisdiction, or to do whatever is necessary and proper to effectuate the exercise of their judicial authority.

Unlike with the Supreme Court, there are solutions to the inherent power dilemma in the lower courts. The most obvious is the assignment of judges from other courts to replace recused judges. Judicial assignments render complete recusal all but impossible, thereby protecting the inherent power of courts to decide cases against the threat of complete recusal. I therefore do not suggest, as I did with regard to the Supreme Court, that Congress is prohibited from setting substantive recusal standards for the lower federal courts. The primary contribution of framing lower court recusal as a constitutional question is instead to show how the separation of powers makes the assignment of judges a constitutional necessity. Rather than treat assignment as a matter of legislative discretion, the power to reassign judges must reside within the judicial branch. This is a (modest) change in the current understanding of both legislative power over judicial assignments and the power of the courts. The existing legislative power must be shared with the courts. Congress may, for example, create procedural requirements or limitations regarding judicial assignments, such as who within the judicial branch should make them and which judges are available for assignment in a given circumstance, but in cases where complete recusal is a possibility, the courts must be able to go beyond the standards set by Congress to protect their decisional prerogative over the case at hand. This is critical to maintaining the appropriate balance between the branches, but it is lost without taking the crucial first step of recasting recusal as a constitutional issue.

A Constitutional Look at State Supreme Court Recusal

Federal courts are not the only ones that benefit from a constitutional perspective on recusal. Applying constitutional principles to state recusal law can reveal much about how the structure of government affects the recusal practices of state court judges. The application of constitutional principles to recusal at the state level is, however, a less exacting proposition than at the federal level. Our general theme holds true for state as well as federal courts. Every state in the union employs some form of tripartite government, in which the same separation-of-powers principles that govern our federal arrangement guide the relationship between state legislatures, executives, and courts.[57] From that vantage point, the prospect of legislative recusal standards rendering a court unable to perform its constitutionally assigned judicial function is no less problematic simply because it is a state tribunal. The challenge for pursuing a constitutional approach to recusal at the state level is practical, not theoretical. Each state has its own constitutional arrangement, and each individual state court system has its own idiosyncrasies that may be different from the federal system. There is still much to learn, though, from combining state recusal law and constitutional structure. One way to sidestep the complexity brought on by the diversity among state constitutions is to limit the type of state court under consideration. For that reason, we will focus on the constitutional features of recusal law for the highest courts in a state, generally referred to here as "state supreme courts," and the jurists who sit on them, collectively referred to as "justices."[58] By removing lower state courts from the analysis, it is possible to eliminate several variables both within a given state system and across different systems. As their state's highest court, state supreme courts are most likely to embody—like the U.S. Supreme Court—the greatest degree of constitutional authority within their respective judicial system. This is important for present purposes because when we are trying to gauge the interbranch tensions created by a particular legal rule, for instance, between the legislature and judiciary, it is easiest and most revealing to compare the institutions at the top of each branch.

Another way to simplify the state court analysis is to focus on some features of state supreme courts that are materially different from their federal counterpart and could have a meaningful impact on state recusal law. The remainder of this chapter is dedicated to examining some of those unique aspects of state supreme courts, in particular varying constitutional structures, broader assignments of power to state legislatures, judicial elections and term limits, different jurisdictional constraints, and more lenient constitutional amendment procedures at the state level. This list is of course a generalization. Although they are all common features of state governments, not all states employ these mechanisms, nor are they interdependent—the fact that a state employs one of them does not mean it employs any of the others. The following discussion is thus a largely theoretical exercise. It is not designed to comment on any specific state's treatment of recusal or to answer questions of state constitutional law. It is designed to show how variation in a constitutional arrangement—particularly within the structure and function of the judiciary—can impact the proper division of authority within a separation-of-powers scheme and, in turn, affect the constitutional status of recusal in state supreme courts.

Constitutional Structure at the State Level

State constitutions vary in their approach to the separation of powers and protection of individual rights. Some of these variations are relevant to treating recusal as a constitutional matter for state supreme court justices. The most obvious is a state constitutional provision directly setting recusal standards for the justices. Several states have such a provision, and in those states the question of who decides recusal questions is no longer a matter of separation of powers but of constitutional fiat.[59] Neither the legislature nor the justices have control over recusal under those circumstances. The justices' power to interpret the constitution gives them a leg up on the legislature, but that advantage may be tempered by the legislature's power to orchestrate constitutional amendments. In any event, states that have constitutional provisions setting substantive recusal standards for their justices are effectively outside of the current discussion. Although it may be interesting to talk about which branch can exert the most influence over recusal, there is no real issue as to who has the power to decide.

States with constitutional recusal standards must still reconcile recusal with the other constitutional forces at play. As with federal recusal, the most likely of those forces to influence state recusal are due process and free speech protections. Because states are also bound by the federal Constitution, we can assume that state constitutional provisions addressing due process and free speech are at least as rigorous as the federal Due Process Clause and the First Amendment. This could cause a state due process clause to require recusal more frequently than the federal probability-of-bias test, but because the outcome is ultimately a product of judicial interpretation, the separation-of-powers calculus still favors the judiciary over the legislature. The same is true of the effect of state free speech provisions. The fact that a state free speech clause could protect only as much or more judicial speech than the First Amendment substantively favors the justices by making recusal less common, but the important question for separation-of-powers purposes is that the scope of the state provision is primarily entrusted to the justices, who retain control over whatever effect state free speech law would have on judicial recusal. State legislatures have a countervailing power over constitutional amendments, but a cumbersome process like amendment is no real match for the power to interpret the constitution. To the extent that state constitutions deal directly with recusal, the separation-of-powers question either is irrelevant, as neither the judicial nor the legislative branch has any impact on the justices' substantive recusal standards, or slightly favors the justices, as any structural issues affecting recusal, like due process and free speech, will be largely under judicial control.

Broader Legislative Authority under State Constitutions

In states without a constitutional provision regarding recusal, the separation-of-powers balance shifts toward state legislatures, which have a much wider range of legislative authority than Congress. This difference in the scope of legislative power at the state and federal level has consequences for understanding recusal as a constitutional issue. Federal legislative power is famously limited by the enumerated powers in Article I of the Constitution. The outer limits of those powers are represented by the two most sweeping provisions, the Commerce Clause and the Necessary and Proper Clause.[60] Notwithstanding the often expansive interpretations of these clauses by both Congress and the Court,[61] there is no question that federal legislative power is narrower than that of the states.[62] State legislatures are commonly understood to be vested with a general "police power."[63] This police power enables state legislatures to regulate within the vague bounds of the public interest, without having to tie their choices to enumerated categories like interstate commerce. Greater legislative authority in turn affects the constitutional balance between the legislative and judicial branches over recusal. The more extensive the legislature's authority, the easier it is to justify using that authority to impact the activities of a coordinate branch. This does not necessarily mean that a state legislature may use its police power to encroach on the core powers and responsibilities of the judicial branch, but only that greater legislative authority tends to shift the balance of power away from the judiciary.

Broader legislative authority could cut both ways in the conversation about recusal. On one hand, a legislature's constitutional authority may—explicitly or implicitly—include the power to regulate recusal. If the state constitution explicitly empowers the legislature to enact recusal standards for the supreme court, then there is no constitutional debate. There is no *constitutional* problem in designing a scheme in which the legislature is empowered by the constitution itself to require recusal under certain conditions. The problem arises—and this book has been dedicated to exploring—when there is a close or unresolved constitutional question about recusal power. At that point, it is important, yet until now rare, to consider all of the constitutional issues surrounding legislative regulation of recusal. Explicit constitutional vesting of recusal authority in the legislature does not amount to a close or unresolved question deserving of further exploration.

Rather than being explicitly assigned by the constitutional text, legislative power over recusal may be implied from the text of the state constitution itself or when considered in the context of the larger constitutional arrangement. Implied power in this context results from more than just a reasonable interpretation of the constitutional language. It refers to a grant of power that directly implicates recusal without necessarily saying as much. For example, consider a constitutional provision that empowers the legislature to "ensure the ethical functioning of all public institutions." This rather clearly includes the power to regulate recusal, without being so direct as to use the word "recusal" or so vague as to imply a power over recusal within a broad grant of power to create the entire judicial system. The biggest challenge for this brand of implied legislative authority over recusal is its potential to interfere with the judiciary's core power to decide cases by triggering complete recusal. The conflict between legislative standards and judicial power depends on an assumption—well established in the federal constitutional context—that courts remain independent in their ability to decide cases properly before them. But for states with different constitutional arrangements, for instance, states with judicial elections and term limits, one could infer that judicial independence is less of a priority than for systems with lifetime judicial appointments. When a state's legislature is vested with a general police power, and its constitutional structure suggests that judicial independence is less of a priority than at the federal level, it becomes easier to understand how statutory recusal standards could fit into the overall state constitutional scheme without unduly infringing on the power of the courts. So in cases of explicit or implicit assignment of recusal power to the state legislature, the constitutional question is answered for that state, and legislative recusal standards are, as a constitutional matter, largely unproblematic.

They may still raise important questions about the wisdom of infringing on judicial independence and the legislature's lack of institutional expertise regarding recusal, but in terms of the impact on constitutional structure, an assignment of legislative power that includes the authority to regulate recusal does not raise any further constitutional questions.

On the other hand, a general police power that does not clearly include the power to regulate recusal (either explicitly or implicitly) does not necessarily grant the legislature any more power over state supreme court recusal than Congress enjoys over the U.S. Supreme Court. The legislature's exercise of its police power has the same critical implications for the separation of powers and judicial independence, and thus makes just as strong a case for courts retaining the ability to protect themselves from a powerful legislative branch as at the federal level. Assuming some measure of judicial independence under a state separation of powers system,[64] and in turn that judicial independence includes at least the narrow judicial prerogative of deciding cases properly before them, there is no obvious reason to interpret a general police power to override courts' inherent authority. In the context of recusal, this means allowing courts to take control over their own substantive recusal decisions to protect themselves against legislative infringement of their core functions.

Judicial Elections

Judicial elections are a controversial feature of state courts, including state supreme courts. They promote democratic transparency and accountability at the highest level of the judiciary by forcing justices to earn and retain the trust of the voting public in order to keep their positions on the bench. In the process of making the judiciary more transparent and accountable, however, elections potentially threaten judicial independence. Justices who are publicly held to account for their decisions could feel pressure to tailor those decisions to the will of the electorate. The threat of political pressure was a driving force behind the Founders' decision to grant life tenure to federal judges,[65] and it is a persistent theme of critics of judicial elections.[66] Yet despite the ongoing debate over their value, judicial elections remain a common feature of state court systems. Twenty-one states elect their supreme court justices. Seven states, including Illinois, Texas, and Pennsylvania, use contested, partisan elections. The remaining fourteen, which include

Michigan and Ohio, hold nonpartisan elections.[67] Twenty-nine states appoint justices to serve on their highest court, but seventeen of them require justices to participate in retention elections to remain in office after their initial appointment period has expired. All told, thirty-eight states use elections in at least some capacity to select or retain their supreme court justices.

A common feature of judicial elections is the presence of term limits. As a theoretical matter, the choice to elect judges does not have to include term limits; the voters could elect a justice to serve for life. This would still have democratic benefits, as judges seeking office would have to appeal to the voting public to obtain their position, but it would not likely promote accountability. Once elected, justices would have no incentive to be responsive to the needs and wants of the electorate because they would be protected from public influence by life tenure. Perhaps for these reasons, in practice elections and term limits go hand in hand. All of the twenty-one states that elect the members of their highest court have some limitation on how long that justice can serve before facing reelection.[68] Conversely, the absence of judicial elections does not logically exclude term limits. Appointed judges can be, and frequently are, appointed for specified terms. After their initial appointment, they are often subject to periodic, uncontested retention elections, through which the voting public can determine whether that justice should retain her seat. This has the benefit of protecting judicial independence at the appointment stage and seeking to promote accountability through public review of a justice's performance. Because retention elections are unopposed and overwhelmingly successful for the sitting justice,[69] there is less pressure to conform to public opinion than in a contested election. Accountability is therefore promoted without applying too much political pressure to a sitting justice. Only three states utilize judicial appointments without term limits or retention elections—Massachusetts, New Hampshire, and Rhode Island (although Massachusetts and New Hampshire have a mandatory retirement age of seventy).[70] This approach most closely resembles the federal system and puts a much higher premium on independence than on democratic pedigree or accountability.

Understanding that each state has its own constitutional dynamics and its own approach to choosing its supreme court justices, we can begin to flesh out the prevailing issues associated with recusal and judicial elections. The politicization of our legal system has raised public concern about judges' ideological preferences tainting their decision making.[71] Does the existence of judicial elections affect our understanding of "who decides" recusal questions under the separation of powers? One way to get at this question is to consider how judicial elections potentially affect the balance of power between the legislative and judicial branches. Judicial elections are designed to promote judicial accountability and democratic government, but they often do so at the expense of judicial independence. Prior to taking the bench, justices could feel indebted to people or organizations that provide financial or other support to their judicial campaigns.[72] This was the issue in *Caperton*, when the Supreme Court found a due process violation in the decision by a West Virginia Supreme Court justice to participate in a case involving his largest (by a wide margin) campaign donor.[73] Once on the court, justices with term-limited positions may feel pressure from influential members of their constituency in the period leading up to their reelection. Much as powerful interest groups can assert their interests with members of Congress, those same groups could seek to sway an elected justice by threatening to use their influence to oppose that justice's retention or reelection. Imagine an analogous situation to *Caperton*, where a wealthy member of the business community threatens to withhold a pending contribution or, in cases where justices face contested reelection campaigns, redirect her contribution to a competitor if the justice does not rule in ways favorable to that party in the months and years leading up to her reelection. The most explicit examples of such conduct may well run afoul of state public integrity or anticorruption statutes, but the point for present purposes—and the one made quite clearly by the Supreme Court in *Caperton*—is that judicial elections make justices more vulnerable to external biases in ways that could be relevant to their constitutional power over recusal.[74]

Recusal is designed to protect the integrity of the judicial process and of the courts themselves. That is without question an admirable goal and one that in general seems to fall within the governing prerogative of the legislature. The constitutional issue arises, of course, when an attempt to set substantive recusal standards interferes with some other, constitutionally protected function of the judicial branch. Assume that state supreme courts perform a similar core function as the federal courts—to decide cases properly before them. This was the understanding of the judicial power at common law and as such would have been familiar not only to the people who drafted the federal Constitution but also to those who designed (at least the earliest) state judicial systems.[75] To the extent that legislative recusal standards cause a state supreme court to be unable to decide a case properly before it due to recusal of a critical number of justices, the constitutional argument against those legislative recusal standards is the same at the state level as it is at the federal. But is it possible that the additional pressures on elected state supreme court justices create reasons for legislative involvement that could change the balance between legislative and judicial power over recusal? The answer, I suggest, is probably.

The best argument for even considering the additional pressures created by judicial elections is that elections at minimum implicate the constitutional principle of separation of powers and often rise to the level of state constitutional law itself. Judicial elections are mandated by state constitutions,[76] and they implicate judicial independence and accountability, both of which are common concerns of the constitutional separation of powers.[77] Because the rationales and mechanisms for judicial elections operate at a constitutional level, it is easier to justify also treating the effects of those elections as a matter of constitutional significance. When we do that, we see a potentially meaningful difference between the recusal decisions of elected versus appointed justices.

The additional political pressure faced by elected state supreme court justices makes it more difficult to leave recusal decisions entirely in their hands. Political influences can bias justices or make them appear biased, either of which is a detriment to both litigants and the court.[78] The supreme court's legitimacy is a critical feature of any state government. It depends on the court's ability to persuade those subject to its authority to follow its commands without result to force.[79] It is reasonable to conclude that an elected court will have greater difficulty maintaining its persuasiveness if it is also the sole authority over its own recusal decisions. If the biggest concern about elected justices is that they will be partial toward their political supporters, allowing them full latitude to make their own recusal decisions does nothing to reduce the likelihood of partiality and may even enhance it. This is especially true under American recusal law, where judges make their own recusal decisions, and in the case of state supreme courts, where the justices' decisions are generally unreviewable.[80] Perhaps the trade-off for the increased accountability of elected justices is to empower a separate branch of government—the legislature—to set recusal standards for them. This gives the legislature at least one means of protecting litigants and the court from the negative consequences of the increased political pressures felt by elected justices.

This point also works in reverse. There seems to be less need for legislative control over the recusal of appointed justices, especially those subject to term limits. Appointed justices do not experience the same amount of political pressure as elected justices because they are not beholden to the will of the electorate. A 2013 empirical study from Princeton University found that appointed state supreme court justices are more likely to overcome preconceived biases about a case than their elected counterparts.[81] Additional studies into the effect of judicial elections on the legitimacy of state supreme courts found that people who live in states with appointed justices have more confidence in their judicial system.[82] Even if appointed justices feel some pressure to meet the expectations of the person or entity responsible for appointing them, sufficiently long term limits can help alleviate that problem through government turnover during a justice's term. Because most state supreme court justices serve for longer terms than their elected representatives, an appointed justice may be less influenced by those responsible for her reappointment because she will be unable to accurately predict who that will be.[83] Moreover, if appointed justices serving fixed terms do engage in questionable recusal practices, they are still answerable to the political branches of government for their choices.[84] Legislatures and governors have greater resources and incentive to make informed judgments about judicial candidates than do members of the voting public. A bad decision about a judicial appointee not only will populate the bench with an unworthy candidate but also could jeopardize a governor's or legislator's own reelection. State officials' personal and professional incentive to provide at least some check on the recusal practices of appointed justices helps offset the cost of empowering those justices to set their own recusal standards. Although this is not as compelling as the power to direct recusal decisions in real time, executive and legislative branches with reappointment power have more control over judicial conduct than the president or Congress has over the federal courts, suggesting that if federal legislative recusal standards are not required by the separation of powers, neither are state standards.

Taken together, these arguments support thinking about recusal for elected and appointed justices differently. The increased pressure to favor political supporters makes it harder to justify allowing elected justices to set their own recusal standards and easier to defend shifting power over recusal to the legislative branch, where it can be used as a check against potentially biased, elected justices. Conversely, appointed justices' greater sense of political freedom is a reason to entrust them with more power over their own recusal decisions—with less political pressure to play favorites, appointed justices are more likely to be reliable judges of their own partiality.

This perspective on judicial elections favors recusal statutes for elected justices but not appointed ones. But there is another way to look at the question of how judicial elections affect the constitutional balance over recusal in state supreme courts. While elections do increase political pressure on the justices, they could also serve as a deterrent against biased decision making. The greater democratic investment and accountability from judicial elections could offer their own protection against actual or apparent bias, thereby negating the argument for additional legislative control over the recusal of elected justices. This argument is advanced by proponents of judicial elections and has significant intuitive appeal, especially in a country like the United States that has such faith in the sanitizing power of democracy.[85] In the context of recusal, however, the increased public scrutiny from elections is not enough to protect against the potentially corrupting influences of judicial politics.

For starters, elections can act as deterrents against bad recusal decisions only for justices who are already on the bench at the time of the election. First-time judicial candidates will not have made any prior recusal decisions for the voting public to evaluate. This means that recusal can only be an issue for a justice's reelection, or where a first-time supreme court candidate previously held some other judicial office. For candidates who have previously held some other judicial office, their ambition may have caused them to pay closer attention to their recusal decisions in the lower court. Those decisions will likely be poor predictors of their behavior on the supreme court, however, as the unique features and responsibilities of a supreme court make the comparison between recusal decisions in the lower court versus those at the supreme court difficult. The potential lack of substitute justices and role of the court as the final arbiter of important and controversial issues of state law could, as they do at the U.S. Supreme Court, cause state justices to approach recusal differently than they may have when serving on a lower court that is subject to appellate review and open to replacement judges. This difference is magnified in the eleven states where litigants have an appeal as of right to their supreme court.[86] In those states, justices may be even more reluctant than normal to recuse because complete recusal has even greater consequences—it not only may interfere with the court's authority to decide cases but also may preclude a litigant from pursuing her individual right to a particular forum. For former lower court judges running for a position on the state supreme court, a judicial election is unlikely to have much if any effect on their recusal practices while on the supreme court because of the inherent differences between the two tribunals.

Sitting justices facing reelection or retention votes may be incentivized to take their recusal obligations more seriously simply because of a pending election. If a justice refused to recuse herself from a case involving her largest campaign donor, that decision could have serious consequences when that justice's position is later subjected to a vote. There are, however, several problems with this argument that are relevant to how judicial elections affect our constitutional understanding of recusal law.

One problem with relying on elections to deter recusal violations by supreme court justices is the inherent difference in timing between recusal decisions and judicial elections. Recusal is a backward-looking decision with immediate consequences. It looks at past facts and circumstances and determines whether a judge is qualified to decide a case immediately before her. Elections are essentially a forward-looking enterprise. They consider past behavior but are designed primarily to select someone for future service, not judge her for past acts. A justice claiming to have changed her ways in response to criticism of past conduct, for instance, could win an election on that basis alone. She could not, however, survive a recusal motion on the grounds that she will not repeat the act or omission that arguably requires her recusal. Elections are also a poor remedy for recusal offenses because they can occur long after those offenses. State judicial terms are typically in the range of six to twelve years.[87] While there are good reasons to have longer terms for supreme court justices—to benefit from their accumulated experience, to grant them a greater degree of independence, and so forth—the long time between elections makes those elections poor deterrents for discrete events like controversial recusal decisions. A justice who improperly fails to recuse at the beginning of her term will not be accountable to the public until her term ends.[88] Even for shorter terms, this could still be on the order of years and may well have failed to hold the public's attention in a way that could make it an issue on reelection. This problem is magnified for longer terms and is joined by the possibility that longer terms may result in fewer reelection bids—justices choosing not to seek reelection or retention will never have to account to the electorate for a poor recusal decision.

Another problem with relying on elections to protect against recusal missteps is the apparent low level of interest in judicial elections. Typically, judicial elections are "low-information" contests, in which "a large share of the voters go to their polling place without having assimilated much (or any) information about these contests."[89] Even though judicial elections are often included on a ballot containing the full slate of state races for that year, "many voters are not aware that these contests exist until they see the ballot."[90] As a result, these voters are more likely to abstain from casting a vote in a judicial contest. This phenomenon, called "roll-off," is common in judicial elections: "From 1980 through 1995, an average of about one-quarter of all people who went to the polls skipped a given contest for a supreme court seat."[91] The percentage of roll-off was higher in nonpartisan and retention elections but remained above 20 percent for every type of contest.[92] When combined with the general trend of low turnout, roll-off compounds the participation problem in judicial elections.[93]

Nevertheless, the deterrent effect of an election is dependent not on the number of voters but on how they vote. If a large enough percentage of even the smallest voting pool decides to hold a justice accountable for a past recusal decision, then a judicial election has served its deterrent purpose. Far more telling, then, is the nature of the election and the likelihood of a justice being replaced as a result. Generally speaking, justices seeking to retain their offices face either a contested election or an uncontested retention vote. Retention votes are not likely to be effective deterrents, mostly because they are such notoriously unexciting affairs. Nineteen states, including Florida, have uncontested retention elections for justices.[94] In Florida, as in many states, judges are included on the ballot with the rest of the state's candidates for office in that year. There were no supreme court justices facing retention elections in Florida in 2014. In 2012, the turnout rate among eligible voters for the presidential election was approximately 71 percent.[95] Despite the voters being closely divided over many of the candidates, especially the presidential candidates (the two principle candidates for president were separated by a margin of about 1 percent), the retention of judicial officers was seemingly totally uncontroversial.[96] One hundred percent—each of the three state supreme court justices and fifteen appellate court judges—were retained. The supreme court justices each received more than 67 percent of the votes, and the appellate court judges were retained with between 61 and 78 percent of the vote.[97] In 2010, a midterm election, only about 49 percent of eligible voters came to the polls, and the judicial retention rate was again 100 percent—all four justices and all twenty-seven appellate court judges on the ballot were retained in uncontested elections.[98] This overall lack of suspense in retention votes is consistent with a national average of 99 percent retention between 1964 and 1998,[99] and reflects at minimum a low threshold for retention, and at worst a lack of voter interest in the matter. In either event, the overwhelming probability of success for the incumbent justice makes retention elections poor deterrents. If justices do not think the electoral outcome is in serious doubt, their choices will not be influenced by the prospect of a negative public reaction. Moreover, the majoritarian nature of elections further decreases their value as actual deterrents. Judicial elections are not single-issue contests. Recusal may well be a significant issue in a given election, but it will almost certainly be lumped together with other, more high-profile issues of, for instance, judicial and political ideology. In order for a reelection campaign to be thwarted by a candidate's recusal practices, a majority of voters not only must be aware of those practices but also must consider them significant enough to sway their vote. In cases of retention elections, the bar is even lower—a sitting justice must only convince voters that she is preferable to leaving her seat on the supreme court (at least temporarily) vacant.

Contested reelections, which are also used in nineteen states,[100] are more promising deterrents, in part because they pose a greater threat to sitting justices. They present the public with a choice between candidates, rather than the choice in a retention election between keeping a justice in office and creating a vacancy on the court, and are typically closer contests than retention elections.[101] Justices facing a contested reelection may thus be more inclined to take public perception into account when making recusal decisions, on the theory that a controversial decision could sway public opinion enough to affect the outcome of the election. This likely benefits both the litigants and the court as a whole, as it increases the chances of a justice making a responsible recusal decision that in turn leads to an impartial outcome that the public will accept as democratically legitimate. The deterrent effect of contested reelections suffers, however, from the timing problem and the problems of low voter turnout and information discussed earlier. It is also limited by the fact that judicial elections are about more than recusal. At best, it stands to reason that recusal is just one of many issues that could be of equal or greater importance to voters. So while the presence of an adversary may help preserve issues that the public may otherwise have forgotten about, the nature of judicial elections means those issues could still be several years old and of limited public interest by the time reelection becomes an issue for a sitting justice.

Finally, the increased accountability created by judicial elections is not likely to compensate for the potential bias they cause in individual cases. The effects of bias are felt acutely by individual litigants in individual cases, not just as a long-term drain on the legitimacy and reputation of the judicial system. Because the costs of bias or its appearance are felt immediately and locally, solutions like elections that seek to remedy the problem after the fact are more likely to miss the mark. Deterrence could, however, be seen as a real-time solution. If elections encourage good recusal practices, they do in fact provide an immediate benefit for litigants. While this may be true in theory, it overvalues the deterrent effect of elections, which as discussed earlier really only attaches to contested reelections, and undervalues the cost to litigants of the prospect that one or more of the elected justices in their case may have reason not to treat them impartially. Deterrence is an attenuated approach to possible bias, whereas the costs of that bias to litigants are quite direct.

In sum, the presence of judicial elections in state supreme courts does have some potential consequences for recusal law. Although contested reelection contests are more likely to create meaningful limits on a justice's recusal practices than uncontested retention elections, in general the prospect of seeking reelection is not likely a powerful enough deterrent against bad recusal practices to leave recusal entirely in the hands of state supreme court justices. Judicial elections are too far removed in time, are too widely focused, and do not generate enough substantive interest from the voting public to effectively deter justices from abusing their recusal power. By contrast, the increased pressures put on justices by campaigns and constituents with a vested interest in the justice's rulings may create enough of a threat to the integrity and fairness of the judicial system to justify some degree of legislative intrusion into the core power of the supreme court to decide cases. Put another way, legislative control over recusal is more easily justified for elected state supreme court justices than for appointed ones. At the extreme, judicial elections may create a toxic enough environment in some cases to justify complete recusal at the hands of the legislature. Practically speaking, as in *Caperton*, due process concerns may force the justices' hand without the need for any legislative involvement. But because recusal decisions are by their very nature fact-specific, it is difficult to construct a clear constitutional doctrine that is neither over- nor underinclusive for the problem at hand. (A case in point is the principled balancing approach advocated for Supreme Court recusal in chapter 5.) Imagine a case in which a party before the state supreme court is also a prominent (although not the most prominent) donor to a majority of the sitting justices' campaigns. Under *Caperton*, it is not at all clear that simply having a significant donor as a party would require recusal under the Due Process Clause. It would, however, create pressures that are unique to (some) state supreme courts, and thus should be treated as unique within the context of a constitutional review of recusal. It may be that the state legislature should be allowed to craft standards that would protect against that case being decided by the beneficiary justices, even if it would potentially conflict with the justices' view of recusal in that case and the court's core constitutional power to decide cases properly before it. If it did, it would be important from a separation-of-powers standpoint for the state legislature to focus any recusal standards that could lead to complete recusal on the problems posed by judicial elections. Nevertheless, the presence of elections might have enough of an effect on state justices' recusal practices to merit a shift away from the federal dynamic of very limited legislative involvement toward a more probing, albeit targeted, approach to regulating recusal in state supreme courts.

Judicial elections are neither the dispositive nor even the most important factor in determining who decides recusal questions for state supreme courts. They are, however, another relevant variable in the broader constitutional analysis of judicial recusal. Without providing any definitive answers to whether state recusal law should be reordered to better accommodate judicial elections, merely considering the constitutional impacts of those elections identifies a feature of state supreme courts that may provide additional insight into how the separation of powers can help us understand who decides questions of recusal.

State Courts as Courts of General Jurisdiction

Another distinctive and relevant feature of state supreme courts is their more generalized jurisdiction. The U.S. Supreme Court has wide-ranging appellate jurisdiction over cases involving issues of federal law or originating in the lower federal courts, but the lower federal courts are restricted in their ability to hear cases by both the Constitution and federal statutes. State supreme courts, by contrast, have access to all manner of state and federal disputes, limited only by the narrow set of cases that Congress or the Constitution has assigned exclusively to the federal courts, such as cases involving ambassadors or admiralty and patent disputes.[102] Most important, whereas state supreme courts have concurrent jurisdiction over the vast majority of cases that could appear in the federal courts, the converse is not true. State supreme courts have responsibility for the full panoply of state court disputes—about 95 percent of all cases in the American judicial system.[103] We can envision this as a Venn diagram, in which the circle representing state supreme courts not only is far larger than that for the federal courts but also overlaps with all but the smallest subset of it—the portion representing exclusive federal court jurisdiction.

But what does this broader authority mean for the constitutional features of state recusal law? The large number of cases that are not eligible for federal review leave state courts in the position of being the sole stewards over much of the law that matters to their citizens. Legislative limits on the courts' ability to decide state law claims could thus raise a due process problem.[104] The core due process requirement that litigants have some neutral forum in which to litigate their case dictates that state legislatures may not restrict state court jurisdiction in such a way as to deprive litigants of such a forum.[105] The specter of complete recusal thus carries a second-level significance for state courts, including state supreme courts. In addition to threatening a court's ability to fulfill its own constitutional responsibility to decide cases properly before it, it implicates the due process rights of litigants by threatening to leave them with no place to resolve their cases. This is particularly true in the eleven states without intermediate appellate courts,[106] or in states that follow the U.S. Supreme Court's guidance in favor of preserving some avenue of appeal to the highest court even when the legislature seems inclined to prevent it. To the extent that a lack of concurrent federal jurisdiction over much of state law threatens a litigant's access to a competent court to resolve her dispute, state legislative recusal standards seem at least as constitutionally suspect as federal ones.

This conclusion raises the practical question of how much the lack of concurrent federal jurisdiction over state law claims actually affects recusal in state supreme courts. One way to measure this effect is to contrast it with the effects of concurrent state court jurisdiction. Does concurrent state court jurisdiction actually protect a federal litigant experiencing a recusal issue at the U.S. Supreme Court? Assuming complete recusal at the Court, is there any procedural mechanism by which a litigant could "move" the case to state court to get the review that has been made effectively unavailable in federal court? If not, then any recusal problems at the state and federal level are arguably the same—state courts hear a wider array of cases than federal courts, but if a federal litigant facing complete recusal cannot benefit from concurrent state jurisdiction, then the lack of concurrent federal jurisdiction over state claims will likewise have no effect on state recusal.

The answer is that at the supreme court level, there is likely no benefit to concurrent state jurisdiction. A litigant facing complete recusal by the Supreme Court could not go to state court to have her case heard. There would be no basis for the case to originate in the state supreme court, and a lower state court would almost certainly be barred from reaching an independent conclusion on the merits of the case. Complete recusal in the lower federal courts, especially the federal trial courts, may be remedied by state courts, as a litigant could abandon her federal case (through motions to dismiss or otherwise) and refile in state court. There would likely not be any preclusion problem in that case, as no judgment had been entered by the federal court, and the state supreme court may be part of the solution, especially in cases where it is the only appellate court in the state. So for complete recusal problems in the lower federal courts, concurrent state jurisdiction is a potential remedy, thereby presenting at least a limited argument for greater judicial control over recusal standards at the state level. State legislatures forcing recusals of state supreme court justices could imperil litigants' due process rights to a judicial resolution of their state law claims. By contrast, federal recusal standards are protected against due process violations (at least in the majority of cases) by concurrent state jurisdiction.

This distinction is unlikely to have any significant impact, however, due to the current system of judicial assignment in the federal courts. Judicial assignment makes complete recusal in the lower federal courts, and thus the need for state courts to relieve such a complete recusal problem, extremely unlikely. Rather than make this exercise superfluous, this serves as a reminder of the importance of judicial assignment systems to the constitutional balance over recusal. As long as such systems are in place, there will be no need to move federal claims to state courts in order to solve a recusal problem in federal court. Similarly, state assignment systems can alleviate recusal problems that could threaten the due process rights of state litigants to access their supreme court. Most states have some system by which judges from one state court are permitted to temporarily fill a vacancy on another court in that state.[107] Unlike the U.S. Supreme Court, state supreme courts are not necessarily constitutionally precluded from utilizing the services of replacement or retired justices. The North Dakota Supreme Court, for example, may assign cases to a temporary "Court of Appeals" that may be staffed by, among others, "retired Supreme Court justices" appointed by the chief justice.[108] For state supreme courts, judicial assignment is thus a more powerful remedy, but no less of a constitutional necessity, than in the federal courts. It helps protect against the separation of powers and due process concerns raised by over-recusal of state supreme court justices at the hands of the legislature. For that reason, it is important that judicial assignment be included in the calculus of judicial authority under a state's constitution. If the ultimate ability to replace recused justices resides anywhere but the courts, the judiciary loses its power to counteract complete recusal issues caused by legislative recusal standards.

In short, broader jurisdictional authority of state supreme courts, coupled with the lack of concurrent federal jurisdiction, tells us two things about the constitutional nature of state recusal law. First, state supreme courts must be protected not only against recusal statutes that interfere with their power to decide cases but also against the limited, but real, potential for due process deprivations of litigants whose claims are not cognizable in federal courts. Second, judicial assignment, including at the supreme court level, can serve as an effective safeguard against constitutional problems raised by recusal, but only if the power to assign rests within the judiciary and is viewed as part of the constitutional structure of government.

State Constitutional Amendments

A final difference between the state and federal systems that could have ramifications for recusal is the constitutional amendment process. Amending the U.S. Constitution is extremely difficult. An amendment must be proposed either through a convention called by two-thirds of the states, which has never happened, or by a vote of two-thirds of the members of both houses of Congress. Once proposed, an amendment must be ratified by three-fourths of the states before it can become part of the Constitution.[109] There have been only twenty-seven amendments to the Constitution, and eleven of those were proposed, and ten ratified, within two years of the original document.[110] By contrast, state constitutional amendments are far more frequent and can be achieved in a variety of ways. Amendments can be initiated by voters, state legislatures, constitutional conventions, or, in rare cases, referral from a public commission.[111] State constitutions are thus more dynamic and detailed documents than the federal Constitution. The Maryland State Constitutions Project reported in 2000 that "there have been almost 150 state constitutions, they have been amended roughly 12,000 times, and the text of the constitutions and their amendments comprises about 15,000 pages of text."[112] To provide some perspective on the high rate of amendment in state constitutions, if each of the states amended its constitution as often as the federal Constitution, there would have been only around 1,350, or one-ninth, the number of state constitutional amendments during that time period. This high rate of amendment, like judicial elections, broader state court jurisdiction, and increased legislative power, impacts the constitutional calculus surrounding recusal in state supreme courts.

Precisely how it affects recusal, however, is a more complicated question. An easier amendment process alleviates some concerns about misinterpreting state constitutions; any unworkable interpretations can be remedied by simply altering the constitutional text. Decisions about who decides questions of supreme court recusal are thus more likely to be part of an active political debate at the state level than at the federal, where the virtual impossibility of amendment means that the separation-of-powers debate over recusal is a matter of interpreting a static document, not altering or updating a dynamic one. It is important not to overstate this point, as while state constitutions are unquestionably easier to amend than the federal Constitution, it is not the equivalent of merely sharpening one's pencil and rewriting a state's highest law. Amendment is a serious matter for all constitutional governments, including states, and should not be taken lightly, no matter how frequently it occurs. We are focused on the differences between the constitutional features of state and federal recusal law. Because the comparative ease of state amendments offers useful insight into those differences, it is an important point of departure, even if state constitutions are not altered as easily as, for example, state statutes.

The greater flexibility of state constitutions makes recusal a question of presumptions and framing more than anything else. The fact that a state constitution can be more readily changed does not say anything about what the status quo should look like. What ultimately matters is whether to approach the question of recusal from the perspective of the legislature or judiciary. One way to find the proper perspective is to compare the constitutional principles at work when substantive recusal standards are vested in the legislative versus the judicial branch. Legislative recusal standards reflect a presumption toward democratic control over a largely unaccountable judiciary. Even when state supreme court justices are elected, they are held accountable only when their terms expire, which can be as rarely as every twelve years.[113] Empowering the state legislature to control recusal practices at the supreme court could bolster judicial accountability by limiting the number of biased justices presiding over individual cases. Leaving recusal in the hands of the justices prioritizes judicial independence. Protecting the justices from interference by the legislature insulates their decisions from unwanted political influences. This is true regardless of how the justices achieve their positions in the first place, or how they keep them in states with judicial term limits.

Several reasons for leaving recusal to the justices emerge when we think of how different constitutional amendment procedures affect the balance between legislative and judicial control over recusal. First, historical practices favor judicial control. At common law, the default position regarding recusal was that judges would make their own decisions, reviewable only by other judges.[114] This position has since been altered by multiple recusal statutes. But in terms of trying to identify a starting point for constitutional authority over recusal, the fact that the judicial branch enjoyed that power pre-Constitution is at least relevant. Second, as Justice Brennan warned, judicial independence is a "prophylactic" concept designed to protect judges and individuals in the long term from legislative and other political interference.[115] By contrast, legislative reforms offer benefits that are "immediate, concrete, and easily understood."[116] When the two are pitted against one another, Justice Brennan argued, "the balance is weighted against judicial independence."[117] The more immediate political appeal of legislative recusal standards is a reason to create a countervailing presumption of judicial control. Assuming judicial independence and democratic control are both laudable goals, we can argue that the goal with less inherent political appeal should be the default, else the more politically seductive option will become inevitable. Put slightly differently, if the political playing field is tilted toward legislative reforms, leveling that field by creating a presumption in favor of judicial independence allows for the amendment process to work to its full potential. Starting with the instant gratification of political control will make it all but impossible for the less alluring—but equally defensible—principle of judicial independence to prevail.

The preservation of a level playing field between judicial independence and democratic control becomes even more important when we recall that every state in the Union allows for the legislature to participate in the amendment process, but none includes its supreme court justices in that process.[118] Legislative input into the amendment process provides an institutional reason to establish a presumption of judicial control over recusal. The legislature will have self-interested reasons to use the amendment process to enhance its institutional authority and will be pitted against a coequal branch of government that is entirely powerless to resist. Furthermore, because amendments generally trump any prior inconsistent precedent, the power to amend potentially overrides the judiciary's most powerful means of protecting itself from the encroachment of other branches—its interpretive authority. Because legislatures often play a role in the amendment process, and because an amendment overrides any existing judicial rulings, it is important that the justices retain, at least as a starting point, authority over their own recusal practices, subject to whatever constitutional changes the people and their legislature choose to impose on them.

* * *

A constitutional perspective on state recusal law does not yield perfectly clear results or prescriptions. It does, however, help to consolidate the full range of questions about who sets substantive recusal standards under state constitutional regimes. With the understanding that each state government is unique, there are at least five features of state governments and, in particular, state supreme courts that make them materially different from federal courts with regard to recusal. By balancing the effects of these features, we can get an overall sense—generalized to cut across varied state systems—of how the constitutional approach to recusal may differ in state supreme courts. More specifically, we see whether the structure of state government gives state legislatures a stronger claim to set substantive recusal standards for state justices than Congress has to set standards for the U.S. Supreme Court. State legislatures' general police power cannot, by itself, justify recusal standards that threaten to impede the courts' core power to decide cases, but where such power is constitutionally entrusted, either explicitly or implicitly, to the legislature, the constitutional balance shifts to the legislature. Judicial elections create a keen enough prospect of bias that, despite the increased accountability they offer in the form of periodic review of a justice's performance, they may justify more legislative involvement in state supreme court recusal than the lifetime appointment regime of the federal courts. State supreme courts' broader jurisdiction weighs in favor of judicial control over recusal. The wider range of cases and lack of concurrent federal court jurisdiction imperil judicial supervision over critical issues of state law and litigants' access to neutral forums to resolve their disputes. They also highlight the importance of supreme courts retaining power over judicial assignments as a way of keeping courts open when large-scale recusals do occur. Finally, more lenient and accessible state constitutional amendment provisions support a presumption in favor of judicial control over recusal because the more open amendment process tends to favor legislative power and creates a responsibility for drafters to be clear about alterations to fundamental principles of the separation of powers like judicial independence.

The differences between state supreme courts and their federal counterparts do not lead to a clear recipe for how to design a recusal system that properly accommodates all of the constitutional issues at play. Judicial elections encourage more legislative involvement, but the scope of state court jurisdiction and the fluidity of state constitutions argue for increased judicial control. The endgame requires, as expected, a state-specific analysis of how the various features of its constitutional system operate on recusal at its highest court. The preceding exercise brings to light the issues likely to be most influential on that analysis and offers a short introduction to how they may come to bear on the ultimate constitutional question of who controls the justices' recusal practices. More important, it shines additional light on the importance of treating recusal as a matter of constitutional structure and power. This constitutional approach is not limited, however, to matters of recusal. As we will see in the next (and final) chapter, the model we have used for evaluating the constitutional aspects of recusal law can be used to gain new perspectives on other common and controversial issues involving the separation of powers.

7 | A Lesson in Structure

There are several reasons to examine recusal through a constitutional prism. Most directly, this approach uncovers several underappreciated aspects of American recusal law that can benefit both Congress and the courts. It also offers an analogy to other interbranch conflicts that can help shed light on broader separation-of-powers questions. This concluding chapter will serve as a brief survey of the foregoing discussion of Supreme Court recusal and the Constitution, while offering examples of how each of the analytical moves made with regard to recusal can be applied to other, sometimes more high-profile, separation-of-powers issues. The point of this is not to resolve any new constitutional debates, or to claim any novel approach to other separation-of-powers issues, but to try to use what we have learned about judicial recusal at the highest level of American government to shed new light on some old questions.

Inherent Power and Constitutional Questions

First among these sources of light is the fact that congressional attempts to prescribe the substantive standards for recusal at the Supreme Court unlawfully infringe on the Court's core constitutional responsibility to decide the cases before it. A constitutional approach to who decides questions of federal law requires an inquiry into the most fundamental functions of each branch of government, and into the effects that the actions of one branch can have on the core features of another. Under the Constitution's separation-of-powers regime, the branches need not be, in the words of Chief Justice Roberts, "hermetically sealed" from one another.[1] They must, however, retain some measure of their own identity. Otherwise, the division of power threatens to become a myth, and the branch with the broadest explicit power—Congress—could threaten to overwhelm the other branches.[2] For recusal, this means that Congress cannot use its own broad legislative authority to force recusals that could leave the Supreme Court without enough justices to decide a case over which it has jurisdiction.

The relationship between recusal and inherent judicial power is relevant to other exercises of legislative authority that affect the judiciary. For example, legislative control over quorum requirements at the Supreme Court has long been understood to be within Congress's authority under the Necessary and Proper Clause. As alluded to in chapter 3, an inherent power perspective could change that view. Much like the recusal statute, quorum requirements for the Supreme Court could render the Court powerless to decide a case over which it has jurisdiction. When viewed purely in light of Congress's affirmative authority under Article I, this potential interference with a core feature of the Article III judicial power is easy to miss. When cast as a separation-of-powers issue, however, it becomes clear that Congress's choices about quorum could encroach on an inherent power of the judicial branch. This is not likely when the quorum threshold remains at its historic level at or slightly above a bare majority of the justices.[3] But that does not mean that legislative power over quorum requirements could not raise serious constitutional questions. Imagine a scenario in which Congress raised the quorum requirement to seven justices to ensure, quite reasonably, that a close case could not be decided without at least four justices granting their approval. Imagine further that two or three justices fell ill or retired, leaving six or seven justices on the Court pending additional Senate confirmations. Congress would have several choices as to how to responsibly exercise its legislative authority in that situation, but those choices should be informed by the fact that the Court cannot perform its core constitutional function of deciding cases without some congressional action.

A similar, and also previously discussed, example is the Exceptions Clause of Article III. While it undoubtedly provides Congress with some affirmative authority to limit the jurisdiction of the Court, the Court itself has interpreted it with its own constitutional existence and responsibilities in mind, repeatedly implying that Congress's power does not extend to the total eradication of Supreme Court review.[4] The Court has likewise rejected Congress's attempts to use its lawmaking power to reopen cases already decided by the Court, on the grounds that it would unconstitutionally interfere with the Court's core power to decide.[5] Both of these instances reflect the Court's reliance on its inherent power to thwart an otherwise textually supported exercise of legislative authority under the Constitution.

The inherent power model is useful in understanding Congress's relationship with the executive as well. The common wisdom on executive appointments is that the president has virtually unbounded authority to choose who to nominate, and the Senate has equally unbounded power to confirm or reject the president's nominees.[6] But when we look at the relationship from an inherent power perspective, we see that neither branch's discretion can be totally unlimited. The president may well have an obligation to fill certain vacancies, particularly when they impair his ability to execute the laws under Article II. This is unlikely to ever occur because the president's power to choose the nominee creates little if any incentive to leave a position vacant. But from the Senate's view, obstruction of federal nominees is both politically advantageous and increasingly common, especially with respect to high-level agency positions.[7] The 2014 elimination of the Senate filibuster rules for presidential nominees could provide some relief,[8] but not in cases where the Senate is controlled by the opposing party.

A powerful tool for the president to combat the Senate's refusal to confirm a nominee is the Recess Appointments Clause, which permits the president to temporarily fill a vacancy without Senate approval. Recess appointments are only permitted, according to the clause, while the Senate is in recess. In *NLRB v. Noel Canning*, the Court severely limited the scope of the Recess Appointments Clause.[9] *Noel Canning* involved the recess appointments of three members of the National Labor Relations Board. Each of the three members had nominations pending before the Senate for at least several weeks (and one as long as a year) when the president appointed them as recess appointees during a break between sessions of Congress. During that period, however, the Senate had arranged for pro forma sessions to take place every three days. The pro forma proceedings were conducted in an "almost empty" chamber and under a Senate resolution that no new business would be conducted.[10] The Court held that recess appointments are only permitted when the Senate determines that it is in recess, and that the Senate can create a presumption that it is not in recess by scheduling pro forma proceedings at least once every ten days.[11] The Court relied on the Senate's own rules that permit business to be conducted despite a resolution to the contrary and presume a quorum is present "unless a present Senator questions it."[12] It concluded that the Senate was not in recess during the pro forma sessions, and therefore that the president was unable to make recess appointments during that period. The Court also recognized the House of Representatives' power to thwart recess appointments. Pursuant to Article I, "Neither House . . . shall, without the Consent of the other, adjourn for more than three days."[13] According to the Court, the House of Representatives can prevent a Senate recess by simply refusing to give its consent for the Senate to adjourn for longer than three days.[14] After *Noel Canning*, it will be exceedingly difficult for a president to fill vacant positions in the executive or judicial branches without Senate consent. Whether this is a good result in its own right, it represents a potentially significant shift in power over federal appointments from the president to the Senate.

The upshot of Congress's ability to scuttle executive appointments is that it can result in a legally mandated agency being unable to perform its statutory function due to lack of staffing. More important for present purposes, it could interfere with the president's constitutional duty to execute the laws. If a statute creates an agency within the executive branch and then Congress refuses to confirm people to work in that agency, Congress has arguably infringed the president's fundamental constitutional responsibility to "take Care that the Laws be faithfully executed."[15] It is one thing for Congress to repeal or amend the statute creating the agency. It is quite another to indirectly eviscerate the agency by refusing to confirm its members and blocking the president's ability to do so temporarily via recess appointment. There are a wide range of choices for Congress to avoid such a scenario, including providing for acting agency officials by statute,[16] and it is not important here to choose among them. The core point is that looking beyond affirmative grants of power like appointment to the interaction of that power with the inherent features of the coordinate branches is critical to preserving our constitutional structure.

Structural Solutions

The second revelation from our recusal analysis is that any resolution of an interbranch conflict must take structural concerns into account by seeking to protect the democratic legitimacy and integrity of both of the conflicting branches. In the recusal context, this refers to the need for Congress to repeal its substantive recusal standards for the Supreme Court, rather than requiring the Court to continue to defy, elude, or invalidate those standards on its own. As discussed in chapter 4, assuming a colorable argument that legislative recusal standards unduly impinge on the Court's inherent power under Article III, the Court has no good options for relieving the tension created by a statutory mandate that it feels neither required nor inclined to abide by. If it states publicly that it is not constitutionally bound by the statute or designates the conflict as nonjusticiable under Article III, it risks exacerbating the appearance of dysfunction and obstinacy between the branches. This could threaten public confidence in the integrity of the Court and, in turn, its legitimacy. If the Court simply rules that the statute is unconstitutional as applied to the justices, it gains procedural integrity at the cost of creating the impression that it is above the law or, at minimum, that a group of unelected, life tenured justices is willing to make an unreviewable and final legal decision promoting its own interests over those of a coequal branch of government. This is deeply problematic for future relations between the branches and fuels democratic concerns about judicial supremacy. Interbranch comity, integrity, and democratic legitimacy point to Congress as the best candidate to alleviate its tension with the Court over recusal.

This focus on structural solutions to interbranch conflicts also applies outside of recusal. In the judicial context, congressional investigations of judges could raise the type of conflict that should be resolved with the separation of powers in mind. Imagine an investigation in which Congress subpoenas a judge to testify. This happened in 1953, when a House subcommittee subpoenaed federal district judge Louis Goodman to testify about alleged judicial interference with a grand jury investigation into misconduct by officials of the Bureau of Internal Revenue.[17] Judge Goodman appeared but refused to testify about matters relating to the grand jury investigation. He cited grand jury secrecy rules and judicial independence, and the committee did not press the matter any further.[18] But what if Judge Goodman had refused to testify and Congress threatened to bring contempt proceedings against him? Congress unquestionably has the power to investigate, so the decision to seek information from Judge Goodman is not constitutionally problematic. A legislative decision to sanction a judge for not testifying, however, is far less clear as a constitutional matter.[19] In a similar case, a federal district court struck a portion of a federal reporting statute that required judges to provide Congress with detailed information on their decisions to sentence defendants below the range suggested by the federal sentencing guidelines.[20] The court held that the reporting requirement "stifles judicial independence" in violation of "the separation of powers."[21] If a reporting requirement can violate the separation of powers, it stands to reason that a contempt proceeding could as well. For that reason alone, a court may not be willing to entertain such a proceeding against a federal judge. It could resolve the issue by simply ignoring the subpoena or by ruling it unconstitutional under Article III. Either path could, however, have serious consequences for the reputation and perceived legitimacy of the federal courts. A self-serving ruling by the courts could seem inconsistent with the checks and balances inherent in the separation of powers. By contrast, congressional acquiescence to the core tenets of judicial independence would convey respect for the prerogatives of a coequal branch. This would project an air of legitimacy and integrity around a difficult question of governmental authority that a judicial resolution could not. It suggests that Congress should take responsibility for resolving any impasse between itself and the courts over the subpoena.

Structural solutions also apply to conflicts between Congress and the executive. One example is in the war powers area, where conflicts frequently arise between Congress and the president over whether to use military force. The president relies on his power as commander in chief of the armed forces and as the primary organ of foreign affairs under Article II to decide when to deploy military force, while Congress relies on its power to declare war under Article I to argue that military engagement requires congressional approval.[22] The federal courts are extremely reluctant to get involved, almost always classifying issues of military control as nonjusticiable political questions. It is not at all uncommon for tension between Congress and the president to become public, such as when President Obama ordered air strikes against perceived threats in Libya and Syria without congressional approval, let alone a declaration of war. President Obama's decision was similar to his predecessors', including President Richard Nixon, whose military choices in Southeast Asia during the Vietnam conflict prompted Congress to enact the War Powers Resolution.[23] There is no easy way to resolve the persistent and historic tension between the legislative and executive branches over the use of military force. One thing that is still critical to consider, and that is reflected in our discussion of recusal, is that any solution must take into account its impact on the integrity and legitimacy of the entities involved. This does not portend any particular outcome. Whether the president orders the use of force against Congress's will or refuses to do so under congressional pressure, scenarios exist in which both branches could be forced to take responsibility in order to protect their integrity and legitimacy.

Picture a situation in which the president wants to engage militarily and Congress disagrees. Institutional expertise and responsiveness should be taken into account to protect the core functions and powers of each branch. Presidents have a more powerful reason to defer to Congress's powers to declare war and to control the nation's purse strings where military engagement is likely to be long-running or extremely costly. The same is true where military engagement is not particularly urgent. It may be in the national interest to bring military pressure to bear on an enemy that is oppressing a segment of its own population, but if that enemy has been engaged in the same conduct for a long time and there has been no recent escalation, the presidential imperative to act without congressional involvement becomes weaker. By contrast, Congress should consider deferring to the president where military engagement is designed to be short-lived or is a matter of national emergency. If the president proves wrong on either count, the democratic process can act as a check by voting him out of office; a single actor subject to national election is easier to hold accountable for a military decision than a group of 535 individual legislators. Congress should also defer to the president in cases of overwhelming public support for prompt military action. A single national perspective on the problem is preferable in that context to one based on local and regional constituencies, and the president is therefore best equipped to respond to public demands to employ military force. One could argue that a direct mandate from the people is sufficient to bypass the inevitable delays and political trading brought on by congressional involvement, and that Congress should respect that mandate in deference to the president's role as the primary representative of our national interests.

A similar approach works where Congress wants to engage militarily and the president resists.[24] For the president, a declaration of war should act as a mandate to pursue military action, as to do otherwise would threaten to eviscerate one of Congress's express constitutional powers. A formal declaration of war triggers presidential deference because it requires the assent of both houses of Congress and, historically, has proved a high hurdle for the legislature to overcome.[25] When Congress commits to a course of action as severe as declaring war, presidential opposition threatens the integrity and legitimacy of both Congress and the president in a way that the separation of powers should seek to avoid. Congressional enthusiasm for military engagement should be tempered, however, by respect for the president's power as commander in chief, including his (and, by extension, the armed forces') relative expertise in military affairs. Congress should consider giving way to presidential prerogative when military involvement would be logistically or strategically complex or uncertain, when it is not a matter of national emergency, and when it is lacking public support.

At first glance, this may seem like just a repackaging of ideas about prudent policy making or institutional expertise, for example, that military action should not be taken without a declaration of war except in cases of national emergency. Whereas in some cases the outcome may be consistent with these approaches, it is not tied solely to the substantive quality of the decision or to whether it is in the hands of the most capable decision maker. Rather, by focusing on how an interbranch conflict over war powers impacts the democratic legitimacy of each branch, an extra layer is added to the analysis. Concerns about public perception play an important role in promoting public confidence in the integrity of government decisions. A statute forbidding the president to militarily resist an imminent armed invasion (like a collection of hostile troops on an American border) until after the first aggressive strike against the United States would almost certainly create a conflict between the two branches. The president would not be inclined to follow the statute if he felt he could prevent American casualties by acting first, but a decision not to would amount to a statutory violation. There may be strong moral, social, and political arguments on each side for how the conflict should be resolved in a given case, but they do not answer the question of which branch should take the initiative in the interest of government integrity and comity. Recusal offers additional perspective on the broader consequences of interbranch conflict resolution. Even if one were to disagree with the suggested outcome in the preceding examples, disputes between coequal branches of government must be resolved in a way that maximizes their democratic legitimacy by honoring interbranch comity and cooperation as well as the core constitutional powers of each branch.

Independent Constitutional Constraints

Constitutional analyses that focus on the core powers and legitimacy of the branches are useful in identifying the boundaries of constitutional authority and in resolving interbranch conflicts. They are also potentially dangerous, as they threaten to leave one branch relatively unchecked. This problem is present in Supreme Court recusal once we conclude that legislative recusal standards violate Article III and that any dispute between Congress and the Court over recusal must be resolved through congressional acquiescence to the justices' authority. At this point it is unclear what, if any, boundaries exist for the justices' recusal decisions. The answer—and one that has application outside of the recusal context—is a reminder to look beyond competing claims from the other branches to independent constitutional restraints. For recusal, this restraint is the Due Process Clause, as balanced against the First Amendment. The result of this balance is a framework for Supreme Court recusal decisions that protects the justices' inherent constitutional authority without allowing it to go unchecked.

An analogous situation involving the judicial branch is impeachment. It is generally accepted that impeachment is part of Congress's inherent constitutional power, and thus that the procedures and standards by which judges are impeached are left to the legislature.[26] This is consistent with separation-of-powers principles, and there is not a competing claim to authority over impeachments by any other branch of government. In fact, the Supreme Court has already held that the procedures used to try impeachments are the sole province of the Senate and are not reviewable by the courts.[27] Notwithstanding the Court's ruling, there remains a strong argument that Congress should feel bound, and abide, by independent constitutional restrictions on its authority. In the case of impeachment, as with recusal, the restriction that comes most readily to mind is the Due Process Clause. Federal judges unquestionably have a property interest in their job, and Congress is no less bound by the Fifth Amendment's obligation to provide fair and impartial hearings than are the federal courts. Justice David Souter hinted at this limitation in his *Nixon* concurrence when, despite agreeing that the case at hand did not lend itself to judicial resolution, he stated that he could "envision different and unusual circumstances that might justify a more searching review of impeachment proceedings."[28] Regardless of whether another branch, in this case the judiciary, can require Congress to meet the requirements of due process, it is important that legislators be aware of their constitutional obligations in order to avoid unjust or arbitrary decisions.

Interactions between Congress and the president also highlight the importance of taking independent constitutional limits seriously when one branch has exclusive control over a particular area of law. The president is widely understood to have sole authority to remove cabinet members and other at-will executive officials; Congress may not impose any limits on that authority.[29] Reserving this power to the president, however, does not remove all boundaries to his conduct. There are no due process requirements for dismissing at-will employees because they do not have a legal entitlement to their employment. But they are covered by the free speech protections of the First Amendment. Although the scope of constitutional protection may vary where the speaker is a government employee, constitutional protections exist that could create freestanding limits on what would otherwise be a purely executive decision to remove. The Supreme Court has not taken up a case involving a cabinet member, and if it did, it may well support the president's decision to remove for political and prudential reasons, but that does not mean the First Amendment should be ignored when addressing separation-of-powers questions.

Immigration offers a mirror image of the removal example. Congress has sweeping power over immigration policy. Acting alone, it could institute immigration restrictions or travel bans on citizens from certain countries or regions free of executive or, most likely, judicial interference.[30] If it could be shown that Congress's decisions were based on the race or religious affiliation of the excluded individuals, the statute would be a violation of the Constitution's guarantee of equal protection of the laws. The fact that it was an exercise of an exclusive legislative power would be irrelevant. The overarching lesson is that it is important to acknowledge that some issues are committed to a lone constitutional actor, but that once that actor is identified, it is equally important to apply the full range of constitutional limitations to help contain their otherwise unchecked authority. Put another way, the true scope of one branch's authority over an issue can only be fully understood by remembering the limitations provided by other constitutional provisions.

Constitutional Contingencies

A final lesson from recusal is that, even where one branch has complete authority over a given issue, that authority may be contingent on its exercising or withholding other powers. This is true for questions of lower court recusal. Congress unquestionably has greater authority over lower federal courts than over the Supreme Court, but its power to regulate lower court recusal must still be weighed against those courts' inherent power to decide cases under Article III. Unlike the Supreme Court, whose justices are irreplaceable and thus highly vulnerable to complete recusal, replacement judges are readily available in the lower courts. This distinction is critical to understanding the constitutional limits on Congress's ability to regulate lower court recusal. But it depends on Congress's power over judicial assignment being contingent on avoiding complete recusal. The best and easiest way to do this is for Congress to share its constitutional authority over judicial assignments with the judiciary. If the courts do not have any power to guarantee judicial assignments, the threat of complete recusal from a recusal statute is simply replaced by the threat of complete recusal from congressional failure to fill judicial vacancies. To protect the courts' inherent authority, Congress must share the power to assign judges with the courts so they can prevent complete recusal on their own, independent of Congress.

This constitutional contingency idea applies to several issues involving congressional control over the judicial branch. As we discussed earlier in this chapter in connection with inherent powers, Congress has uncontested and sole authority to set quorum requirements for the justices, but there is a structural limit on where that quorum number may be set. Quorum cannot, in light of the Court's inherent power to decide cases, be set at a number higher than the number of seats on the Court itself. During an extended vacancy, it may even be unconstitutional to have a quorum requirement above the actual composition of the Court. In either of these cases, Congress may be constitutionally obligated to exercise another of its constitutional powers to help remedy the problem. An extended vacancy could create a contingent constitutional obligation on Congress to confirm enough candidates to ensure that quorum is obtainable. Where the quorum requirement equals the number of sitting justices, Congress may need to, as advocated here, eliminate any statutory recusal standards that could force the disqualification of justices needed to reach a quorum.

A similar phenomenon arises with Congress's power to set the qualifications for justices to serve on the Court. Congress is the lone source of those qualifications, but I contend it would be constitutionally precluded from setting them in such a way as to prevent an adequate number of candidates from being available. Imagine Congress requiring that all Supreme Court justices be former federal appellate judges who served in a former president's cabinet. Even if these are relevant qualifications for a Supreme Court justice, it is possible that the pool of available candidates would not be large enough to fill the Court, even with a 100 percent confirmation rate. If these examples seem far-fetched, there are two responses. One is that our discussion of complete recusal shows that even though a situation at first seems highly unlikely, closer examination may reveal external forces that prevent it from happening in a way that merely masks, rather than disproves, its potential. The other is that even if the examples are a bit extreme, they reinforce the point that simply being the sole repository of constitutional authority over a particular issue does not necessarily provide carte blanche to address that issue. The inherent powers of the coordinate branches must still be protected from encroachment by another branch, and that protection may take the form of additional constitutional limitations on, or prerequisites to, the way the encroaching branch exercises its constitutional authority.

The same circumstances arise outside of the judiciary. Take funding of the executive branch. Congress controls the federal purse strings and has wide-ranging authority regarding whether and how to allocate funds to executive departments. The president has an inherent duty to execute the laws. Now think what would happen if Congress eliminated the president's funding for enforcement, say for all violations of existing securities laws. No other branch is empowered to change Congress's decision, but it may be that the power to appropriate funds is limited by the legal responsibilities of the other branches, such that Congress is constitutionally obligated to either provide funding or to suspend or repeal the unenforceable federal law until it does. When Congress's funding power runs up against another constitutional requirement, certain contingencies may emerge that rise to the level of constitutional mandates.

These examples are not meant to be exhaustive or to take a position on a specific issue involving the separation of powers. They are included here to represent the universality of the themes at work in Supreme Court recusal. The role of inherent power, interbranch comity, and contingent constitutional authority all translate to other, sometimes more high-profile, areas of constitutional law. Projecting Supreme Court recusal onto a constitutional stage has brought these issues into the light in a way that traditional ethical approaches to the justices' recusal practices could not.

* * *

Who thought all of this could come from Supreme Court recusal? What until now has been largely a matter of judicial ethics has turned into a discourse on constitutional government. For essentially the first time, these two legal disciplines that stretch back over a millennium, and that have been interacting in the United States since its Founding, have been formally introduced. In the process, we have uncovered a host of ideas about how to manage both the ethical behavior of our highest court and the sharing of power among competing, yet coordinate, branches of government.

Some of these ideas will be inherently controversial because they seem to prioritize theoretical notions of government structure over important questions of judicial ethics and good judging. As the foregoing analysis no doubt reveals, I am less inclined to think of those things as mutually exclusive. The separation of powers is far more than a theory. It is a practical approach to governance that seeks to assign power where it belongs and then to keep that same power under control by balancing it against equal, and potentially opposite, sources of power. In addition to encouraging better decisions from a balanced government, the separation of powers has the added and critical effect of legitimizing our institutions, especially the judiciary. This is where it has the most in common with judicial recusal. The separation of powers gives us confidence in the judgments of unelected, life-tenured judges and justices because it creates limits on their otherwise unchecked power. Recusal gives us confidence in the judiciary by ensuring that the binding decisions we expect and rely on from our courts will be the product of fair and impartial judges. When we think of them as legitimizing forces, rather than just user's manuals for government conduct, it should come as no surprise that recusal, like the separation of powers, comes with the same full slate of challenges and possibilities as any other constitutional doctrine. In addition to spurring interbranch conflict and controversy, it has the potential to make our government institutions stronger both in practice and in the eyes of the governed. The trick, until now, has been in recognizing that potential. This book seeks to do that by sketching out a constitutional framework for recusal at the Supreme Court that also serves as a template for larger lessons about the way the coordinate branches interact in our constitutional system.

Notes

Introduction

1. *The Federalist* No. 78 (A. Hamilton).
2. 505 U.S. 833, 866 (1992).
3. "Recusal" is used interchangeably to include both the terms "disqualification," which traditionally refers to involuntary removal of a judge from a case, and "recusal," which has historically referred to a judge's voluntary decision to withdraw from a case. Richard E. Flamm, *Judicial Disqualification: Recusal and Disqualification of Judges* § 1.1, at 4 (2d ed. 2007).
4. This viewpoint is not unique to the American judicial system. It is a common feature of most stable and effective judicial systems, and certainly of the common law regimes that served as examples for the formation of America's constitutional structure.
5. *The Federalist* No. 78 (A. Hamilton).
6. Michael J. Gerhardt, *The Federal Impeachment Process: A Constitutional and Historical Analysis* 94 (1996).
7. Several examples of such behavior are discussed in greater detail in chapter 2.
8. David Paul Kuhn, "The Incredible Polarization and Politicization of the Supreme Court," *The Atlantic,* June 29, 2012, http://www.theatlantic.com/politics/archive/2012/06/the-incredible-polarization-and-politicization-of-the-supreme-court/259155/.
9. Stern v. Marshall, 131 S. Ct. 2594, 2620 (2011).
10. Adam Liptak, "Justices Get Out More, but Calendars Aren't Open to Just Anyone," *N.Y. Times,* June 1, 2015, http://www.nytimes.com/2015/06/02/us/politics/justices-get-out-more-but-calendars-arent-open-to-just-anyone.html?_r=0.

1. The Evolution of American Recusal Law

1. Richard E. Flamm, *Judicial Disqualification: Recusal and Disqualification of Judges* § 1.2, at 5 (2d ed. 2007), citing *The Code of Maimonides,* bk. XIV, ch. 23, 68–70 (trans. A Hershman 1949).
2. Codex of Justinian, lib. III, title 1, no. 16, cited in Harrington Putnam, "Recusation," 9 *Cornell L.Q.* 1, 3 (1923).

3. Id., translated in Putnam, "Recusation," at 3n10.

4. Putnam, "Recusation," at 5–6.

5. Harvard Law School Library, "Bracton Online," http://bracton.law.har vard.edu/index.html.

6. Id. at vol. 4, 281.

7. Flamm, *Judicial Disqualification*, § 1.2, at 5.

8. Adrian Vermeule, "Contra Nemo Iudex In Sua Causa: The Limits of Impartiality," 122 *Yale L.J.* 384, 386n1 (2012). The question was complicated for medieval lawyers by the common practice of private parties being granted the judicial franchise by the Crown. D. E. C. Yale, "Iudex in Propria Causa: An Historical Excursus," 33 *Cambridge L.J.* 80, 96 (1974).

9. Yale, "Index in Propia Causa," at 81.

10. Id. at 96.

11. 77 Eng. Rep. 638 (1608). Prior to 1875, there were three high common law courts in England: the King's Bench, the Court of Common Pleas, and the Court of the Exchequer. Each had its own chief justice. Sir Edward Coke served as chief justice of both the King's Bench and the Court of Common Pleas. Lord Coke served as lord chief justice of the Common Pleas from 1605 to 1613, when he was appointed lord chief justice of the King's Bench. He served in that role until 1616.

12. Id.

13. 77 Eng. Rep. 1390 (1613).

14. The Earl of Derby in this case was a successor to William, the judge forced to recuse himself in the *Earl of Derby's Case* discussed earlier.

15. 145 Eng. Rep. 569 (1679).

16. Anonymous, 91 Eng. Rep. 343 (1700).

17. 16 Geo. 2, c. 18 (1742), reprinted in Sir John Comyns and Anthony Hammond, 3 *A Digest of the Laws of England* 659 (1822).

18. United States v. Will, 449 U.S. 200, 213 (1980) (citing Y. B. Hil. 8 Hen. IV, f. 19 pl. 6).

19. H. Rolle, 2 *An Abridgment of Many Cases and Resolutions at Common Law* 93 (1668) (translation).

20. William Blackstone, 3 *Commentaries on the Laws of England* 361 (1768).

21. Id.

22. Id.

23. District of Columbia v. Heller, 554 U.S. 570, 593–594 (2008).

24. Daniel J. Boorstin, *The Mysterious Science of the Law* 3 (1941).

25. The Framers' understanding of the law was heavily influenced by the "business of the Colonial courts and the courts of Westminster when the Constitution was framed." Joint Anti-Fascist Refugee Comm. v. McGrath, 341 U.S. 123, 150 (1951) (Frankfurter, J., concurring); Evan Caminker, "Allocating the Judicial Power in a 'Unified Judiciary,'" 78 *Tex. L. Rev.* 1513, 1518 (2000).

26. Raoul Berger, "Doctor Bonham's Case: Statutory Construction or Constitutional Theory?," 117 *U. Pa. L. Rev.* 521, 522 (1969).

27. Daniel J. Boorstin, "Preface to the Beacon Press Edition," in *The Mysterious Science of the Law* (1958).

28. Flamm, *Judicial Disqualification*, § 1.4, at 8.

29. 1 Stat. 275, 278–279 (1792).

30. Flamm, *Judicial Disqualification*, § 23.1, at 670.

31. 3 Stat. 643 (1821).

32. 26 Stat. 826 (1891). This 1891 statute has since been codified as amended at 28 U.S.C. § 47 and reads, in pertinent part, "No judge shall hear or determine an appeal from the decision of a case or issue tried by him."

33. 36 Stat. 1090 (1911).

34. Flamm, *Judicial Disqualification*, § 23.1, at 670.

35. Id.

36. John P. Frank, "Disqualification of Judges," 56 *Yale L.J.* 605, 627 (1947) (emphasis added).

37. Flamm, *Judicial Disqualification*, § 33.1, at 988.

38. Frank, "Disqualification of Judges," at 628.

39. 41 U.S. 230 (1921).

40. Id. at 36.

41. Frank, "Disqualification of Judges," at 629. Section 21 of the 1911 act was recodified in 1948 in almost precisely the same form. 28 U.S.C. § 144 (1998). Section 144's definition of "bias and prejudice" continues to be narrowly construed by the courts and applies only to federal district judges. In terms of its impact on current recusal law, section 455 "has frequently been referred to as the 'principal' or 'comprehensive' federal judicial disqualification statute. . . . In fact, some courts have issued decisions which appear to reflect the belief that § 455 is the *only* federal disqualification statute." Flamm, *Judicial Disqualification*, § 23.1, at 678.

42. Flamm, *Judicial Disqualification*, § 29.4, at 915.

43. David Pietrusza, *Judge and Jury: The Life and Times of Judge Kenesaw Mountain Landis* 197 (1998).

44. Id. The bill was defeated in the Senate by a tie vote. "Bill Aimed at Landis Fails," *N.Y. Times*, July 19, 1921, at 13.

45. Report of the Forty-Fourth Annual Meeting of the American Bar Association 61–68 (1921). The ABA's censure of Judge Landis was reprinted in "Bar Meeting Votes Censure of Landis," *N.Y. Times*, September 2, 1921, at 1.

46. The other canons that are relevant to judicial recusal were far less revolutionary. For example, Canon 13 explained that a judge "should not act in a controversy where a near relative is a party," and Canon 29 explained that a judge should avoid presiding over cases "in which his personal interests are involved." American Bar Association, 1924 Canons of Judicial Ethics, http://www.americanbar.org/content/dam/aba/migrated/cpr/pic/1924_canons.authcheckdam.pdf.

47. Debra Lyn Bassett, "Judicial Disqualification in the Federal Appellate Courts," 87 *Iowa L. Rev.* 1213, 1229 (2002).

48. In 1974, for example, Congress codified a provision of the ABA's Model Code of Judicial Conduct that required recusal "'in any proceeding in which [the judge's] impartiality might reasonably be questioned.'" Flamm, *Judicial Disqualification*, § 23.1, at 677.

49. As discussed earlier, courts have construed section 144 extremely narrowly, making it effectively useless for litigants seeking to recuse an otherwise unwilling judge. Section 47 prohibits judges from serving as appellate judges in cases where they also served as the trial judge. 28 U.S.C. § 47. Although there is no evidence that the courts have sought to unduly limit the application of section 47, the fact that it is explicitly limited to cases where judges are hearing appeals from their own cases is both narrowing in its own right and potentially redundant with the reasonableness standard of section 455: "Any justice, judge, or magistrate judge of the United States shall disqualify himself in any proceeding in which his impartiality might reasonably be questioned."

50. 28 U.S.C. § 455 (1948).

51. Id.

52. Id.

53. Id.

54. Federal Judicial Center, Judicial Disqualification: An Analysis of Federal Law 6 (2010), http://www.fjc.gov/public/pdf.nsf/lookup/judicialdq.pdf/$file/judicialdq.pdf.

55. 334 F.2d 360 (1964).

56. Id. at 362n2.

57. Id.

58. Id.

59. Laird v. Tatum, 409 US 824, 837 (1972).

60. John A. Jenkins, *The Partisan: The Life of William Rehnquist* 90–91 (2012).

61. Robert Shogan, *A Question of Judgment: The Fortas Case and the Struggle for the Supreme Court* 195 (1972).

62. There is evidence, for instance, that soon after he was elected, President Richard Nixon saw the controversies surrounding Justice Fortas as an opportunity to force the justice's resignation and appoint his own nominee to the Court, and that members of his administration, including Attorney General John Mitchell, brought additional pressure to bear on Justice Fortas and his family to encourage his resignation. Attorney General Mitchell reportedly reopened an old Justice Department investigation involving Justice Fortas's wife, Carolyn Agger, and his former law partner, Paul Porter. He also threatened to submit a formal report to the House of Representatives calling for the justice's impeachment. Neither the investigation nor the threat of impeachment ever came to fruition. Jenkins, *The Partisan*, at 93.

63. Henry J. Abraham, *Justices, Presidents, and Senators* 10 (1999).

64. Id.

65. Irving R. Kaufmann, "Lions or Jackals: The Function of a Code of Judicial Ethics," 35 *Law & Contemp. Probs.* 3, 3 (1970).

66. The 1972 ABA Model Code of Judicial Conduct (hereinafter 1972 Model Code), including Canon 3C, was reprinted in Note, "Disqualification of Judges and Justices in the Federal Courts," 86 *Harv. L. Rev.* 736, 743–744 (1973). The code also mandated recusal where a judge was personally biased; had served as a lawyer in the controversy; had a financial interest in the outcome of the case;

or was within the third degree of relationship with a party, lawyer, interested person, or material witness in the case.

67. American Bar Association, Canons of Judicial Ethics, Canon 4 (1924), http://www.americanbar.org/content/dam/aba/migrated/cpr/pic/1924 _canons.authcheckdam.pdf.

68. 1972 Model Code, Canon 3C.

69. 3 Blackstone, *Commentaries on the Laws of England* 361.

70. 1972 Model Code, Canon 3C.

71. 409 U.S. 824 (1972). Justice Rehnquist was sworn in as chief justice on September 26, 1986, and held that position until his death on September 3, 2005.

72. 408 U.S. 1 (1972). This citation reflects the Court's opinion on the merits of *Tatum*. The previous citation is to Justice Rehnquist's memorandum explaining his decision not to recuse in the case, which was published separately from the merits opinion.

73. Id. at 4–5. The riots in Detroit took place from July 23 to 27, 1967. They were precipitated by a police raid on an unlicensed bar. Confrontations between the police, bar patrons, and observers led to five days of violence and civil unrest. Dr. Martin Luther King Jr. was assassinated on April 4, 1968. His death triggered a week of rioting and violence in several cities across the United States, including Washington, DC. In both cases, President Lyndon Johnson called upon the military to help restore order. Earl Caldwell, "Martin Luther King Is Slain in Memphis; A White Is Suspected; Johnson Urges Calm," *N.Y. Times*, April 5, 1968, at A1; Robyn Meredith, "5 Days in 1967 Still Shake Detroit," *N.Y. Times*, July 23, 1997, http://www.nytimes.com/1997/07/23/us/5 -days-in-1967-still-shake-detroit.html.

74. Tatum, 408 U.S., at 2n1 (1972).

75. Tatum, 409 U.S., at 824–825 (1972).

76. The Model Code provisions ostensibly applying to Justice Rehnquist's decision were not legally binding in the formal sense, as they had yet to be codified.

77. 28 U.S.C. § 455 (1948).

78. 1972 Model Code, Canon 3C (1972).

79. Tatum, 409 U.S., at 825. Justice Rehnquist's mention of the Model Code may be an indication that the justices consider the guidelines in the code to include members of the Court. As discussed later, however, any potential impact of the Model Code on Supreme Court recusal practice has been at best minimal.

80. Id. at 828.

81. Id. at 833, 835.

82. Id. at 837.

83. "Proceedings of the Judicial Conference of the United States," April 5–6, 1973, at 10, http://www.uscourts.gov/FederalCourts/JudicialConference/Pro ceedings/Proceedings.aspx?doc=/uscourts/FederalCourts/judconf/proceed ings/1973-04.pdf.

84. 28 U.S.C. § 331 (2014).

85. 175 F.R.D. 364, 365–373 (1998).

86. It would be overly simplistic to attribute Congress's amendment of section 455 wholly to Justice Rehnquist's *Tatum* memorandum. Federal recusal law had not been meaningfully updated in several decades, and several high-profile events such as the controversies surrounding Justice Fortas and Judge Haynsworth and, in turn, the reactions of professional organizations like the ABA and the Judicial Conference of the United States no doubt functioned as important catalysts for legislative reform. Nevertheless, the closeness in time and the fact that the amended statute appears to respond directly to some of the arguments raised by Justice Rehnquist in his *Tatum* memorandum make the case for at least some causal relationship between Justice Rehnquist's actions in *Tatum* and the 1974 amendments to section 455.

87. 28 U.S.C. § 455(b)(4), (d)(4) (1974).

88. Id. at § 455(a).

89. Federal Judicial Center, Judicial Disqualification: An Analysis of Federal Law, at 7.

2. *Recusal and the Supreme Court*

1. The Court has since explained that due process, like the Supreme Court's recusal practices, "'is not a technical conception with a fixed content unrelated to time, place, and circumstances. [It] is flexible and calls for such procedural protections as the particular situation demands.'" Mathews v. Eldridge, 424 U.S. 319, 334 (1976) (internal citations omitted). My proposal for incorporating due process principles into Supreme Court recusal is the primary focus of chapter 5.

2. Jean Edward Smith, *John Marshall: Definer of a Nation* 1–3 (1996).

3. 5 U.S. (1 Cranch) 137 (1803).

4. 5 U.S. (1 Cranch) 299 (1803).

5. 14 U.S. (1 Wheat.) 304 (1816).

6. John Marshall served as both secretary of state and chief justice of the United States from January 27, 1801, when he was confirmed as chief justice, until the close of President Adams's term on March 4, 1801. Smith, *John Marshall*, at 15–16.

7. Louise Weinberg, "Our Marbury," 89 *Va. L. Rev.* 1235, 1237 (2003).

8. James Bradley Thayer, *John Marshall: An Address* 32 (1901).

9. 5 U.S. (1 Cranch) 299 (1803).

10. Kathryn Turner, "The Midnight Judges," 109 *U. Pa. L. Rev.* 494 (1961).

11. Smith, *John Marshall*, at 301–311.

12. Stuart, 5 U.S. at 299–300.

13. Id. at 303.

14. Sanford Levinson and Jack Balkin, "What Are the Facts of *Marbury v. Madison?*" 20 *Const. Comm.* 255, 261 (2003).

15. Stuart, 5 U.S. at 307.

16. Smith, *John Marshall*, at 315.

17. Levinson and Balkin, "What Are the Facts of *Marbury*," at 260; 1 Stat. 275, 278–279 (1792).

18. 14 U.S. 304 (1816).

19. Smith, *John Marshall*, at 164–168.

20. Id.

21. 11 U.S. 603 (1812).

22. Smith, *John Marshall*, at 15–16.

23. Thayer, *John Marshall*, at 32.

24. Id.

25. Levinson and Balkin, "What Are the Facts of *Marbury*?" at 260.

26. The relationship between the Court's approach to recusal and due process is explored in detail in chapter 5.

27. Jeffrey W. Stempel, "Rehnquist, Recusal, and Reform," 53 *Brook. L. Rev.* 589, 621 (1987).

28. Joseph M. Cormack, "The Legal Tender Cases—A Drama of American Legal and Financial History," 16 *Va. L. Rev.* 132, 141–142 (1929).

29. 79 U.S. 457 (1870).

30. Henry J. Abraham, *Justices, Presidents, and Senators* 97 (1999).

31. Id.

32. James L. Moses, "William O. Douglas and the Vietnam War: Civil Liberties, Presidential Authority, and the 'Political Question,'" 26 *Pres. Stud. Q.* 1019, 1019 (1996).

33. 399 U.S. 267 (1970). The case was ultimately dismissed by the Court for lack of appellate jurisdiction over Justice Douglas's, and others', objection.

34. Letter from Representative F. Edward Hébert to Chief Justice Warren E. Burger, August 8, 1969, reprinted in "Final Report" by the special subcommittee on H. Res. 920 of the House Judiciary Committee, 91st Cong., 2d Sess. 61 (1970).

35. Letter from Representative F. Edward Hébert to Solicitor General Erwin N. Griswold, September 2, 1969, reprinted in "Final Report" by the special subcommittee on H. Res. 920 of the House Judiciary Committee, 91st Cong., 2d Sess. 62 (1970).

36. John Frank, "Conflict of Interest and U.S. Supreme Court Justices," 18 *Am. J. Comp. L.* 744, 748 (1970).

37. Stempel, "Rehnquist, Recusal, and Reform," at 622.

38. Donald G. Morgan, "Mr. Justice William Johnson and the Constitution," 57 *Harv. L. Rev.* 328, 33–35, 37 (1944).

39. Frank, "Conflict of Interest and U.S. Supreme Court Justices," at 747.

40. Alpheus Thomas Mason, *Harlan Fiske Stone: Pillar of the Law* 270 (1956); Alpheus Thomas Mason, *William Howard Taft: Chief Justice* 138–157 (1965).

41. Laird v. Tatum, 409 U.S. 824, 832 (1972).

42. Philip Elman and Norman Silber, "The Solicitor General's Office, Justice Frankfurter, and Civil Rights Litigation, 1946–1960: An Oral History," 100 *Harv. L. Rev.* 817 (1987).

43. James E. St. Clair and Linda C. Gugin, *Chief Justice Fred Vinson of Kentucky* 190–191 (2002).

44. Id. at 191.

45. Id. at 145, 156.

46. 343 U.S. 579 (1952).

47. St. Clair and Gugin, *Chief Justice Fred Vinson*, at 216–217; Robert J. Donovan, *Tumultuous Years: The Presidency of Harry S. Truman, 1949–1953* (1983).

48. Abraham, *Justices, Presidents, and Senators*, at 216.

49. Id.

50. Id. Professor Abraham also noted that "in his biography of Fortas, Bruce A. Murphy counted a total of 254 contacts between LBJ and Fortas from October 1966 to December 1968." Id.

51. A. Fortas, *Concerning Dissent and Civil Disobedience* (1968).

52. Abraham, *Justices, Presidents, and Senators*, at 216–217.

53. Justices Melville Fuller, Wills Van Devanter, and Pierce Butler, for example, all participated in cases in which a former client was a party. Stempel, "Rehnquist, Recusal, and Reform," at 623–624.

54. 325 U.S. 161 (1945).

55. Jewell Ridge, 325 U.S. at 897.

56. Edwin M. Yoder Jr., "Black vs. Jackson: A Study in Judicial Enmity," in *The Unmasking of a Whig and Other Essays in Self-Definition* 47 (1990).

57. Id.

58. Stempel, "Rehnquist, Recusal, and Reform," at 608.

59. United States v. Darby, 312 U.S. 100 (1941).

60. Laird v. Tatum, 409 U.S. 824, 832 (1972).

61. Nathaniel L. Nathanson, "Book Review: The Extra-judicial Activities of Supreme Court Justices: Where Should the Line Be Drawn?," 78 *Nw. U. L. Rev.* 494, 501, 522 (1983).

62. Stempel, "Rehnquist, Recusal, and Reform," at 626.

63. William Blackstone, 3 *Commentaries on the Laws of England* 361 (1768); 28 U.S.C. § 455 (1948).

64. 28 U.S.C. § 455 (1948).

65. The NAACP describes itself as the nation's oldest civil rights organization, with a mission "to ensure the political, educational, social, and economic equality of rights of all persons and to eliminate race-based discrimination." National Association for the Advancement of Colored People, http://www.naacp .org/pages/our-mission. The LDF was founded by Thurgood Marshall in 1940 as the "country's first and foremost civil and human rights law firm." National Association for the Advancement of Colored People Legal Defense and Educational Fund, http://www.naacpldf.org/history. In terms of his recusal practices, Justice Marshall did not distinguish between the two organizations when deciding whether to remove himself from a case. Ross E. Davies, "The Reluctant Recusants: Two Parables of Supreme Judicial Disqualification," 10 *Green Bag* 2d 79, 80n5 (2006).

66. Brown v. Board of Educ., 347 U.S. 483 (1954).

67. Memorandum to the Conference of the Supreme Court of the United

States from Justice Thurgood Marshall, October 4, 1984, reprinted in "NAACP Recusals," 10 *Green Bag* 2d 93, 93–99 (2006).

68. Id. at 95, 98–99.

69. Id. at 100–107.

70. Statement of Recusal Policy, reprinted in Richard E. Flamm, *Judicial Disqualification: Recusal and Disqualification of Judges* App. D at 1101 (2d ed. 2007). Justices Blackmun and Souter did not sign the policy. Id.

71. Id. at 1101. The chief justice took that position in connection with Brutsche v. Cleveland-Perdue, No. 89-1167, cert. denied, 111 S. Ct. 368 (1990).

72. Statement of Recusal Policy, at 1102–1103.

73. Id. at 1102.

74. Id. at 1103.

75. Sherrilyn A. Ifill, "Do Judicial Appearances Matter? Judicial Impartiality and the Supreme Court in *Bush v. Gore*," 61 *Md. L. Rev.* 606, 626 (2002).

76. 530 U.S. 1301 (2000).

77. Id. at 1302.

78. Id. at 1303.

79. 541 U.S. 913 (2004).

80. Id. at 915.

81. Id. at 926–927.

82. Id. at 916.

83. Justice Scalia cited decisions by Justices Byron White and Jackson not to recuse themselves despite their close friendships with high-ranking members of the governing administration. Cheney, 541 U.S. at 924–926. Justice Jackson's decision occurred in 1942, six years before the federal recusal statute was amended to include members of the Court. 28 U.S.C. § 455 (1948).

84. Id. at 927.

85. Id.

86. Jennifer Senior, "In Conversation: Antonin Scalia," *N.Y. Mag.*, October 6, 2013, http://nymag.com/news/features/antonin-scalia-2013-10/#.

87. Letter from Senator Patrick Leahy and Senator Joseph I. Lieberman to Chief Justice William H. Rehnquist, January 22, 2004, reprinted in "From the Bag: Irrecusable and Unconfirmable," 7 *Green Bag* 2d 277, 277–280 (2004).

88. Id. at 278.

89. Id. at 279.

90. Id.

91. Letter from Chief Justice William H. Rehnquist to Senator Patrick Leahy, January 26, 2004, reprinted in "From the Bag: Irrecusable and Unconfirmable," 7 *Green Bag* 2d 277, 280 (2004).

92. Id.

93. Id.

94. The Judicial Conduct and Disability Act Study Committee, "Implementation of the Judicial Conduct and Disability Act of 1980—A Report to the Chief Justice," September 2006, at 131, http://www.fjc.gov/public/pdf.nsf/lookup /breyero6.pdf/$file/breyero6.pdf.

95. Id. at 2.

96. Antonin Scalia, "Originalism: The Lesser Evil," 57 *U. Cin. L. Rev.* 849, 863 (1989).

97. 530 U.S. 1301 (2000).

98. There is always the possibility that the chief justice cited precedent purely to justify the desired outcome in that case. Such cynicism is not necessary, however, as a good faith argument for precedent leads to the same conclusion regarding the constraining effect (or lack thereof) of section 455 on Supreme Court recusal.

99. Caperton v. A. T. Massey Coal Co., 556 U.S. 868 (2009).

100. The full name and citation for the act is the Patient Protection and Affordable Care Act, Pub. L. No. 111-148, 124 Stat. 119 (2010). It has been codified in scattered sections of the U.S. Code.

101. John Gibeaut, "Sitting This One Out," *ABA J.*, March 2012, at 18; David Jackson, "Obama Health Care Politics Hits High Court," *USA Today*, November 15, 2011, http://content.usatoday.com/communities/theoval/post/2011/11/obama-health-care-politics-hits-high-court/1; Michael B. Mukasey, "The Obama-Care Recusal Nonsense," *Wall St. J.*, December 5, 2011, at A17.

102. 132 S. Ct. 2566, 2577 (2012).

103. Huma Khan, "Should Supreme Court Justices Clarence Thomas, Elena Kagan Sit Out Health Care Case?," ABC News, February 10, 2011, http://abcnews.go.com/Politics/supreme-court-justice-clarence-thomas-sit-health-care/story?id=12878346.

104. Mark Sherman, "Sen. Hatch: Kagan Should Sit out Health Care Case," *USA Today*, February 5, 2011, http://usatoday30.usatoday.com/news/topstories/2011-02-04-3661380121_x.htm.

105. Id.; "Groups Target Thomas' Wife's Work to Force Him to Sit Out High Court Rulings on Health Care," Fox News, May 30, 2011, http://www.foxnews.com/politics/2011/05/30/groups-target-thomas-wife-seek-ouster-high-court-rulings/#ixzz1Vm5MKEdD. For a better understanding of the scope of the public dialogue on the topic, see Joan Biskupic, "Justices Face Conflict of Interest Questions," *USA Today*, April 18, 2011, http://abcnews.go.com/Politics/justices-face-conflict-interest-questions/story?id=13396040; editorial, "The Court's Recusal Problem," *N.Y. Times*, March 15, 2011, http://www.nytimes.com/2011/03/16/opinion/16wed3.html; editorial, "Supreme Court Ethics," *L.A. Times*, May 25, 2011, http://articles.latimes.com/2011/may/25/opinion/la-ed-judges-20110525; editorial, "Cloud over the Court," *N.Y. Times*, June 22, 2011, http://www.nytimes.com/2011/06/23/opinion/23thu4.html; Dahlia Lithwick, "Ethics Are for Other People," *Slate*, April 15, 2011, http://www.slate.com/id/2290726/; Herman Schwartz, "SCOTUS Needs an Ethics Code," *Politico*, May 13, 2011, http://dyn.politico.com/printstory.cfm?uuid=879EA44D-9C9E-4253-B17F-C3580641 2FF1; Russell Wheeler, "Regulating Supreme Court Justices' Ethics—'Cures Worse Than the Disease?'" Brookings Inst., March 22, 2011, http://www.brookings.edu/research/opinions/2011/03/21-justices-ethics-wheeler.

106. Nan Aron, "An Ethics Code for the High Court," *Wash. Post*, March 14,

2011, at A19; Nina Totenberg, "Bill Puts Ethics Spotlight on Supreme Court Justices," NPR, August 17, 2011, http://www.npr.org/2011/08/17/139646573 /bill-puts-ethics-spotlight-on-supreme-court-justices.

107. Mike McIntire, "The Justice and the Magnate," *N.Y. Times,* June 19, 2011, at A1.

108. Totenberg, "Bill Puts Ethics Spotlight on Supreme Court."

109. Justices Breyer, Ginsburg, and Sotomayor were connected with the American Bar Association, the American Sociological Association, and the American Civil Liberties Union, respectively. "The Justices' Junkets," *Wash. Post,* February 21, 2011, at A14.

110. The Supreme Court Transparency and Disclosure Act of 2011, H.R. 862, 112th Cong., 1st Sess. § 3(a)(2), (b) (2011), http://www.govtrack.us/congress /bill.xpd?bill=h112–862.

111. Letter from 132 Law Professors to the House and Senate Judiciary Committees, March 17, 2011, http://www.afj.org/judicial_ethics_sign_on_letter.pdf, at 1.

112. Supreme Court Transparency and Disclosure Act of 2011, at § 3(a)(2), (b). Using circuit court judges to review Supreme Court recusal decisions may appeal to those concerned with the ethical ramifications of current Supreme Court recusal practices, but there are significant constitutional problems with such an arrangement, including Article III's mandates that there be only "one supreme Court" and that Congress have power to create only "inferior Courts." U.S. Const., Art. III, § 1.

113. Eileen Malloy, "Supreme Court Justices Already Comply with Ethics Rules, Kennedy, Breyer Say," 79 *U.S.L.W.* 2389 (April 19, 2011).

114. Id.

115. Id.

116. Id.

117. Id. at 2390.

118. "Considering the Role of Judges under the Constitution of the United States," hearings before the Senate Committee on the Judiciary, 112th Cong., 1st Sess. (2011).

119. Id. at 27.

120. Id. at 28.

121. Id.

122. Id.

123. John G. Roberts Jr., 2011 Year-End Report on the Federal Judiciary 4 (2011), http://www.supremecourt.gov/publicinfo/year-end/2011year-endreport.pdf.

124. Id. at 7.

125. Id. at 7–8.

126. Id. at 5.

127. Federal judges may voluntarily submit their decisions for review by their peers on the court. In re United States, 158 F.3d 26, 34 (1st Cir. 1998). Some states such as Alaska, California, Michigan, Oklahoma, and Texas have adopted procedures whereby a judge's decision not to recuse may be reviewed by the other members of the same court. Alaska Stat. Ann. § 22.20.020(c) (West

2012); Cal. Civ. Proc. Code § 170.3(c)(5) (West 2012); MCR 2.003(D)(3)(b) (West 2012); Okla. Stat. Ann. tit. 12, Ch. 2, App. Rule 15(b) (West 2012); Tex. R. Civ. P. 18a(f), (g) (West 2012).

128. 28 U.S.C. §§ 291–297. The process of judicial assignment in the lower courts is discussed in greater detail in chapter 6.

129. 2011 Year-End Report, at 9.

130. Letter from Senators Leahy, Blumenthal, Durbin, Franken, and Whitehouse to Chief Justice John G. Roberts, February 13, 2012 (hereafter Letter from Five Senators to Chief Justice Roberts), http://sblog.s3.amazonaws.com /wp-content/uploads/2012/02/Senators-letter-on-SCt-ethics-2-13-12.pdf.

131. Letter from Chief Justice John G. Roberts to Senator Patrick J. Leahy, February 17, 2012, http://www.washingtonpost.com/r/2010–2019/Washington Post/2012/02/21/National-Politics/Graphics/Ltr_to_Chairman_Leahy.pdf.

132. "Supreme Court Ethics Act of 2013," H.R. 2902, 113th Cong., 1st Sess. (2015). The act was originally introduced in 2013 only to die in committee.

133. "Hearing on the Supreme Court Budget," hearings before the Financial Services and General Government Subcommittee of the House Appropriations Committee, 114th Cong., 1st Sess. (2015).

134. Id. at 14–15.

135. Id. at 14.

136. Steven Lubet, "Stonewalling, Leaks, and Counter-leaks: SCOTUS Ethics in the Wake of NFIB v. Sebelius," 47 *Val. U. L. Rev.* 883, 893 (2013).

137. Jacob Gershman, "Justice Ginsburg Comments on Abortion Law Stir Recusal Debate," *Wall St. J.*, October 1, 2014, http://blogs.wsj.com/law /2014/10/01/justice-ginsburg-comments-on-abortion-law-stir-recusal-de bate/; Tony Mauro, "Ginsburg Faulted for Comment on Texas Abortion Law," *Nat'l L.J.*, September 30, 2014, http://www.nationallawjournal.com/legaltimes /id=1202671814033/Ginsburg-Faulted-for-Comment-on-Texas-Abortion -Law?slreturn=20140922151944. The Court granted certiorari in the case, *Whole Woman's Health v. Cole*, on November 13, 2015. 84 *U.S.L.W.* 3111 (U.S. Nov. 13, 2015) (No. 15-274).

138. Alison Frankel, "Should Scalia Step Aside in Gay Marriage Cases?," Reuters, December 12, 2012, http://blogs.reuters.com/alison-frankel/2012/12/12 /should-scalia-step-aside-in-gay-marriage-cases/.

139. Mark Joseph Stern, "No Justice, Liberal or Conservative, Should Be Recused from the Gay Marriage Cases," *Slate*, January 26, 2015, http://www.slate .com/blogs/outward/2015/01/26/justices_shouldn_t_recuse_themselves _from_gay_marriage_cases.html; Emma Margolin, "Calls Increase for Ginsburg to Recuse Herself from Same-Sex Marriage Case," MSNBC.com, February 17, 2015, http://www.msnbc.com/msnbc/calls-increase-ginsburg-recuse-herself -same-sex-marriage-case.

140. Erwin Chemerinsky, "It's Time to Reform the Supreme Court—Here Are Five Ways to Do It," BillMoyers.com, July 21, 2014, http://billmoyers .com/2014/07/15/its-time-to-reform-the-supreme-court-here-are-five-ways-to -do-it/; Tony Mauro, "Sitting Out: Recusals Mount among Justices," *Nat'l L.J.*,

January 27, 2014, http://www.nationallawjournal.com/id=1202639866149
/Sitting-Out-Recusals-Mount-Among-the-Justices.

141. Louise M. Slaughter, "We Need a Code of Conduct for the Supreme Court," *Roll Call*, October 7, 2015, http://www.rollcall.com/news/we_need_a _code_of_conduct_for_the_supreme_court_commentary-244096-1.html. The only interested entity that appears to reject greater congressional regulation is the Court itself. Cheney v. United States District Court, 541 U.S. 913 (2004); Laird v. Tatum, 409 U.S. 824 (1972); Ruth Bader Ginsburg, "An Open Discussion with Ruth Bader Ginsburg," 36 *Conn. L. Rev.* 1033, 1039 (2004).

142. Professor Stempel explained that "the Court also lacks any formal rule, mechanism, or custom of permitting fact development in aid of a recusal motion. . . . [L]itigants questioning the impartiality of a Supreme Court Justice have never been permitted to develop the facts of the alleged conflict under the auspices of the Court." Stempel, "Rehnquist, Recusal, and Reform," at 642. He went on to point out that "occasionally, as in *Tatum*, a Justice will offer a version of the facts in answer to the motion, which hardly passes as meaningful discovery or even scrutiny." Id. A similar lack of factual development occurred in connection with Justice Scalia's decision not to recuse in *Cheney*. Amanda Frost, "Keeping Up Appearances: A Process-Oriented Approach to Judicial Recusal," 53 *U. Kan. L. Rev.* 531, 576 (2005).

143. Stempel, "Rehnquist, Recusal, and Reform," at 644; Frost, "Keeping Up Appearances," at 591–592.

144. 2011 Supreme Court Transparency and Disclosure Act, at § 3(b) (emphasis added). The prospect of allowing lower court judges to review Supreme Court recusal decisions potentially runs afoul of the constitutional requirement that there be "one supreme Court." U.S. Const., Art. III, § 1.

145. 2011 Supreme Court Transparency and Disclosure Act, at § 3(a)(2); Letter from 132 Law Professors, at 2.

146. Debra Lyn Bassett, "Recusal and the Supreme Court," 56 *Hastings L.J.* 657, 695 (2005).

147. William Yeomans and Herman Schwartz, "Roberts to America: Trust Us," *Politico*, January 24, 2012, http://www.politico.com/news/stories/0112/71895 .html.

148. Justin McCarthy, "Americans Losing Confidence in All Branches of U.S. Government," Gallup, June 30, 2014, http://www.gallup.com/poll/171992 /americans-losing-confidence-branches-gov.aspx.

149. Whether the Court is in fact politicized—or even a clearer understanding of what that phrase means—is a complicated and controversial question that is beyond the scope of this project. All that is presently required is to understand that the public is indeed concerned about the political motivations of the justices and that is relevant to their feelings about, and the justices' responsibilities regarding, the Court's recusal practices. David Paul Kuhn, "The Incredible Polarization and Politicization of the Supreme Court," *The Atlantic*, June 29, 2012, http://www.theatlantic.com/politics/archive/2012/06/the -incredible-polarization-and-politicization-of-the-supreme-court/259155/.

150. "Supreme Court Update: 26% Rate Supreme Court's Performance Positively," *Rasmussen Reports*, May 27, 2014, http://www.rasmussenreports.com /public_content/politics/mood_of_america/supreme_court_update.

151. United States v. Will, 449 U.S. 200, 213 (1980); Flamm, *Judicial Disqualification*, § 20.2.1, at 589–590.

152. Sir Frederick Pollock, *A First Book of Jurisprudence: For Students of the Common Law* 269 (5th ed. 1923).

153. 28 U.S.C. §§ 291, 292, 294 (2006). I argue in chapter 6 that Congress's provision for substitute judges may be a constitutional prerequisite for its setting recusal standards for the lower federal courts.

154. U.S. Const., Art. III, § 1.

155. Letter from Chief Justice Hughes to Senator Wheeler, March 22, 1937, http://newdeal.feri.org/court/hughes.htm; Russell Wheeler, "What's So Hard about Regulating Supreme Court Justices' Ethics?—A Lot," Brookings Inst., November 30, 2011, at 2, http://www.brookings.edu/research /papers/2011/11/28-courts-wheeler. Some highly respected commentators have argued that retired Supreme Court justices could, in some circumstances, sit in review of active justices' recusal decisions. Chemerinsky, "It's Time to Reform the Supreme Court"; Michael C. Dorf and Lisa T. McElroy, "Coming Off the Bench: Legal and Policy Implications of Proposals to Allow Retired Justices to Sit by Designation on the Supreme Court," 61 *Duke L.J.* 81, 104 (2011).

156. Cheney v. United States District Court, 541 U.S. 913, 915 (2004); Statement of Recusal Policy, at 1103.

157. Cheney, 541 U.S. at 915.

158. Steven Lubet described this phenomenon as the "certiorari conundrum." Steven Lubet, "Disqualification of Supreme Court Justices: The Certiorari Conundrum," 80 *Minn. L. Rev.* 657, 661–665 (1996).

159. U.S. Const., Art. III, § 2. The problem of multiple recusals is taken up in detail in chapter 3.

160. This phenomenon is considered by many to be the driving force behind the calls for Justices Kagan and Thomas to recuse themselves from cases reviewing the Affordable Care Act. Mukasey, "The ObamaCare Recusal Nonsense," at A17.

161. Cheney, 541 U.S. at 928.

162. Malloy, "Supreme Court Justices Already Comply," at 2389.

163. Id.

164. 2011 Year-End Report, at 7.

165. Flamm, *Judicial Disqualification*, § 29.4, at 916–917; Bassett, "Recusal and the Supreme Court," at 682–693; Ifill, "Do Judicial Appearances Matter?," at 619.

166. Letter from Chief Justice John G. Roberts to Senator Patrick J. Leahy.

167. 2011 Year-End Report, at 9.

168. Id. at 7.

169. Dorf and McElroy, "Coming Off the Bench," at 99. Due to her serving as solicitor general immediately prior to joining the Court, Justice Kagan recused herself from "about half of the [first] 54 cases" on the Court's docket for the

2010 term. Times Topics, "Elena Kagan," *N.Y. Times*, October 4, 2010, http://topics.nytimes.com/top/reference/timestopics/people/k/kagan_elena/index.html.

170. Frost, "Keeping Up Appearances," at 569.

171. Ifill, "Do Judicial Appearances Matter?," at 622.

172. Stempel, "Rehnquist, Recusal, and Reform," at 642.

173. Eric A. Posner and Adrian Vermeule, "Constitutional Showdowns," 156 *U. Pa. L. Rev.* 991, 997 (2008).

3. The Constitutionality of Supreme Court Recusal Standards

1. Montesquieu, *The Spirit of the Laws*, bk. XI, ch. 6 (trans. Thomas Nugent, 1949). Montesquieu's views regarding the separation of powers were explicitly relied upon by several of the convention delegates. 1 Max Farrand, *The Records of the Federal Convention of 1787*, at 391 (1911) (remarks of Butler); 2 Farrand at 34 (remarks of Madison).

2. 131 S. Ct. 2594, 2608 (2011).

3. Id. at 2609.

4. Linda Jellum, "'Which Is to Be Master,' the Judiciary or the Legislature? When Statutory Directives Violate Separation of Powers," 56 *UCLA L. Rev.* 837, 861 (2009).

5. Felix Frankfurter and James Landis, "Power of Congress over Procedure in Criminal Contempts in 'Inferior' Federal Courts—A Study in Separation of Powers," 37 *Harv. L. Rev.* 1010, 1012–1013 (1924); Jellum, "Which Is to Be Master," at 870.

6. Peter L. Strauss, "The Place of Agencies in Government: Separation of Powers and the Fourth Branch," 84 *Colum. L. Rev.* 573, 617 (1984); William W. Van Alstyne, "The Role of Congress in Determining Incidental Powers of the President and of the Federal Courts: A Comment on the Horizontal Effect of the Sweeping Clause," 40 *Law & Contemp. Probs.* 102, 107 (1976).

7. Constitutional structure is a form of interpretation that refers to the document as a whole to discern the meaning of a given provision.

8. U.S. Const., Art. III, § 1.

9. U.S. Const., Art. I, § 8, cl. 3.

10. James S. Liebman and William F. Ryan, "'Some Effectual Power': The Quantity and Quality of Decisionmaking Required of Article III Courts," 98 *Colum. L. Rev.* 696, 708 (1998).

11. U.S. Const., Art. III, § 1; William F. Ryan, "Rush to Judgment: A Constitutional Analysis of Time Limits on Judicial Decisions," 77 *B.U. L. Rev.* 761, 767 (1997); Frankfurter and Landis, "Power of Congress over Procedure," at 1018.

12. Joint Anti-Fascist Refugee Comm. v. McGrath, 341 U.S. 123, 150 (1951) (Frankfurter, J., concurring); Evan Caminker, "Allocating the Judicial Power in a 'Unified Judiciary,'" 78 *Tex. L. Rev.* 1513, 1518 (2000); Frankfurter and Landis, "Power of Congress over Procedure," at 1017.

13. Robert J. Pushaw Jr., "The Inherent Powers of Federal Courts and the Structural Constitution," 86 *Iowa L. Rev.* 735, 822 (2001).

14. Richard E. Flamm, *Judicial Disqualification* §§ 1.2–1.4, at 5–8 (2d ed. 2007).

15. This is consistent with historical accounts of the importance placed on the independence of judges in the period. Scott Douglas Gerber, *A Distinct Judicial Power: The Origins of an Independent Judiciary, 1606–1787*, at 34–37 (2011).

16. Flamm, *Judicial Disqualification*, § 1.2, at 6; John P. Frank, "Disqualification of Judges," 56 *Yale L.J.* 605, 611–612 (1947).

17. United States v. Will, 449 U.S. 200, 213 (1980); Flamm, *Judicial Disqualification*, § 20.2.1, at 589–590.

18. Frank, "Disqualification of Judges," at 609–610.

19. Flamm, *Judicial Disqualification*, § 1.2, at 6.

20. Id. at § 1.4, at 8.

21. 1 Stat. 278. A detailed historical account of American recusal law is provided in chapter 1.

22. Flamm, *Judicial Disqualification*, § 32.1, at 669.

23. Id.

24. Frank, "Disqualification of Judges," at 612.

25. 1 Stat. 278.

26. Frankfurter and Landis, "Power of Congress over Procedure," at 1018.

27. 343 U.S. 579 (1952).

28. Id. at 635–638 (Jackson, J., concurring).

29. Id. at 610–611 (Frankfurter, J., concurring).

30. 17 U.S. 316 (1819).

31. 1 Charles Warren, *The Supreme Court in United States History* 504–505 (rev. ed. 1926).

32. U.S. Const., Art. I, § 8, cl. 18.

33. McCulloch, 17 U.S. at 401.

34. Id. at 401, 402.

35. Id. at 402.

36. 272 U.S. 52 (1926).

37. Id. at 164.

38. Id. at 163; Rebecca Brown, "Tradition and Insight," 103 *Yale L.J.* 177, 193 (2003).

39. Myers, 272 U.S. at 163.

40. Id. at 176.

41. Brown, "Tradition and Insight," at 193.

42. 279 U.S. 655 (1929).

43. U.S. Const., Art. I, § 7, cl. 2.

44. Pocket Veto Case, 279 U.S. at 672.

45. Id. at 691.

46. Id.; Brown, "Tradition and Insight," at 194.

47. 453 U.S. 654 (1981).

48. Id. at 686.

49. 236 U.S. 459 (1915).

50. Id. at 471.

51. 50 U.S.C. §§ 1541–1548.

52. Campbell v. Clinton, 203 F.3d 19 (D.C. Cir. 2000). The majority opinion in *Campbell* was authored by Judge Laurence Silberman and held that the congressman seeking to challenge President Bill Clinton's use of force in Yugoslavia lacked standing to do so. In a separate concurrence to his own majority opinion, Judge Silberman added that the challenge was also outside the courts' authority because it amounted to a nonjusticiable "political question." Id. at 24–25 (Silberman, J., concurring).

53. Jack Goldsmith, "War Power: The President's Campaign against Libya Is Constitutional," *Slate*, March 21, 2011, http://www.slate.com/id/2288869/; David B. Rivkin Jr. and Lee A Casey, "Why Our Libya Strikes Don't Require Congressional Approval," *Wash. Post*, March 24, 2011, http://www.washington post.com/opinions/why-obamas-libya-strikes-dont-require-congressional-ap proval/2011/03/24/ABgnxMQB_story.html; Charlie Savage, "Attack Renews Debate over Congressional Consent," *N.Y. Times*, March 21, 2011, http://www .nytimes.com/2011/03/22/world/africa/22powers.html.

54. 501 U.S. 32 (1991).

55. Id. at 38, 41.

56. Id. at 40.

57. Id. at 47.

58. 370 U.S. 626 (1962).

59. Id. at 631–632 (1962).

60. 514 U.S. 211 (1995).

61. Id. at 230.

62. Scholars have argued—quite convincingly—that the use of long-standing practice to discern constitutional meaning is far more difficult to justify in individual rights, as opposed to separation of powers, cases. Brown, "Tradition and Insight," at 195–196. But see INS v. Chadha, 462 U.S. 919, 944–945 (1983) (arguing that frequent reliance on legislative veto provisions does not insulate Congress from searching judicial inquiry into their constitutionality).

63. Frank, "Disqualification of Judges," at 612. The review notes of section 455 explained that its predecessor, "Section 24 of Title 28, U.S.C., 1940 ed., applied only to district judges. The revised section is made applicable to all justices and judges of the United States." 28 U.S.C. § 455 rev. notes.

64. 28 U.S.C. § 455(a).

65. "Testimony of Chief Justice Stone," hearings before House Committee on the Judiciary on H.R. 2808, 78th Cong., 1st Sess. 24 (1943).

66. 327 U.S. 686 (1946).

67. Sherrilyn A. Ifill, "Do Judicial Appearances Matter? Judicial Impartiality and the Supreme Court in *Bush v. Gore*," 61 *Md. L. Rev.* 606, 620 (2002). "The 'historic practice' of the United States Supreme Court has always been to refer motions for recusal to the Justice whose disqualification is sought. Thus . . . the actual procedure by which the decision is made is truly a creature of tradition." R. Matthew Pearson, Note, "Duck, Duck, Recuse? Foreign Common Law Guidance & Improving Recusal of Supreme Court Justices," 62 *Wash. & Lee L. Rev.* 1799, 1813 (2005).

68. This is even more telling when compared with legislative enactments like Title VI of the Ethics in Government Act, which applied direct pressure to the executive branch by creating the position of "independent counsel" to investigate and prosecute criminal activity by certain high-ranking members of that branch. 28 U.S.C. §§ 591–599 (1982). The portion of the act dealing with the independent counsel expired in 1999.

69. A detailed account of the Court's resistance to the two bills is included in chapter 2.

70. 28 U.S.C. § 455.

71. Debra Lyn Bassett, "Recusal and the Supreme Court," 56 *Hastings L.J.* 657, 676–680 (2005).

72. 409 U.S. 824 (1972).

73. Id. at 829–830.

74. Id. at 831.

75. Id. at 833. Chief Justice Rehnquist made the identical argument in his memorandum explaining his decision not to recuse in *Microsoft v. United States:* "Here . . . there is no way to replace a recused Justice. Not only is the Court deprived of the participation of one of its nine Members, but the even number of those remaining creates a risk of affirmance of a lower court decision by an equally divided court." 530 U.S. 1301, 1303 (2000).

76. 541 U.S. 913 (2004). A more thorough discussion of Justice Scalia's decision in *Cheney* is included in chapter 2.

77. Id. at 924–926.

78. Justice Scalia was concerned that more stringent recusal standards for the Court could "give elements of the press a veto over participation of any Justices who had social contacts with . . . a named official" and encourage "so-called investigative journalists to suggest improprieties and demand recusals." Id. at 927.

79. Statement of Recusal Policy, reprinted in Flamm, *Judicial Disqualification,* App. D at 1101.

80. Bassett, "Recusal and the Supreme Court," at 681; Ifill, "Do Judicial Appearances Matter?," at 625, 626.

81. 79 *U.S.L.W.* 2389 (April 19, 2011).

82. John G. Roberts Jr., 2011 Year-End Report on the Federal Judiciary 7, 9 (2011), http://www.supremecourt.gov/publicinfo/year-end/2011year-endre port.pdf.

83. Letter from Chief Justice John G. Roberts to Senator Patrick J. Leahy, *Wash. Post,* February 17, 2012, http://www.washingtonpost.com/r/2010–2019 /WashingtonPost/2012/02/21/National-Politics/Graphics/Ltr_to_Chair man_Leahy.pdf.

84. It is well established that the Supreme Court is not subject to regulation by the lower courts or the Judicial Conference of the United States, so only another coequal branch of government would have the constitutional authority to influence the justices' recusal practices. 28 U.S.C. § 331 (2014).

85. U.S. Const., Art. III, § 1.

86. U.S. Const., Art. I, § 1; Art. II, § 1.

87. U.S. Const., Art. III, § 1.

88. U.S. Const., Art. III, § 2.

89. Livingston v. Story, 34 U.S. (9 Pet.) 632, 656 (1835).

90. The relationship between the Ordain and Establish Clause and legislative recusal standards for the lower courts is discussed in greater detail in chapter 6.

91. Tara Leigh Grove, "A (Modest) Separation of Powers Success Story," 87 *Notre Dame L. Rev.* 1647, 1652 (2012).

92. Liebman and Ryan, "'Some Effectual Power,'" at 708.

93. Reed Elsevier, Inc. v. Muchnick, 130 S. Ct. 1237, 1243 (2010).

94. The one notable exception is *United States v. Klein*, 80 U.S. (13 Wall.) 128 (1872), which is discussed in the following paragraphs.

95. 518 U.S. 651 (1996).

96. Id. at 662.

97. Ex Parte Yerger, 75 U.S. (8 Wall.) 85 (1868); Ex Parte McCardle, 74 U.S. (7 Wall.) 506 (1868).

98. 80 U.S. at 128.

99. Id. at 145–147.

100. Id. at 146.

101. Id. at 147.

102. The Court reached a similar conclusion when it announced that Congress may not reopen its final decisions in *Plaut.* The hypothetical jurisdiction-stripping statute currently under discussion does not reopen a final decision, but it does potentially dictate the substantive result in a case before the Court.

103. 327 U.S. 686 (1946).

104. John Frank, "Disqualification of Judges: In Support of the Bayh Bill," 35 *Law & Contemp. Probs.* 43, 44 (1970).

105. 2011 Year-End Report, at 8–9.

106. U.S. Const., Art. I, § 2, cl. 5; U.S. Const., Art. I, § 3, cl. 6.

107. This analysis does not consider the text or structure of Article II because there is no clearly articulated executive power that could conceivably interfere with the Supreme Court's adjudication of specific cases. The president does not have the power to remove Supreme Court justices because they are not executive officers, and any suggestion to the contrary would be preempted by the Impeachment Clauses. Any attempt to thwart Supreme Court adjudication through assertions of executive privilege or national security concerns would ultimately be considered legal issues for the justices to decide. United States v. Nixon, 418 U.S. 683, 705 (1974).

108. U.S. Const., Art. III, § 1.

109. U.S. Const. Art. I, § 2, cl. 5; U.S. Const., Art. I, § 3, cl. 6.

110. Saikrishna Prakash and Steven Smith argue from historical evidence that the "good Behaviour" requirement in Article III allows for the removal of federal judges from office for conduct less egregious than high crimes and misdemeanors, and by procedural mechanisms less cumbersome than impeachment by the House and conviction by the Senate. Saikrishna Prakash and Steven D. Smith, "How to Remove a Federal Judge," 116 *Yale L.J.* 72 (2006).

111. Michael J. Gerhardt, *The Federal Impeachment Process: A Constitutional and Historical Analysis* 83–84 (1996).

112. Id. at 85, 86.

113. Congress does of course have the authority to create official positions within the federal government that function as at-will employment (individuals who serve at the pleasure of the president) or that expire after a term of years, in the case of many independent agencies. In these cases, however, the separation-of-powers calculus is different in that the officials being removed by means other than impeachment are not constitutionally guaranteed to hold those offices "during good Behaviour." U.S. Const., Art. III, § 1.

114. Michael C. Dorf and Lisa T. McElroy, "Coming Off the Bench: Legal and Policy Implications of Proposals to Allow Retired Justices to Sit by Designation on the Supreme Court," 61 *Duke L.J.* 81, 99 (2011).

115. Karl Llewellyn famously made this point by documenting the counter-maxim for many well-known maxims of statutory interpretation. Karl Llewellyn, *The Common Law Tradition* App. C (1960).

116. 28 U.S.C. § 455 (2014).

117. Flamm, *Judicial Disqualification*, § 33.1, at 986–987.

118. It is possible that recusal was designed as a system of self-punishment and deterrence, but that would still make it distinct from impeachment, which is quite explicitly a punitive system driven by external forces.

119. U.S. Const., Art. II, § 1.

120. Gerhardt, *The Federal Impeachment Process*, at 85.

121. U.S. Const., Art. I, § 2, cl. 5.

122. U.S. Const., Art. I, § 3, cl. 6; U.S. Const., Art. II, § 4; U.S. Const., Art. III, § 1.

123. Peter Shane, "Who May Discipline or Remove Federal Judges? A Constitutional Analysis," 142 *U. Pa. L. Rev.* 209, 218–219 (1993).

124. U.S. Const., Art. I, § 8, cl. 18.

125. Id.

126. U.S. Const., Art. II, § 1; U.S. Const., Art. III, § 1.

127. City of Boerne v. Flores, 521 U.S. 507, 519 (1997).

128. This was, in a nutshell, the position taken by a majority of the Court in Plaut v. Spendthrift Farm, Inc., 514 U.S. 211 (1995).

129. Chambers v. NASCO, 501 U.S. 32, 47 (1991); Michaelson v. United States, 266 U.S. 42, 66 (1924); United States v. Klein, 80 U.S. (13 Wall.) 128, 146 (1871); United States v. Hudson, 11 U.S. (7 Cranch) 32, 34 (1812).

130. Pushaw, "The Inherent Powers of Federal Courts," at 739–740; Amy Cohen Barrett, "Procedural Common Law," 94 *Va. L. Rev.* 813, 817–820 (2008); Frankfurter and Landis, "Power of Congress over Procedure"; Elizabeth T. Lear, "Congress, the Federal Courts, and *Forum Non Conveniens:* Friction on the Frontier of the Inherent Power," 91 *Iowa L. Rev.* 1147, 1162–1163 (2006).

131. David E. Engdahl, "Intrinsic Limits of Congress' Power Regarding the Judicial Branch," 1999 *BYU L. Rev.* 75, 103.

132. A. Leo Levin and Anthony Amsterdam, "Legislative Control over Judicial Rulemaking: A Problem in Constitutional Revision," 107 *U. Pa. L. Rev.* 1, 30 (1958); Frankfurter and Landis, "Power of Congress over Procedure," at 1020–1023; Pushaw, "The Inherent Powers of Federal Courts," at 741; Van Alstyne, "The Role of Congress," at 107.

133. Pushaw, "The Inherent Powers of Federal Courts," at 760–782.

134. Missouri v. Holland, 252 U.S. 416, 434 (1920).

135. Liebman and Ryan, "'Some Effectual Power,'" at 771. At least one commentator takes the position that inherent judicial power of the federal courts only attaches in the face of congressional silence. Benjamin Barton, "An Article I Theory of the Inherent Powers of the Federal Courts," 61 *Cath. Univ. L. Rev.* 1 (2011).

136. Chambers v. NASCO, Inc., 501 U.S. 32, 43 (1991); Pushaw, "The Inherent Powers of Federal Courts," at 738.

137. 514 U.S. 211 (1995).

138. U.S. Const., Art. III, § 1.

139. U.S. Const., Art. III, § 2, cl. 2.

140. Flamm, *Judicial Disqualification*, § 33.1, at 983–984.

141. 28 U.S.C. § 455(a)(2014).

142. Cheney v. United States District Court, 541 U.S. 913, 916 (2004).

143. The more complex but likely scenario is where recusal leaves an even number of justices to decide a case and the final vote is a tie, resulting in a mandatory affirmance of the decision below without precedential value. Cheney, 541 U.S. at 915; Note, "Disqualification of Judges and Justices in the Federal Courts," 86 *Harv. L. Rev.* 736, 749 (1973). From October 2005 through July 2014, an average of 20 percent of the Court's merits opinions were 5–4 decisions, meaning that a single recusal could create a real possibility for a tie in about one in every five cases before the Court. Kedar S. Bhatia, "Stat Pack for October Term 2013," ScotusBlog, July 3, 2014, http://sblog.s3.amazonaws.com/wp-content/uploads/2014/07/SCOTUSblog_Stat_Pack_for_OT13.pdf. This increased likelihood, however, is not necessary to the larger point that expanding recusal standards by definition increases the likelihood that recusals could interfere with the Court's inherent authority to completely decide the cases before it.

144. The Supreme Court Transparency and Disclosure Act of 2011.

145. Monroe H. Freedman, "Duck-Blind Justice: Justice Scalia's Memorandum in the *Cheney* Case," 18 *Geo. J. Legal Ethics* 229, 232 (2004).

146. Cheney, 541 U.S. at 916.

147. Id. at 916–917.

148. That number could even be argued down to two. Justice Ginsburg initially attended Harvard Law School—the alma mater of five of her current colleagues—but graduated from Columbia Law School, raising the total number of law schools attended by the current Court to three.

149. 28 U.S.C. §§ 1, 2109.

150. Six of those cases occurred between 1950 and 2007. United States v. Hatter, 519 U.S. 801 (1996); Haig v. Bissonette, 485 U.S. 264 (1988); Arizona v. United States District Court, 459 U.S. 1191 (1983); Arizona v. Ash Grove Cement Co., 459 U.S. 1190 (1983); Sloan v. Nixon, 419 U.S. 958 (1974); Prichard v. United States, 339 U.S. 974 (1950). They all involved the minimum number of recusals (four) necessary to defeat a quorum. The remaining twelve cases were all before the Roberts Court. Eleven of them named sitting Supreme Court

justices as defendants. Smith v. Scalia, 84 *U.S.L.W.* 3215 (U.S. Nov. 30, 2015); Missud v. California, 136 S. Ct. 36 (2015); Sibley v. Supreme Court, 133 S. Ct. 393 (2012); Johnson v. Obama, 132 S. Ct. 398 (2011); Murphy v. Kollar-Kotelly, 132 S. Ct. 76 (2011); Jones v. Supreme Court, 131 S. Ct. 1824 (2011); Smith v. Thomas, 131 S. Ct. 1614 (2011); Henderson v. Sony Pictures, 561 U.S. 1020 (2010); Sibley v. Alito, 559 U.S. 965 (2010); Awala v. Five United States Supreme Court Justices, 552 U.S. 1088 (2008); Sibley v. Breyer, 552 U.S. 987 (2007). The remaining case, from 2008, involved an extensive list of major corporations as defendants and resulted in the recusal of four justices, thereby defeating a quorum. American Isuzu Motors, Inc. v. Ntsebeza, 553 U.S. 1028 (2008).

151. Haig v. Bissonette, 485 U.S. 264 (1988).

152. Emily Chertoff, "Occupy Wounded Knee: A 71-Day Siege and a Forgotten Civil Rights Movement," *The Atlantic*, October 23, 2012, http://www.theatlantic.com/national/archive/2012/10/occupy-wounded-knee-a-71-day-siege-and-a-forgotten-civil-rights-movement/263998/. The grievances by the occupants of Wounded Knee were more numerous and more complicated, but the alleged failure of the United States to live up to its treaty obligations was significant among them. Id.

153. Id.

154. Bissonette, 485 U.S. at 264.

155. Tony Mauro, "When the Justices Sit on the Side," *Nat'l L.J.*, October 19, 2015, http://www.nationallawjournal.com/id=1202740010412/When-the-Justices-Sit-On-the-Side?slreturn=20151104155113.

156. 253 U.S. 245 (1920).

157. U.S. Const., Art. III, § 1.

158. 314 U.S. 583 (1941).

159. 320 U.S. 708 (1943).

160. Id.

161. The current version of that statutory requirement can be found at 28 U.S.C. § 2109.

162. 327 U.S. 686 (1946).

163. Id.; Frank, "Disqualification of Judges," at 626.

164. Id.

165. 449 U.S. 200 (1980).

166. U.S. Const., Art. III, § 1.

167. Will, 449 U.S. at 212.

168. Id. at 213, 214.

169. Id. at 216.

170. Id. at 217.

171. Id. The lower courts continue to share this view. In 2015, the Ninth Circuit relied on the rule of necessity to hold, in a case in which a plaintiff sued every judge in the District of Montana, that "where a litigant sues all the judges" in a district or circuit, "none of the judges are required to recuse." Glick v. Edwards, 803 F.3d 505, 509 (9th Cir. 2015).

172. Will, 449 U.S. at 213–214.

173. "Considering the Role of Judges under the Constitution of the United States," hearings before the Senate Committee on the Judiciary, 112th Cong., 1st Sess. 28–29 (2011).

174. Id. at 29.

175. Id.

176. Ginsburg, "An Open Discussion with Ruth Bader Ginsburg," 36 *Conn. L. Rev.* 1033, 1039 (2004).

177. Dorf and McElroy, "Coming Off the Bench," at 107–112.

178. Id.

179. The distinction between retired and resigned justices hinges on the idea that once they have resigned, a justice no longer holds his commission to serve on the Court. A retired justice, by contrast, has just ceased to be an active member of the Court, much like a lower court judge who assumes senior status.

180. Dorf and McElroy, "Coming Off the Bench," at 111.

181. Jeffrey W. Stempel, "Rehnquist, Recusal, and Reform," 53 *Brook. L. Rev.* 589, 656–661 (1987).

182. U.S. Const., Art. III, § 1.

183. 28 U.S.C. § 2109 (2014).

184. The same charge of unconstitutionality would adhere if the president failed to appoint enough candidates.

185. United States v. Will, 449 U.S. 200 (1980); Evans v. Gore, 253 U.S. 245 (1920).

186. 327 U.S. 686 (1946).

187. The Supreme Court Transparency and Disclosure Act of 2011; Bassett, "Recusal and the Supreme Court," at 693–697.

188. Caminker, "Allocating the Judicial Power," at 1519; Engdahl, "Intrinsic Limits of Congress' Power," at 89–90, 101–103; Ryan, "Rush to Judgment," at 798.

189. Bassett, "Recusal and the Supreme Court," at 695.

190. "Hearing on the Supreme Court Budget," hearings before the Financial Services and General Government Subcommittee of the House Appropriations Committee, 114th Cong., 1st Sess. 14 (2015).

191. Stempel, "Rehnquist, Recusal, and Reform," at 644.

192. Jewell Ridge Coal Corp. v. Local No. 6167, United Mine Workers of Am., 325 U.S. 897 (1945); Dennis J. Hutchinson, "The Black-Jackson Feud," 1988 Sup. Ct. Rev. 203.

193. 2011 Year-End Report, at 9.

194. Letter from Thomas Jefferson to John B. Colvin, reprinted in 9 *The Writings of Thomas Jefferson* 279 (Paul Leicester Ford ed., 1892–1899).

195. 337 U.S. 1, 37 (1949).

196. Letter from 132 Law Professors.

197. The Supreme Court Transparency and Disclosure Act of 2011, § 3(b).

198. William Blackstone, 3 *Commentaries on the Laws of England* 361 (1768).

199. Stempel, "Rehnquist, Recusal, and Reform," at 642; Dorf and McElroy, "Coming Off the Bench," at 99.

200. Jonathan L. Entin, "Separation of Powers, the Political Branches, and the Limits of Judicial Review," 51 *Ohio St. L.J.* 175, 226 (1990).

201. Kevin Hopkins, "Supreme Court Leaks and Recusals: A Response to Professor Steven Lubet's Supreme Court Ethics in the Wake of *NFIB v. Sebelius*," 47 *Val. U. L. Rev.* 925, 932 (2013).

202. The Court articulated this principle in *City of Boerne v. Flores*, when it explained that "Congress does not enforce a constitutional right by changing what the right is. It has been given the power 'to enforce,' not the power to determine what constitutes a constitutional violation." 521 U.S. 507, 519 (1997). A more detailed discussion of how due process principles should shape the justices' recusal practices is included in chapter 5.

4. *Constitutional Solutions*

1. Stern v. Marshall, 131 S. Ct. 2594, 2620 (2011). Chief Justice Roberts borrowed this quote from Justice Black's opinion more than fifty years earlier in Reid v. Covert, 354 U.S. 1, 39 (1957).

2. Michael Doyle, "A Flurry of Briefs as Supreme Court's Same-Sex Marriage Case Looms," McClatchyDC.com, March 6, 2015, http://www.mcclatchy dc.com/2015/03/06/258938/a-flurry-of-briefs-as-supreme.html.

3. John Dorfman, "What Enron, WorldCom, Tyco Fiascos Can Teach Us," Bloomberg, March 2, 2004, http://www.bloomberg.com/apps/news?pid=news archive&sid=aqrJ2FjoXJjo.

4. Free Enterprise Fund v. Public Co. Acct. Oversight Bd., 510 U.S. 477 (2010).

5. Anthony J. Franze and R. Reeves Anderson, "Commentary: The Court's Increasing Reliance on Amicus Curiae in the Past Term," *Nat'l L.J.*, August 24, 2011, at 1, http://www.arnoldporter.com/resources/documents/Arnold &PorterLLP_NationalLawJournal_8.24.11.pdf.

6. 134 S. Ct. 2550 (2014).

7. District of Columbia v. Heller, 554 U.S. 570 (2008).

8. United States v. Windsor, 133 S. Ct. 2675 (2013); National Fed. Indep. Bus. v. Sebelius, 132 S. Ct. 2566 (2012); Obergefell v. Hodges, 135 S. Ct. 2584 (2015).

9. Peter L. Strauss, "The Place of Agencies in Government: Separation of Powers and the Fourth Branch," 84 *Colum. L. Rev.* 573, 617 (1984).

10. Robert C. Post and Reva B. Siegel, "Legislative Constitutionalism and Section Five Power: Policentric Interpretation of the Family and Medical Leave Act," 112 *Yale L.J.* 1943, 1966 (2003).

11. 12 *The Papers of James Madison* 238 (William T. Hutchinson et al., eds., 1962–1991); *The Federalist* No. 49 (J. Madison).

12. Letter from Thomas Jefferson to Mrs. John Adams, September 11, 1804, reprinted in 11 *The Writings of Thomas Jefferson* 49, 50 (Andrew A. Lipscomb ed., 1905).

13. President Jackson's Veto Message to the Senate, July 10, 1832, reprinted in 2 *Messages and Papers of the Presidents* 576, 582 (James D. Richardson ed., 1908).

14. 418 U.S. 683, 703 (1974).

15. Symposium, "The Most Disparaged Branch: The Role of Congress in the Twenty-First Century, Panel III: Is Congress Capable of Conscientious Responsible Constitutional Interpretation?," 89 *B.U. L. Rev.* 499 (2009); Louis Fisher, "Constitutional Interpretation by Members of Congress," 63 *N.C. L. Rev.* 707 (1985); Abner Mikva, "How Well Does Congress Support and Defend the Constitution?" 61 *N.C. L. Rev.* 587, 590 (1983).

16. Elizabeth Garrett and Adrian Vermeule, "Institutional Design of a Thayerian Congress," 50 *Duke L.J.* 1277 (2001).

17. Larry Alexander and Frederick Schauer, "On Extrajudicial Constitutional Interpretation," 110 *Harv. L. Rev.* 1359 (1997).

18. James Bradley Thayer, "The Origin and Scope of the American Doctrine of Constitutional Law," 7 *Harv. L. Rev.* 129 (1893).

19. Id. at 136.

20. Alexander and Schauer, "On Extrajudicial Constitutional Interpretation," at 1359–1360. See also Michael Stokes Paulsen, "The Most Dangerous Branch: Executive Power to Say What the Law Is," 83 *Geo. L.J.* 217, 343–345 (1994); Mark V. Tushnet, "The Hardest Question in Constitutional Law," 81 *Minn. L. Rev.* 1, 25–28 (1996).

21. Jonathan L. Entin, "Separation of Powers, the Political Branches, and the Limits of Judicial Review," 51 *Ohio St. L.J.* 175, 226 (1990).

22. Clinton v. Jones 520 U.S. 681, 702, 703 (1997); Youngstown Sheet & Tube Co. v. Sawyer, 343 U.S. 579 (1952) (Jackson, J., concurring).

23. Paulsen, "The Most Dangerous Branch," at 228–229.

24. Id.

25. David Pozen refers to such considerations by the coordinate branches as "separation-of-powers conventions." David E. Pozen, "Self-Help and the Separation of Powers," 124 *Yale L.J.* 2, 34–35 (2014).

26. Letter from Senators Leahy, Blumenthal, Durbin, Franken, and White-house to Chief Justice John G. Roberts, February 17, 2012, http://sblog.s3 .amazonaws.com/wp-content/uploads/2012/02/Senators-letter-on-SCt-eth ics-2–13–12.pdf.

27. William Yeomans and Herman Schwartz, "Roberts to America: Trust Us," *Politico*, January 24, 2012, http://www.politico.com/news/stories/0112/71895 .html.

28. Sherrilyn Ifill, "The Chief Strikes Out," *Concurring Opinions*, January 4, 2012, http://www.concurringopinions.com/archives/2012/01/sherrilyn-ifills -the-chief-strikes-out.html.

29. Supreme Court Ethics Act of 2013, H.R. 2920, 113th Cong, 1st Sess. (2013).

30. Ifill, "The Chief Strikes Out."

31. There are several justiciability doctrines that have arisen from Article III's statement that the courts may resolve "cases" and "controversies." U.S. Const.,

Art. III. § 1. The most common is standing doctrine, in which the Court asks if the plaintiff has been personally harmed such that an actual case or controversy exists for the court to resolve. Lujan v. Defenders of Wildlife, 504 U.S. 555 (1992). The justiciability doctrine most directly implicated by interbranch disputes like that between Congress and the Court over recusal is the political question doctrine, which prevents courts from resolving cases that are more appropriately committed to the political branches. The Court has explained, "'In determining whether a question falls within (the political question) category, the appropriateness under our system of government of attributing finality to the action of the political departments and also the lack of satisfactory criteria for a judicial determination are dominant considerations.'" Baker v. Carr, 369 U.S. 186, 210 (1962).

32. 50 U.S.C. §§ 1541–1548 (2014).

33. Members of Congress raised concerns under the War Powers Resolution during President Clinton's bombing of Kosovo in 1999 and President Barack Obama's bombing of Libya in 2011, and in both instances there was much public and scholarly debate over the constitutional basis for those objections. Geoffrey S. Corn, "Clinton, Kosovo, and the Final Destruction of the War Powers Resolution," 42 *Wm. & Mary L. Rev.* 1149 (2001); Jack Goldsmith, "War Power: The President's Campaign against Libya Is Constitutional," *Slate*, March 21, 2011, http://www.slate.com/id/2288869/. In neither case, however, was there any serious threat of legal action by Congress to enforce the requirements of the resolution.

34. U.S. Const., Art. II, § 2.

35. Jeffrey K. Tulis, "On Congress and Constitutional Responsibility," 89 *B.U.L. Rev.* 515, 516–517 (2009); John Hart Ely, *War and Responsibility: Constitutional Lessons of Vietnam and Its Aftermath* 49 (1993); Louis Fisher, *Presidential War Power* 192 (1995); Harold Hongju Koh, *The National Security Constitution* 39–40, 123 (1990).

36. Charles A. Shanor, *American Constitutional Law: Structure and Reconstruction* 208 (4th ed. 2009); Campbell v. Clinton, 203 F.3d 19 (D.C. Cir. 2000), cert. denied, Campbell v. Clinton, 531 U.S. 815 (2000).

37. Russell Wheeler, "Regulating Supreme Court Justices' Ethics—'Cures Worse Than the Disease?'" Brookings Inst., March 3, 2011, http://www.brookings.edu/opinions/2011/0321_justices_ethics_wheeler.aspx?p=1; Michael C. Dorf and Lisa T. McElroy, "Coming Off the Bench: Legal and Policy Implications of Proposals to Allow Retired Justices to Sit by Designation on the Supreme Court," 61 *Duke L.J.* 81, 107–112 (2011).

38. Marbury v. Madison, 5 U.S. (1 Cranch) 137, 177 (1803).

39. There has been much discussion of the "antimajoritarian difficulty" presented by judicial review of validly enacted statutes. Alexander Bickel, *The Least Dangerous Branch: The Supreme Court at the Bar of Politics* (1962).

40. 272 U.S. 52 (1926).

41. 39 U.S.C. § 31 (1876).

42. Myers, 272 U.S. at 52.

43. Fisher, *Presidential War Power*, at 60–64.

44. Humphrey's Executor v. United States, 295 U.S. 602 (1935).

45. Id.

46. Free Enterprise Fund v. Public Co. Acct. Oversight Bd., 130 S. Ct. 3138 (2010).

47. U.S. Const., Art. III, § 2, cl. 2. The scope of Congress's power under the Exceptions Clause is discussed in detail in chapter 3.

48. Felker v. Turpin, 518 U.S. 651 (1996); Ex Parte Yerger, 75 U.S. (8 Wall.) 85 (1869); Ex Parte McCardle, 74 U.S. 7 (Wall.) 506 (1869).

49. 80 U.S. 128 (1871).

50. U.S. Const., Art. III, § 1; U.S. Const., Art. II, § 2, cl. 1. The *Klein* Court went on to explain that "it is clear that the legislature cannot change the effect of [] a pardon any more than the executive can change a law. Yet this is attempted by the provision under consideration. . . . This certainly impairs the executive authority and directs the court to be instrumental to that end." Klein, 80 U.S. at 147–148.

51. Felker, 518 U.S. at 651; Ex Parte McCardle, 74 U.S. at 506.

52. Klein, 80 U.S. at 128.

53. 133 S. Ct. 1138 (2013).

54. Id. at 1146–1147.

55. Id.

56. Id. at 1147.

57. 488 U.S. 361 (1989).

58. Id. at 371.

59. 487 U.S. 654 (1988).

60. Id. at 682–683.

61. Id. at 684–685.

62. 520 U.S. 681 (1997).

63. Id. at 701.

64. 418 U.S. 683 (1974).

65. The Court held that the due process rights of the criminal defendants outweighed the separation-of-powers consequences of ordering the president to produce the requested documents, which did not implicate matters of foreign relations or national security. Id.

66. Id. at 708.

67. Bruce G. Peabody and John D. Nugent, "Toward a Unifying Theory of the Separation of Powers," 53 *Am. U. L. Rev.* 1, 40 (2003).

68. Pozen, "Self-Help," at 2.

69. Michael J. Gerhardt, *The Federal Impeachment Process: A Constitutional and Historical Analysis* 107 (1996).

70. Nixon v. United States, 506 U.S. 224 (1993).

71. Gerhardt, *The Federal Impeachment Process*, at 82.

72. U.S. Const., Art. III, § 1.

73. Gerhardt, *The Federal Impeachment Process*, at 103.

74. Id. at 106–107.

75. U.S. Const., Art. I, § 8, cl. 11.

76. U.S. Const., Art. I, § 7. The possibility of a congressional override is of course a check on the effectiveness of the president's veto power, but not on his constitutional authority to choose to issue the veto in the first place.

77. U.S. Const., Art. I, § 2, cl. 5; U.S. Const., Art. I, § 3, cl. 6.

78. Report of the National Commission on Judicial Discipline and Removal, 152 F.R.D. 265, 293–296 (1993).

79. The precise opposite motivations could also be true. A justice who is not enamored of a case could make her recusal decision dependent at least in part on how that decision would affect the case's viability, but I think this is a far less likely scenario, especially when the alternative is to vote on the merits of the case.

80. As discussed in chapter 3, quorum standards do not create separation-of-powers problems when they set attainable participation requirements for the justices.

81. This is what happened in *North American Company v. SEC*, 327 U.S. 686 (1946), when Chief Justice Stone originally recused himself from the case, only to reverse his decision when he realized his recusal would defeat a quorum.

82. This authority could also be grounded in the Necessary and Proper Clause of Article I, section 8, but for present purposes the precise constitutional basis is unimportant.

83. Louis J. Virelli III, "The (Un)Constitutionality of Supreme Court Recusal Standards," 2011 *Wis. L. Rev.* 1181, 1223–1225.

84. U.S. Const., Art. II, § 2, cl. 2.

85. Lori A. Ringhand and Paul M. Collins, Jr., "May It Please the Senate: An Empirical Analysis of the Senate Judiciary Committee Hearings of Supreme Court Nominees, 1939–2009," 60 Am. *U. L. Rev.* 589, 632, 633 (2011).

86. Id. at 617–618.

87. "Confirmation Hearing on the Nomination of John G. Roberts, Jr. to Be Chief Justice of the United States," hearings before the Senate Committee on the Judiciary, 109th Cong., 1st Sess. 55 (2005).

88. Dmitry Bam, "Making Appearances Matter: Recusal and the Appearance of Bias," 2011 *B.Y.U. L. Rev.* 943, 983 (2011).

89. U.S. Const., Art. I, § 9, cl. 7.

90. U.S. Const., Art. III, § 1.

91. William P. Marshall, "The Limits on Congress's Authority to Investigate the President," 2004 *U. Ill. L. Rev.* 781, 785.

92. Louis Fisher, *Constitutional Conflicts between Congress and the President* 176 (6th ed. 2014).

93. Todd David Peterson, "Congressional Investigations of Federal Judges," 90 *Iowa L. Rev.* 1, 11 (2004).

94. Eileen Malloy, "Supreme Court Justices Already Comply with Ethics Rules, Kennedy, Breyer Say," 79 *U.S.L.W.* 2389 (April 19, 2011); "Considering the Role of Judges under the Constitution of the United States," hearings before the Senate Committee on the Judiciary, 112th Cong., 1st Sess. (2011).

5. Due Process and the First Amendment

1. Bracy v. Gramley, 520 U.S. 899, 904–905 (1997).

2. Tumey v. Ohio, 273 U.S. 510, 523 (1927); Richard E. Flamm, *Judicial Disqualification: Recusal and Disqualification of Judges* § 2.5.2, at 36–37 (2d ed. 2007).

3. City of Boerne v. Flores, 521 U.S. 507, 519 (1997).

4. Poe v. Ullman, 367 U.S. 497, 542 (1961) (Harlan, J., dissenting).

5. Cheney v. United States District Court, 541 U.S. 913, 923–929 (2004); Laird v. Tatum, 409 U.S. 824, 829–838 (1972).

6. Statement of Recusal Policy, reprinted in Flamm, *Judicial Disqualification*, App. D at 1101; John G. Roberts Jr., 2011 Year-End Report on the Federal Judiciary 4 (2011), http://www.supremecourt.gov/publicinfo/year-end/2011year-endreport.pdf.

7. U.S. Const., Art. VI, § 2.

8. Jewell Ridge Coal Corp. v. Local No. 6167, United Mine Workers of Am., 325 U.S. 897 (1945).

9. Id. (Jackson, J., concurring). As a reminder, the federal recusal statute was not amended to include the Supreme Court justices until 1948. 28 U.S.C. § 455 (1948).

10. 273 U.S. 510 (1927).

11. I am referring to the adoption of the Fifth Amendment's Due Process Clause here because that is the one that governs the federal courts, but there is also no evidence that recusal was discussed in connection with the adoption of the Fourteenth Amendment's Due Process Clause.

12. Tumey, 273 U.S. at 523.

13. Martin v. Hunter's Lessee, 14 U.S. (1 Wheat.) 304 (1816).

14. Stuart v. Laird, 5 U.S. (1 Cranch) 299 (1803).

15. 273 U.S. 510 (1927).

16. Gen. Code, Ohio, § 6212–13 et seq. (1927).

17. Tumey, 273 U.S. at 517.

18. Id. at 517–518.

19. Id.

20. Id. at 518.

21. Id. at 535.

22. Id. at 523.

23. Id. at 524–526.

24. Id. at 523.

25. Id. at 531.

26. Id. at 532.

27. Id.

28. 349 U.S. 133 (1955).

29. Id. at 133.

30. Id. at 139.

31. William Blackstone, 3 *Commentaries on the Laws of England* 361 (1768).

32. Murchison, 349 U.S. at 136.

33. Id.

34. Id.

35. Tumey v. Ohio, 273 U.S. 510, 532 (1927).

36. Murchison, 349 U.S. at 136.

37. 400 U.S. 455 (1971).

38. Id. at 456, 458, 465.

39. Id. at 458.

40. Id. at 465.

41. Id. at 466.

42. Dmitry Bam, "Understanding *Caperton*: Judicial Disqualification under the Due Process Clause," 42 *McGeorge L. Rev.* 65, 72–78 (2010).

43. 409 U.S. 57 (1972).

44. Id. at 57.

45. Id. at 58.

46. Id. at 60.

47. 475 U.S. 813 (1986).

48. Id. at 817. Two of the Alabama Supreme Court justices affirmatively removed themselves from the pending class action suit once they became aware of it. Id. at 818.

49. Id. at 822.

50. Id.

51. Id. at 820, 824.

52. Id. at 825.

53. Id. at 829–830 (Brennan, J., concurring).

54. Not for the Supreme Court, of course, as I contend that such legislative requirements are unconstitutional under Article III. A full defense of this position is available in chapter 3.

55. As this book goes to press, the Court is poised to decide whether due process requires recusal when the allegedly unfit judge, in this case a justice of the Pennsylvania Supreme Court is not the deciding vote in a multimember tribunal. Williams v. Pennsylvania, 105 A.3d 1234, cert granted, 136 S. Ct. 28 (2015).

56. DelVecchio v. Illinois, 494 U.S. 1062 (1990).

57. Id. at 1062.

58. 556 U.S. 868 (2009).

59. Id. at 872–874.

60. Id. at 876.

61. Id. at 876–877 (citations omitted).

62. Id. at 887.

63. Petition for Writ of Certiorari, Williams v. Pennsylvania, 105 A.3d 1234, cert granted, 136 S. Ct. 28 (Oct. 1, 2015) (No. 15-5040).

64. Id. at 2.

65. Id. at 15–20.

66. 28 U.S.C. § 455(a)(1974).

67. In re Murchison, 349 U.S. 133, 136 (1955).

68. Mayberry v. Pennsylvania, 400 U.S. 455, 465, 468 (1971).

69. Murchison, 349 U.S. at 136.

70. Chapter 6 addresses the important constitutional concerns associated with congressional regulation of recusal in lower federal and state supreme courts.

71. 536 U.S. 765, 794 (2002) (Kennedy, J., concurring).

72. DelVecchio v. Illinois Dep't of Corr., 31 F.3d 1363, 1391 (7th Cir. 1994).

73. Planned Parenthood of Se. Pa. v. Casey, 505 U.S. 833, 865–866 (1992).

74. 135 S. Ct. 1656, 1666 (2015) (quoting *The Federalist* No. 78 (A. Hamilton)).

75. U.S. Const., Art. III, § 1.

76. Letter from 132 Law Professors to the House and Senate Judiciary Committees, March 17, 2011, http://www.afj.org/wp-content/uploads/2013/09/judicial_ethics_sign_on_letter.pdf.

77. U.S. Const., Art. I, § 8, cl. 9; U.S. Const., Art. III, § 1.

78. 327 U.S. 686 (1946).

79. Laird v. Tatum, 409 U.S. 824 (1972).

80. Cheney v. United States District Court, 541 U.S. 913 (2004).

81. Tatum, 409 U.S. at 837–838; Cheney, 541 U.S. at 915–916.

82. 28 U.S.C. §§ 291–297 (2014).

83. 347 U.S. 483 (1954).

84. Dennis J. Hutchinson, "Unanimity and Desegregation: Decisionmaking in the Supreme Court, 1948–1958," 68 *Geo. L.J.* 1 (1979).

85. Richard M. Esenberg, "If You Speak Up, Must You Stand Down: *Caperton* and Its Limits," 45 *Wake Forest L. Rev.* 1287, 1323 (2010).

86. Andrey Spektor and Michael Zuckerman, "Judicial Recusal and Expanding Notions of Due Process," 13 *U. Pa. J. Const. L.* 977, 1001–1004 (2011).

87. 536 U.S. 765, 794 (2002) (Kennedy, J., concurring).

88. Michael Dorf, "Incidental Burdens on Fundamental Rights," 109 *Harv. L. Rev.* 1175, 1178 (1996).

89. Spektor and Zuckerman, "Judicial Recusal," at 1001–1002; James Sample and David E. Pozen, "Making Judicial Recusal More Rigorous," 46 *Judges' J.* 17, 19 (2007).

90. 536 U.S. at 796 (Kennedy, J., concurring).

91. Id. at 774.

92. Dorf, "Incidental Burdens," at 1200–1210.

93. Tony Mauro, "Ginsburg Faulted for Comment on Texas Abortion Law," *Nat'l L.J.*, September 30, 2014, http://www.nationallawjournal.com/legaltimes/id=1202671814033/Ginsburg-Faulted-for-Comment-on-Texas-Abortion-Law#ixzz3QFKFg4xo.

94. Ariane de Vogue, "Groups Suggest Elena Kagan, Clarence Thomas Should Be Recused from Health Law Challenge," ABC News, November 16, 2011, http://abcnews.go.com/blogs/politics/2011/11/groups-suggest-elena-kagan-clarence-thomas-should-be-recused-from-health-law-decision/.

95. Erwin Chemerinsky, "Is It the Siren's Call? Judges and Free Speech While Cases Are Pending," 28 *Loy. L.A. L. Rev.* 831, 841, 842–843 (1995); Leonard E. Gross, "Judicial Speech: Discipline and the First Amendment," 36 *Syracuse L. Rev.* 1181 (1986). Chemerinsky suggests that the First Amendment law governing attorney speech applies most sensibly to restrictions on judicial speech

during pending cases, but he acknowledges that the public employee and content-based speech restrictions could also apply. Chemerinsky, "Is It the Siren's Call?," at 841.

96. Caperton v. A. T. Massey Coal Co., 556 U.S. 868, 877 (2009); Mayberry v. Pennsylvania, 400 U.S. 455, 465–466 (1971).

97. During the oral argument in *Caperton*, Justice Ginsburg asked counsel for Massey to "clarify" the difference between probability of bias and a reasonable appearance of impartiality, because "I was taking appearance, likelihood, probability, as all synonyms." Transcript of Oral Argument at 34–35, Caperton v. A. T. Massey Coal Co., 556 U.S. 868 (2009) (No. 08-22).

98. Bam, "Understanding *Caperton*," at 72–76.

99. Turner Broadcasting System v. FCC, 512 U.S. 622, 643 (1994).

100. Washington v. Glucksberg, 521 U.S. 702, 721 (1997).

101. Turner, 512 U.S. at 643. Intermediate scrutiny permits restrictions on speech that "further[] an important or substantial governmental interest [that] . . . is unrelated to the suppression of free expression" and that are "no greater than is essential to the furtherance of that interest." United States v. O'Brien, 391 U.S. 367, 377 (1968).

102. White, 536 U.S. 765, 768 (2002); Minn. Code of Judicial Conduct Canon 5(A)(3)(d)(i) (2000).

103. Republican Party of Minnesota v. White, 536 U.S. at 774–775.

104. Id. at 773.

105. Id. at 776–777.

106. Id. at 777; Kermit Roosevelt, "What Do You Mean by 'Impartial'?," *N.Y. Times*, November 3, 2013, http://www.nytimes.com/roomfordebate/2013/11/03/judges-appearance-of-impartiality/ways-a-judge-should-and-should-not-be-impartial.

107. White, 536 U.S. at 788.

108. 135 S. Ct. 1656 (2015).

109. Id. at 1665.

110. Id. at 1666.

111. Id. at 1668–1672.

112. Id. at 1672.

113. 28 U.S.C. § 144; Berger v. United States, 41 U.S. 230 (1921).

114. Washington v. Glucksberg, 521 U.S. 702, 767 (1997).

115. James S. Liebman and William F. Ryan, "'Some Effectual Power': The Quantity and Quality of Decisionmaking Required of Article III Courts," 98 *Colum. L. Rev.* 696, 771 (1998).

116. Republican Party of Minnesota v. White, 536 U.S. 765, 775–776 (2002). If section 455 also prohibits judges from participating in cases in which there is a reasonable appearance of partiality with regard to the issues, rather than the parties, it could fail the compelling interest requirement of strict scrutiny just like Canon 5(A)(3)(d)(i) did in *White*.

117. Id. at 796 (Kennedy, J., concurring).

118. 391 U.S. 563 (1968).

119. Connick v. Myers, 461 U.S. 138, 143–144 (1983).

120. Pickering, 391 U.S. at 568.

121. Id. at 566.

122. Id. at 566.

123. Id. at 572–573.

124. 461 U.S. 138 (1983).

125. Id. at 141.

126. Id. at 141–142.

127. Id. at 146–147.

128. Id. at 147.

129. Id. at 154.

130. Id. at 138.

131. 547 U.S. 410 (2006).

132. 134 S. Ct. 2369 (2014).

133. Garcetti, 547 U.S. at 426.

134. Lane, 134 S. Ct. at 2374–2376.

135. Id. at 2379.

136. White, 536 U.S. at 796 (Kennedy, J., concurring).

137. U.S. Const., Art. II, § 2.

138. The theoretical and practical differences between impeachment and recusal are discussed in detail in chapter 3.

139. Lower court judges are subject to the traditional standards of appellate review. Amanda Peters, "The Meaning, Measure, and Misuse of Standards of Review," 13 *Lewis & Clark L. Rev.* 233, 243–247 (2009).

140. It is possible that a justice could face a recusal motion based on something she said before taking the bench. If she was a government employee without life tenure when she made the statement in question—like Solicitor General Kagan and her e-mail about the ACA—then the public employee doctrine may apply. This would not likely change the analysis, as the probability-of-bias standard would still govern under the Due Process Clause.

141. David Lat, "Err on the Side of Allowing Speech," *N.Y. Times*, November 4, 2013, http://www.nytimes.com/roomfordebate/2013/11/03/judges-appearance-of-impartiality/err-on-the-side-of-allowing-judicial-speech; Deborah Rhode, "Judges Have a First Amendment Right, Too," *N.Y. Times*, November 4, 2013, http://www.nytimes.com/roomfordebate/2013/11/03/judges-appearance-of-impartiality/judges-have-a-first-amendment-right-too.

142. Pickering v. Board of Educ., 391 U.S. 563, 568 (1968).

143. Caperton v. A. T. Massey Coal Co., 556 U.S. 868, 876 (2009).

144. Pickering, 391 U.S. at 568.

145. Lane v. Franks, 134 S. Ct. 2369, 2379 (2014); Garcetti v. Ceballos, 547 U.S. 410, 426 (2006).

146. Chemerinsky, "Is It the Siren's Call?," at 843.

147. 501 U.S. 1030 (1991).

148. Id. at 1033.

149. Gentile v. State Bar of Nevada, 106 Nev. 60, 61 (1991).

150. Gentile, 501 U.S. at 1034.

151. Id. at 1033. Rule 177 was repealed in 2006.

152. Gentile, 106 Nev. at 63.

153. Gentile, 501 U.S. at 1071.

154. Id. at 1074.

155. Id. at 1075. The Court held that another portion of the state ethics rule was void for vagueness and reversed the Nevada Supreme Court's decision to affirm the disciplinary action against the attorney. Id. at 1048, 1058.

156. The circuit courts are split, for instance, on the broader question of when a court may punish an attorney for speech critical of the court and its judges. Compare the Ninth Circuit's decision in *Standing Comm. on Discipline v. Yagman*, 55 F.3d 1430 (9th Cir. 1995), which permitted punishment for critical comments by an attorney only where actual malice was present, with the Seventh Circuit's holding in *In the Matter of Michael Palmisano*, 70 F.3d 483 (7th Cir. 1995), which permitted an attorney to be punished for false factual statements about the court.

157. The Supreme Court has interpreted the word "speech" in the First Amendment broadly. In a case addressing the First Amendment status of flag burning, the Court concluded that "the First Amendment literally forbids the abridgment only of 'speech,' but we have long recognized that its protection does not end at the spoken or written word." Texas v. Johnson, 491 U.S. 397, 404 (1989).

158. 327 U.S. 686 (1946).

159. 325 U.S. 161 (1945).

6. Beyond the High Court

1. Lower federal courts are defined here as Article III courts other than the Supreme Court. U.S. magistrate or bankruptcy judges are not included in this analysis because they are not life-tenured and thus do not qualify as Article III judges. Because they are not Article III judges, they do not derive their authority from its Vesting Clause and thus cannot claim to be exercising any inherent judicial power within the meaning of Article III.

2. U.S. Const., Art. III, § 1; U.S. Const., Art. I, § 8, cl. 9.

3. Paul M. Bator, "Congressional Power over the Jurisdiction of the Federal Courts," 27 *Vill. L. Rev.* 1030, 1031 (1982).

4. 1 Stat. 73 (1789).

5. This history of early federal recusal legislation is discussed in detail in chapter 1.

6. The fact that it is unfathomable that Congress would eliminate the federal courts at this point in our history is beside the constitutional point that the authority vested in those courts may very well be affected by the fact that Article III gives Congress complete dominion over their formation.

7. Felix Frankfurter and James Landis, "Power of Congress over Procedure in Criminal Contempts in 'Inferior' Federal Courts—A Study in Separation of Powers," 37 *Harv. L. Rev.* 1010 (1924).

8. Id. at 1012.

9. Id. at 1020.

10. Id.

11. Id.

12. James Liebman and William Ryan, "'Some Effectual Power:' The Quantity and Quality of Decisionmaking Required of Article III Courts," 98 *Colum. L. Rev.* 696, 771 (1998).

13. Robert J. Pushaw Jr., "The Inherent Powers of Federal Courts and the Structural Constitution," 86 *Iowa L. Rev.* 735, 847–848 (2001).

14. Id. at 844, 846.

15. Id. at 846.

16. Id. at 847.

17. Id. at 847–848.

18. Id. at 848.

19. Id.

20. Evan Caminker, "Allocating the Judicial Power in a 'Unified Judiciary,'" 78 *Tex. L. Rev.* 1513, 1528 (2000).

21. Id.

22. Id.

23. The Ninth Circuit is entitled to twenty-nine active judges. 28 U.S.C. § 44 (2015). It currently has a full slate of active judges, along with fifteen senior judges. http://www.ca9.uscourts.gov/content/view_seniority_list.php?pk _id=0000000035. The Eastern District of Pennsylvania is entitled to twenty-two active judges. 28 U.S.C. § 133 (2015). It currently has twenty-one active, and seventeen senior, judges. http://www.paed.uscourts.gov/documents/directry /directry.pdf.

24. With only six active judges allotted to it, 28 U.S.C. § 44 (2015), the First Circuit is the smallest of the circuit courts, but it is not an extreme outlier in terms of its vulnerability to complete recusal. The Eighth Circuit and Eleventh Circuit are allotted eleven and twelve circuit judges, respectively. Id. As of March 2015, the Eighth Circuit consisted of eleven active and four senior judges, and the Eleventh Circuit had eleven active and eight senior judges. Current lists of these circuits' judges are available at http://www.ca8.uscourts.gov/active-and -senior-judges, and http://www.ca11.uscourts.gov/eleventh-circuit-judges.

25. Each district is allotted three active judges by federal law, so there were no vacancies in either court as of March 2015. 28 U.S.C. § 133 (2015). Complete lists of judges in each district are available at http://www.wyd.uscourts.gov/ht mlpages/about.html and http://www.rid.uscourts.gov/#.

26. These totals represent the full slate of judges allotted to each district by federal law. 28 U.S.C. § 133 (2015). A complete and current list of the judges in the Southern District of Alabama is available at http://www.als.uscourts.gov /judges/, and of the Southern District of Illinois is available at http://www.ilsd .uscourts.gov/Judges.aspx.

27. The Supreme Court Ethics Act of 2013, H.R. 2902, 113th Cong., 1st Sess. (2013), died in committee in 2013 and was reintroduced in 2015. Tony Mauro, "New Bill Would Force Justices to Adopt Ethics Code," *Nat'l L.J.*, April 23, 2015. It was preceded by the Supreme Court Transparency and Disclosure Act of 2011, H.R. 862, 112th Cong., 1st Sess. (2011).

28. According to the official website of Senator Diane Feinstein, a member of the Senate Judiciary Committee, "Senators recommend individuals to the President to serve as U.S. District Court Judges." http://www.feinstein.senate.gov/public/index.cfm/applications-jud.

29. A 2014 study by the Brennan Center for Justice at New York University School of Law explained that "since 2009, the federal trial courts have experienced unusually high and sustained levels of judicial vacancies." Alicia Bannon, "The Impact of Judicial Vacancies on Federal Trial Courts," Brennan Ctr. for Justice 1 (2014), https://www.brennancenter.org/publication/impact-judicial-vacancies-federal-trial-courts.

30. 9 Stat. 442 (1869).

31. 34 Stat. 1417 (1907).

32. 42 Stat. 837 (1922). That provision was reworded but remained essentially the same in a 1953 amendment. 50 Stat. 753.

33. 28 U.S.C. §§ 291(b), 292(b), 294(c) (1993).

34. 28 U.S.C. §§ 291(a), 292(d) and (e) (active judges); § 294(d) (senior judges).

35. 28 U.S.C. § 294(d) (senior judges).

36. A more complete discussion of the historical and practical roots of judges deciding their own recusal questions is included in chapter 3.

37. U.S. Const., Art. III, § 2.

38. The Judiciary Act of 1789, for example, "did not give the lower federal courts general 'arising under' jurisdiction." Daniel J. Meltzer, "The History and Structure of Article III," 138 *U. Pa. L. Rev.* 1569, 1585 (1990).

39. Liebman and Ryan, "'Some Effectual Power,'" at 708.

40. John Harrison, "The Power of Congress to Limit the Jurisdiction of Federal Courts and the Text of Article III," 64 *U. Chi. L. Rev.* 203, 214–215 (1997).

41. A. Benjamin Spencer, "The Judicial Power and the Inferior Federal Courts: Exploring the Constitutional Vesting Thesis," 46 *Ga. L. Rev.* 1, 48 (2011).

42. Akhil Reed Amar, "A Neo-Federalist View of Article III: Separating the Two Tiers of Federal Jurisdiction," 65 *B.U. L. Rev.* 205 (1985).

43. Id. at 240–246.

44. Id.

45. Id. at 248.

46. U.S. Const., Art. III, § 2, cl. 2.

47. Alden v. Maine, 527 U.S. 706 (1999).

48. Id. at 749.

49. F.D.I.C. v. Meyer, 510 U.S. 471 (1994).

50. U.S. Const., Art III, § 2.

51. Erwin Chemerinsky, *Federal Jurisdiction* 309–312 (6th ed. 2012); Felix Frankfurter, "Distribution of Judicial Power between United States and State Courts," 13 *Cornell L.Q.* 499, 521 (1928); Robert W. Kastenmeier and Michael J. Remington, "Court Reform and Access to Justice: A Legislative Perspective," 16 *Harv. J. on Legis.* 301, 314–317 (1979); Suzanna Sherry, "Against Diversity," 17 *Const. Comment.* 1 (2000).

52. Martin v. Hunter's Lessee, 14 U.S. (1 Wheat.) 304, 331 (1816).

53. U.S. Const., Art. III, § 2.

54. Battaglia v General Motors Corp., 169 F.2d 254 (2d Cir. 1948).

55. Williams-Yulee v. The Florida Bar, 135 S. Ct. 1656, 1668–1672 (2015).

56. U.S. Const., Art I., § 18.

57. Thomas C. Marks and John F. Cooper, *State Constitutional Law* 189–190 (2003); *The Federalist* No. 47 (J. Madison).

58. Some states refer to their highest court by a name other than the supreme court, and the members of that court as something other than justices. For example, the highest court in New York is called the Court of Appeals, and its members are simply called judges. N.Y. Const., Art. VI, §§ 1, 2.

59. For a sample of recusal provisions in state constitutions, see generally Md. Const., Art. IV, § 7; Miss. Const., Art. VI, § 165; Tenn. Const., Art. VI, § 11; Tex. Const., Art. V, § 11.

60. U.S. Const., Art. I, §§ 3, 18.

61. Gonzales v. Raich, 545 U.S. 1 (2004); Wickard v. Filburn, 317 U.S. 111 (1942); McCulloch v. Maryland, 17 U.S. 316 (1819). The Court did begin to scale back on its interpretation of Congress's commerce and necessary and proper powers starting in 1996, but both clauses remain robust sources of congressional power. United States v. Morrison, 529 U.S. 598 (2000); United States v. Lopez, 514 U.S. 549 (1996).

62. State legislative power is limited by constitutional provisions like the Supremacy Clause and the Dormant Commerce Clause but overall includes a much wider range of substantive concerns than are assigned to Congress under even the most permissive reading of Article I.

63. National Fed. of Indep. Bus. v. Sebelius, 132 S. Ct. 2566, 2578 (2013).

64. Scott Douglas Gerber, *A Distinct Judicial Power: The Origins of an Independent Judiciary, 1606–1787* (2011).

65. *The Federalist* No. 78 (A. Hamilton).

66. Adam Skaggs, Maria da Silva, Linda Casey, and Charles Hall, *The New Politics of Judicial Elections 2009–10*, at 21 (2011); Charles Gardner Geyh, "Why Judicial Elections Stink," 64 *Ohio St. L.J.* 43, 58–59 (2003); Joanna M. Shepherd, "Money, Politics, and Impartial Justice," 58 *Duke L.J.* 623, 625 (2009).

67. American Bar Association, "Fact Sheet on Judicial Selection Methods in the States," http://www.americanbar.org/content/dam/aba/migrated/leader ship/fact_sheet.authcheckdam.pdf.

68. Id.

69. As an example, Florida held seventy-one judicial retention elections from 2010 through 2014. The retention elections were for state supreme court justices (seven) and appellate court judges (sixty-four). The retention rate was 100 percent. Florida Division of Elections, "Candidates and Races," http://election .dos.state.fl.us/candidate/Index.asp.

70. American Bar Association, "Fact Sheet."

71. David Paul Kuhn, "The Incredible Polarization and Politicization of the Supreme Court," *The Atlantic*, June 29, 2012, http://www.theatlantic.com /politics/archive/2012/06/the-incredible-polarization-and-politicization-of -the-supreme-court/259155/. In a 2015 speech at the New York Public Library,

Justice Sonia Sotomayor acknowledged that the Court was becoming politicized but attributed it to the "world around" the Court rather than to the justices themselves. Tony Mauro, "Sotomayor: Don't Blame the Justices for Politicization of Supreme Court," *Nat'l L.J.*, April 10, 2015, http://www.nationallawjournal.com/legaltimes/id=1202723165481/Sotomayor-Dont-Blame-the-Justices-for-Politicization-of-Supreme-Court?slreturn=20150414094133.

72. Skaggs et al., *The New Politics of Judicial Elections*, at 21; Shepherd, "Money, Politics, and Impartial Justice," at 625.

73. Caperton v. A. T. Massey Coal Co., 556 U.S. 868 (2009).

74. Id. at 884–886.

75. Liebman and Ryan, "'Some Effectual Power,'" at 771.

76. National Center for State Courts, "Methods of Judicial Selection: Selection of Judges," http://www.judicialselection.us/judicial_selection/methods/selection_of_judges.cfm?state=.

77. *The Federalist* No. 47 (J. Madison); *The Federalist* No. 78 (A. Hamilton); Stephen B. Burbank, "The Architecture of Judicial Independence," 72 *S. Cal. L. Rev.* 315, 339 (1999).

78. Sara C. Benesh, "Understanding Public Confidence in American Courts," 68 *J. Pol.* 697 (2006); Damon M. Cann and Jeff Yates, "Homegrown Institutional Legitimacy: Assessing Citizens' Diffuse Support for State Courts," 36 *Am. Pol. Res.* 297 (2008).

79. Planned Parenthood of Se. Pa. v. Casey, 505 U.S. 833 (1992).

80. John P. Frank, "Disqualification of Judges," 56 *Yale L.J.* 605, 612 (1947).

81. Matias Iaryczower, Garrett Lewis, and Matthew Shum, "To Elect or to Appoint? Bias, Information, and Responsiveness of Bureaucrats and Politicians," 97 *J. Pub. Econ.* 230 (2013).

82. Benesh, "Understanding Public Confidence"; Cann and Yates, "Homegrown Institutional Legitimacy."

83. State supreme court terms vary among the states, but only fifteen even permit a justice to face reelection or reappointment within six years of taking the bench. Of those fifteen, only Missouri and Tennessee require a justice to be reevaluated in less than six years after initially taking the bench. Subsequent terms for justices in those states are twelve and eight years, respectively. American Bar Association, "Fact Sheet." State legislatures, by contrast, all have terms between two and four years. Most states have longer, four-year terms for senators and two-year terms for representatives, but none have a single legislative term longer than four years. National Conference of State Legislators, "Number of Legislators and Length of Terms in Years," March 11, 2013, http://www.ncsl.org/research/about-state-legislatures/number-of-legislators-and-length-of-terms.aspx. Governors all serve four-year terms except in New Hampshire and Vermont, where they serve two-year terms. National Governors Association, "Elections," http://www.nga.org/cms/elections.

84. In three states, South Carolina, Virginia, and Vermont, reappointments are done by legislative "election." National Center for State Courts, "Methods of Judicial Selection: Selection of Judges," http://www.judicialselection.us/judicial_selection/methods/selection_of_judges.cfm?state=. Judicial im-

peachment is also a feature of every state constitutional system except Hawaii and Oregon. National Center for State Courts, "Methods of Judicial Selection: Removal of Judges," http://www.judicialselection.us/judicial_selection/meth ods/removal_of_judges.cfm?state=.

85. Louis D. Brandeis, *Other People's Money, and How the Bankers Use It* 92 (1914).

86. R.I. Gen. Laws § 9–24–11 (2014).

87. National Center for State Courts, "Methods of Judicial Selection: Selection of Judges."

88. Other forms of discipline like impeachment are of course still available, but they do not go to the present question of how judicial elections change the constitutional dynamics of recusal. For one, impeachment and elections involve different actors, procedures, and substantive criteria. State legislatures control impeachments, while the public controls the outcome of elections. Second, impeachment is a factor at both the state and federal levels, so there is likely little difference between the effects of impeachment on state versus federal recusal practices.

89. Lawrence Baum, "Judicial Elections and Judicial Independence: The Voter's Perspective," 64 *Ohio St. L.J.* 13, 19 (2003).

90. Id.

91. Id.

92. Id. at 19–20.

93. Geyh, "Why Judicial Elections Stink," at 53–54.

94. National Center for State Courts, "Methods of Judicial Selection: Selection of Judges."

95. Florida Department of State, Division of Elections, "November 6, 2012 General Election: Official Results," http://election.dos.state.fl.us/elections /resultsarchive/Index.asp?ElectionDate=11/6/2012&DATAMODE=. The national turnout rate for the 2012 presidential election was about 58 percent. United States Election Project, "Voter Turnout Rates, 1787–2012," http://www .electproject.org/home/voter-turnout/voter-turnout-data.

96. Florida Department of State, "November 6, 2012 General Election."

97. Id.

98. Florida Department of State, Division of Elections, "November 2, 2010 General Election: Voter Registration and Turnout," http://election.dos.state .fl.us/elections/resultsarchive/Index.asp?ElectionDate=11/2/2010&DATAM ODE=.

99. Larry Aspin, "Trends in Judicial Retention Elections, 1964–1998," 83 *Judicature* 79 (1999).

100. National Center for State Courts, "Methods of Judicial Selection: Selection of Judges."

101. From 1990 to 2004, state supreme court justices were reelected 91 percent of the time, but only 68 percent of the time when running in partisan reelections. Chris W. Bonneau, "A Survey of Empirical Evidence Concerning Judicial Elections," *Fed. Soc'y*, March 2012, at 11, http://www.fed-soc.org/publi cations/detail/a-survey-of-empirical-evidence-concerning-judicial-elections.

102. 28 U.S.C. §§ 1333 (admiralty), 1338 (patents, copyrights, trademarks), 1351 (ambassadors).

103. R. LaFountain, R. Schauffler, S. Strickland, S. Gibson, and A. Mason, *Examining the Work of State Courts: An Analysis of 2009 State Court Caseloads* 4 (National Center for State Courts 2011); Shepherd, "Money, Politics, and Impartial Justice," at 625.

104. Although each state's constitution may treat its own due process protections slightly differently, the Fourteenth Amendment to the federal Constitution prohibits the states from denying any person "life, liberty, or property, without due process of law." U.S. Const., Amend. XIV.

105. Battaglia v. General Motors Corp., 169 F.2d 254 (2d Cir. 1948).

106. Delaware, the District of Columbia, Maine, Montana, Nevada, New Hampshire, North Dakota, Rhode Island, South Dakota, Vermont, West Virginia, and Wyoming do not have intermediate appellate courts. S. Strickland, R. Schauffler, R. LaFountain, and K. Holt, eds., *State Court Organization*, January 9, 2015, http://data.ncsc.org/QvAJAXZfc/opendoc.htm?document=Public%20 App/SCO.qvw&host=QVS@qlikviewisa&anonymous=true.

107. Conn. Gen. Stat. § 51-50d (2014); Kan. Stat. Ann. § 20-2616 (2014); Ohio Rev. Code Ann. § 2501.14 (2014); Or. Rev. Stat. § 1.300 (2014); R.I. Gen. Laws § 8-15-3 (2014); Tenn. Code Ann. § 17-2-304 (2014); Tex. Gov't Code Ann. § 74.056; Vt. Stat. Ann. Tit. 4, § 22 (2014).

108. N.D. Administrative Rule 27, § 7. The court of appeals does not share the same level of authority as the supreme court but is an example of how state systems are able to utilize a more fluid system for staffing cases that would otherwise be before their highest court because they are not restricted by constitutional provisions like Article III's mandate that there be one Supreme Court. U.S. Const., Art. III, § 1.

109. U.S. Const., Art. V.

110. The eleventh one ended up being the Twenty-Seventh Amendment, which reads, "No law, varying the compensation for the services of the Senators and Representatives, shall take effect, until an election of Representatives shall have intervened." U.S. Const., Amend. XXVII. The text of the amendment was introduced in Congress in 1789 by James Madison, along with the ten amendments that became the Bill of Rights. It was not ratified by the required three-fourths of the states, however, until 1992.

111. Eighteen states have procedures in place by which voters can trigger ballot initiatives leading to constitutional amendments.

112. The NBER/Maryland State Constitutions Project, http://www.statecon stitutions.umd.edu/index.aspx.

113. California, Delaware, Missouri, Virginia, and West Virginia, for example, all have twelve-year terms for their supreme court justices. National Center for State Courts, "Methods of Judicial Selection: Selection of Judges."

114. Richard E. Flamm, *Judicial Disqualification: Recusal and Disqualification of Judges* § 23.1, at 670 (2d ed. 2007).

115. Commodity Futures Trading Comm'n v. Schor, 478 U.S. 833, 863 (1986) (Brennan, J., dissenting).

116. Id.

117. Id.

118. Marks and Cooper, State Constitutional Law, at 300–314. In addition to legislative and popularly initiated amendments, Florida allows for a thirty-seven-member revision commission to hold hearings and make proposals for constitutional amendments every twenty years. The chief justice is one of the members of that commission. Id. at 305–306.

7. A Lesson in Structure

1. Stern v. Marshall, 131 S. Ct. 2594, 2609 (2011).

2. This was a primary concern of Madison, who advocated for constitutional checks on Congress in order to prevent "the legislative department [from] everywhere extending the sphere of its activity, and drawing all power into its impetuous vortex." *The Federalist* No. 48 (J. Madison).

3. 28 U.S.C. § 1 (2014).

4. Ex Parte Yerger, 75 U.S. (8 Wall.) 85 (1868); Ex Parte McCardle, 74 U.S. (7 Wall.) 506 (1868).

5. Plaut v. Spendthrift Farm, Inc., 514 U.S. 211 (1995).

6. U.S. Const., Art. II, § 2.

7. Two recent examples of entities that either could not function or were significantly limited in their function due to Senate intransigence over the appointment process are the National Labor Relations Board and the Consumer Financial Protection Bureau. NLRB v. Noel Canning, 134 S. Ct. 2550 (2014); Danielle Douglas, "Senate Confirms Cordray to Head Consumer Financial Protection Bureau," *Wash. Post,* July 16, 2013, http://www.washingtonpost.com/business/economy/senate-confirms-consumer-watchdog-nominee-richard-cordray/2013/07/16/965d82c2-ee2b-11e2-a1f9-ea873b7e0424_story.html.

8. Jeremy W. Peters, "In Landmark Vote, Senate Limits Use of the Filibuster," *N.Y. Times,* November 21, 2013, http://www.nytimes.com/2013/11/22/us/politics/reid-sets-in-motion-steps-to-limit-use-of-filibuster.html?_r=0.

9. 134 S. Ct. 2550 (2014).

10. Id. at 2575, 2576.

11. Id. at 2574.

12. Id. at 2575.

13. U.S. Const., Art. I, § 5, cl. 4.

14. Noel Canning, 134 S. Ct. at 2566.

15. U.S. Const., Art. II, § 3.

16. In fact, Congress has done just that for some agencies. 5 U.S.C. § 3345. The presence of a statutory solution to a potential constitutional problem, however, only highlights the importance of treating congressional intransigence over appointments as a constitutional matter. To the extent statutory solutions provide adequate relief, Congress's power to alter or amend those statutes must also be viewed as a constitutional issue in order to provide the proper protection to the coordinate branches.

17. Elizabeth B. Bazan, "Congressional Oversight of Judges and Justices," *Cong. Res. Serv. Rep.*, May 31, 2005, at 5, https://www.senate.gov/CRSReports/crs-publish.cfm?pid=%270E%2C*P%2C%3F8%23%40%20%20%0A.

18. Id.

19. Id. at 4–6.

20. United States v. Mendoza, 2004 U.S. Dist. Lexis 1449, at 18 (C.D. Cal. Jan. 12, 2004).

21. Id. at 18.

22. U.S. Const., Art. II, § 2; U.S. Const., Art. I, § 8, cl. 11.

23. 50 U.S.C. §§ 1541–1548 (2014).

24. There have been several examples of such conflicts throughout American history. As Gregory Sidak explained:

> Today, of course, we are so accustomed to thinking of Presidents as more hawkish than Congress that the hypothetical of a dovish President would strike many as preposterous. Yet, history provides a number of commonly ignored examples: John Adams resisted calls for a declaration of war against France in 1798 and instead sought authority for the limited and undeclared Quasi-War; James Madison was ambivalent about declaring war on Britain in 1812; Grover Cleveland in 1896 rebuffed the proposal by various members of Congress to declare war on Spain; William McKinley in 1898 reluctantly conceded to the same war fervor; and Woodrow Wilson successfully campaigned for reelection in 1916 on the slogan, "He kept us out of war."

J. Gregory Sidak, "To Declare War," 41 *Duke L.J.* 27, 85–86 (1991).

25. Congress's last formal declaration of war occurred on June 4, 1942. The Senate unanimously approved a House resolution declaring war with Romania as part of the nation's involvement in World War II. H.J. Res. 321, 77th Cong., 2d Sess. (1942).

26. Nixon v. United States, 506 U.S. 224 (1993); Michael J. Gerhardt, *The Federal Impeachment Process: A Constitutional and Historical Analysis* 40 (1996).

27. Nixon, 506 U.S. at 228–238.

28. Id. at 253 (Souter, J., concurring).

29. Myers v. United States, 272 U.S. 52 (1926).

30. In *Zivotofsky v. Clinton*, 132 S. Ct. 1421 (2013), the Court showed some willingness to become involved in interbranch immigration disputes when it held that it had the power to resolve a conflict between Congress and the president over whether Jerusalem should be described as being part of Israel on an American passport.

Index